The Coal Miner Who Became Governor

THE COAL MINER WHO BECAME GOVERNOR

—

PAUL E.
PATTON

With Jeffrey S. Suchanek

My best to Janet Halloway

Paul E. Patto

UNIVERSITY PRESS OF KENTUCKY

Editorial and Sales Offices: The University Press of Kentucky
663 South Limestone Street, Lexington, Kentucky 40508–4008
www.kentuckypress.com

Cataloging-in-Publication data available from the Library of Congress

ISBN 978-0-8131-9833-0 (hardcover)
ISBN 978-0-8131-9935-1 (paperback)
ISBN 978-0-8131-9834-7 (pdf)
ISBN 978-0-8131-9835-4 (epub)

This book is printed on acid-free paper meeting
the requirements of the American National Standard
for Permanence in Paper for Printed Library Materials.

Manufactured in the United States of America.

Member of the Association
of University Presses

Contents

Preface

Before I left the governor's office, I commissioned Fran Ellers, a prominent Louisville journalist, to write a book she titled *Progress and Paradox: The Patton Years, 1995–2003*. That book was her evaluation of my administration in real time. She interviewed me, members of my staff, and other people who were familiar with our work. I did not exercise editorial control of that book. In the main, it is accurate, although I disagree with a few segments.

At the same time, I asked Mary Lassiter, a member of my staff, to compile the accomplishments of my eight years in the governor's office. That document, printed by the Kentucky state government, is titled *Public Policy Initiatives of the Paul E. Patton Administration*. Again, I did not exercise editorial control; in fact, I did not read it in its entirety until after I left Frankfort in December 2003. As far as I know, that book is factual.

In September 2014 Jeffrey S. Suchanek, an oral historian at the University of Kentucky, began a series of interviews with me that took four years to complete. We recorded a total of approximately 125 interview hours during more than fifty sessions. I donated the audio and video recordings to the University of Kentucky's Louie B. Nunn Center for Oral History. Mr. Suchanek then edited the interviews into a first-person narrative. I approved, edited, and added details to each chapter. Crit Luallen, Jim Ramsey, Skipper Martin, and Carol Jordan, all of whom served as members of my two gubernatorial administrations, reviewed a draft of the manuscript for accuracy. The result is this book. In these pages, I explain what I did and why I did it. My objective was to document the accomplishments of my governorship, as many of these details are not part of the public record. I trust this background will be helpful to scholars who are interested in my personal life, my political career, and the time I spent in public office.

Paul E. Patton

Introduction

The fifty-ninth governor of Kentucky, Paul Edward Patton, was born on May 26, 1937, in the small community of Fallsburg, Kentucky. Fallsburg is located seven and a half miles north of Louisa, the Lawrence County seat, and seventy-three miles north of Pikeville, the economic capital of eastern Kentucky. Nothing in Paul Patton's upbringing suggested that he was destined to become one of the most progressive governors in the state's history.

The son of Ward Patton and Irene Marie (née Borders) Patton, Paul grew up poor by today's standards, but that was true of almost all the hundred or so residents of Fallsburg. His maternal grandfather, Roscoe Borders, was a farmer and coal miner employed for most of his life by the Consolidation Coal Company. He worked the mines in Cabin Creek, West Virginia, and in Van Lear, Harlan, and Jenkins, Kentucky. Roscoe was very active in the fight for unionization of the miners, participating in the event known as "Bloody Harlan" during the 1930s. The Borders family kept pictures of Jesus Christ and labor leader John L. Lewis in their living room. Paul's paternal grandfather, Charles Patton, worked in the oil fields in Magoffin County but spent most of his life in Lawrence County employed by the Ashland Oil Company.

Ward Patton graduated from Louisa High School in 1928 when he was twenty-one years old. After obtaining a teaching certificate, he taught in one-room schools in Lawrence County during the school year and took classes at Morehead State Teachers College during the summer. He met Irene while teaching at a one-room school near Ulysses, Kentucky, where she was a student. They married in 1934 and had three children: Jo Ann, Paul, and Linda. Paul was born in a two-room board-and-batten tenant house constructed out of wood from a torn-down corn silo on his grandfather Patton's farm. The walls of the house were partially insulated with pages from newspapers.

During the Great Depression, Ward was a timekeeper for the Works Progress Administration. He also worked briefly in central Kentucky during construction of the Bluegrass Army Depot. In 1940 he was employed as a

1

laborer on an engineering crew for the state Highway Department and competed in the Democratic primary for state representative, but he lost by seventeen votes to the Elliott County candidate, Joe B. Jerboa. Ward's brother, William Patton, was the postmaster in Louisa and was actively involved in politics. Ward took a correspondence course to become a registered land surveyor, and he worked in that capacity for the Chesapeake and Ohio (C&O) Railroad during World War II, when the railroad laid track in the eastern Kentucky hollows to extract coal required for the war effort. He eventually became the resident engineer for the C&O Railroad in the Big Sandy valley, and Paul worked for the railroad in the summertime when he was in college.

The family moved frequently during Paul's childhood, going wherever Ward could find a teaching position or some other type of employment. In most of the houses in which Paul grew up, the only room with heat was the living room; there was no insulation, so the bedrooms were as cold or as hot as the outdoors. Most of the houses had electricity but no indoor plumbing. Water came from a well, and the bathroom was often a two-hole outhouse. The family took baths once a week on Saturday. Not until Paul was a freshman in high school did he live in a house with indoor plumbing. Through high school, his family never had a telephone. They could not afford a refrigerator or an electric stove until 1948. Irene was a talented seamstress, and she made most of the girls' clothes during their childhood. In 1948, when the four-room schoolhouse in Fallsburg got electricity, the community installed a kitchen and hired Irene as the cook. She made $3 a day and got free lunches for the three kids. Ward bought the family's first car, a black Plymouth, in 1949 when Paul was twelve. In 1950 the Pattons moved to a very nice house about two miles south of Fallsburg. It had two bedrooms and a bathroom, living room, dining room, kitchen, and attached garage; it was also equipped with a natural gas furnace. They lived in that house until Paul graduated from high school in the spring of 1955.

Ward and Irene emphasized the importance of obtaining a good education, and they expected their children to make good grades in school. Paul's favorite subject was math, which played a role in his desire to become an engineer. He graduated third in his class in 1955. His sister Jo had been valedictorian of her class two years earlier. Of the seventy-three students in Patton's graduating class, only seven went to college immediately after high school. Paul's score on the college aptitude test indicated that he could enroll in medical school, law school, or engineering school. He knew he could not afford to stay in college for postgraduate work, so he chose to major in mechanical engineering, a degree he could attain at the University of Kentucky (UK) in four years.

My mother and father were the most influential people in my life. They gave me the right combination of freedom and discipline to allow me to develop into the person I became. (Author's collection)

Paul and a high school friend, David Shortridge, became roommates in UK's brand-new Donovan Hall. They soon discovered that the curriculum was more difficult than what they had encountered in high school, but they buckled down, and Paul's grade point average was 3.75 after the first semester. He and David pledged the Kappa Sigma fraternity during the spring semester of their freshman year.

Early in his sophomore year, Paul got a job as a waiter and busboy at the Kappa Delta sorority house in exchange for free lunch and supper. While working there, he met Carol Cooley, and they married in July 1957. Carol's father, Jake Cooley, a coal operator in Floyd County, rented a house in a subdivision off Southland Drive for the young couple to live in and loaned them $10,000. Paul and Carol lived in married student housing in Cooperstown on the UK campus during his senior year. In his first flirtation with elected office, Paul ran for Student Government Assembly in 1957 but was defeated.

Paul won the Convair Award for outstanding freshman air force ROTC cadet on the UK campus. He enjoyed the ROTC program so much that he decided to remain a cadet and considered making the air force a career. However, after he and Carol had their first child, Nicki, Patton dropped out of the ROTC program and the mandatory four years of active duty.

Upon graduation from UK in May 1959, Paul went to work at his father-in-law's coal mine in McDowell, Kentucky. Jake promised Paul that if he worked hard and learned the coal business from the bottom up, he would help Paul start his own coal mining business. And that is what he did.

From the underground shafts in the coal mines of eastern Kentucky to the governor's office at the state capitol, Paul Patton's life exemplifies triumph through hard work, determination, and perseverance, as well as disappointment and personal failure. In February 1944, while World War II was still raging, George Orwell wrote, "History is written by the winners." Patton was both a winner and a loser politically as well as personally. Historians may judge him to have been a gifted politician and a great but flawed governor. He always considered himself a commoner, no more and no less. In the end, he was a man comfortable in the time in which he lived. And he was able to move Kentucky forward, despite his personal shortcomings. This is his story in his own words.

Jeffrey S. Suchanek

1

Life in the Coal Mines

My father-in-law, J. C. "Jake" Cooley, didn't want his daughter and grand-daughter to move to Detroit. That was my plan after I graduated from the University of Kentucky in the spring of 1959 with a degree in mechanical engineering. I guess he figured I would get a job with one of the automobile companies. He said, "The coal business is tough, but if you'll come and work for me, I'll teach you the business, and I'll help you start your own company. I think you can make a good living at it." I had no particular job prospects at the time, so I agreed to work for him for $400 a month. My family lived on that $400 a month for nine years, even after I opened my own mining operation. Any profit we made I invested back into the company. That is how I got into the coal business. Jake told me it was a "boom or bust" industry, and it turned out to be more bust than boom. He said you might have one good year out of ten, and he was right. I was in the coal business for twenty years, and I had only two good years, but they were *really good* years!

At the same time, my wife's brother, Nick, had just been discharged from the military and had returned to McDowell to work for his father. After Nick and I spent two years performing manual labor, Jake decided it was time for us to get out on our own. He wanted to treat us equally but realized we each needed our own businesses. He proposed that, with his help, Nick and I would start our own mining operations. We would co-own all the mines fifty-fifty, but each of us would control the company we were person-ally managing. Nick and I stuck to that unwritten policy for twenty years.

Jake got us a lease for about five thousand acres of coal property near Virgie in Pike County, signed a note for $10,000 so we could build a coal processing plant (a tipple), and secured a contract for us to sell three thou-sand tons of coal a month to the new Kentucky Power Plant near Louisa for $3.30 a ton. Our operating margin was 30 cents a ton on the contract, or about $900 a month. I paid myself $400 a month and laborer Gabe New-some $160 a month, so we netted close to $340 a month. There were already ten or twelve small mines operating on the property, and we secured their coal to supply the contract. We sold the excess tonnage on the open market for as little as $3 a ton.

Coal mining was a dangerous business in those days. In the 1960s it was very common to have more than one hundred miners killed in US mine accidents every year. During the 1950s Kentucky averaged sixty-nine coal mine deaths each year, and although the average number of mining deaths declined in the 1960s, there were still too many.

My general work ethic has always been to demonstrate to my employees that I would not ask them to do anything I wouldn't do myself. That included working side by side in a mine or a tipple when I was a coal operator, crawling underneath a county-owned truck to fix a clutch or a brake line when I was Pike County judge/executive, or using a ruler to go line by line looking for excesses in the state budget when I was governor. I wanted to demonstrate to my employees that I wasn't above doing any job: the dirtier and more dangerous it was, the more I insisted on being there to help. I think I have always had a good relationship with my employees.

In underground mining, miners are essentially working in a long hole called a "heading" that has been dug into the side of a mountain; the rest of the mountain sits on top of the coal left on each side of the heading. Roof falls and cave-ins were ever-present dangers. Electrocution was another major hazard, and so was the possibility of being crushed by equipment. Two things are always found in underground mines: water and electrical cables. Electrical equipment sometimes malfunctioned, or another piece of equipment accidentally cut a cable, and someone died by electrocution. People are constantly moving back and forth inside a mine, and machines occupy the same limited space. If man and machine meet in a constricted area, the machine wins every time.

Another unpleasant fact is that underground mines are dark and crowded environments. If you are claustrophobic, underground mining is not for you. In the twenty-first century, mining deaths in Kentucky have dwindled to two or three a year, which is still two or three too many.

In the twenty years I was in the coal business, none of my miners lost their lives, but two people were seriously injured. Lonnie Hampton was trying to unblock a crusher, and he had removed the safety guard to gain access. He slipped, his foot landed between the big flywheel and a smaller driving wheel, and the gears sheared his foot off. Lloyd Elswick was working underground and suffered a serious head injury when a slate roof fell on him and fractured his skull. He lost the sight in one eye as a result. Both men recovered and returned to work.

I had more than a few narrow escapes myself in the mines I operated. One incident involved a roof fall. One way to test the solidity of the roof of a mine shaft is with a hammer. When you hit solid rock with a hammer, you hear a pinging sound. If there is a crack in the rock, it makes a hollow sound. One day I was in the mine working alone—which is *never* a good idea. I was setting timbers to shore up a section of roof that I was pretty sure had an unseen crack in it. Suddenly, the roof began to crack and pop, and I realized it was going to fall. I had supported part of the roof, but I was standing underneath the unsupported section, and the rock was cracking right above me. I had to make a split-second decision: run out of there or get underneath the supported part of the roof, which might not hold. I decided to run for it, and the roof caved in right behind me not half a second later. I would have been killed had I decided to stay where I was.

Most of my narrow escapes had nothing to do with the mine itself but with the machinery we used. There was an outdoor shed near the mine entrance where we worked on equipment and stored batteries. One day I was operating an old front-end loader with a manual transmission to move something into the shed in the loader's bucket. The shed had a low steel beam in it, which the loader barely fit underneath. As I was moving into the shed, the machine got stuck in gear. As I got closer and closer to that steel beam, I didn't have anywhere to escape. For whatever reason, Providence shined on me that day. Somehow, I was able to stop the loader with only inches to spare before that steel beam would have cut me in two.

Probably the dumbest thing I ever did to put my life in danger occurred when we were unloading a roll of new conveyor belt from the back of a truck into the bucket of a front-end loader. The truck and the loader were only about ten inches apart, and somehow or other, the new belt became stuck between them. Well, I squeezed myself between the blade of the loader's bucket and the back of the truck to free it. The problem was that the front-end loader was sitting on a little upgrade behind the truck, and it didn't have any brakes. Sammie Hall, who was operating the loader, prevented it from rolling away by keeping the clutch barely in gear. If he had put just a little more pressure on that clutch, or if the clutch had failed, the blade of the front-end loader would have cut me in two. Despite these incidents, I never worried about the danger I was in. I think very few miners worry about it. I was young and invincible and I thought nothing would ever happen to me!

By 1969, I had gotten away from most of the manual labor of coal mining and had become more of a manager, running the business end of my operation. I knew that for coal mining to become a safer occupation, it would require government-mandated safety improvements. Toward that end, I testified in 1969 at a congressional hearing in Washington at the invitation of the National Independent Coal Operators Association (NICOA).

NICOA opposed some but not all of the provisions of the proposed federal Coal Mine Health and Safety Act of 1969, which came on the heels of the Farmington, West Virginia, mine explosion that killed seventy-eight miners on November 20, 1968. I guess the small coal operators thought that since I had a college degree, I would be articulate enough to state their position in language members of Congress could understand. I was nervous about testifying, and when it was over, I thought I had probably made a fool of myself. However, I must have done all right because when I got back to Pikeville, Jerry Sander, a reporter for WSAZ-TV in Huntington, West Virginia, interviewed me about my experience on Capitol Hill. (Sander would later work for many years at a television station in Lexington.) That trip was my first time in Washington and my first time flying in a commercial airliner.

Throughout the 1970s, I spent a lot of time on Capitol Hill testifying on behalf of NICOA. The federal Mine Safety and Health Administration was responsible for writing regulations to implement the new mining laws passed by Congress, and it seemed like the agency held hearings every month. That was when I learned all about federal regulations and the *Federal Register*. It was a real education for me.

In response to the Scotia mine disaster that killed twenty-six miners in Letcher County on March 9, 1976, Governor Julian Carroll created a fifteen-member Deep Mine Safety Commission to investigate what had happened and ensure that it never happened again. I had worked for Carroll's gubernatorial campaign and he knew I was a coal operator, so he appointed me to the commission. We held multiple hearings and analyzed every coal mining death in Kentucky in the past two years, including the Scotia disaster. We discovered that in every case, somebody had violated a law that got a miner killed. In many cases, a careless miner himself was the cause. Charlie Head, who represented the United Mine Workers of America (UMWA), and I insisted that one of the commission's main recommendations should be an emphasis on safety training. We persuaded the Kentucky General Assembly to pass legislation that resulted in the hiring of mine safety analysts who established training programs at each mine and ensured that safety standards were enforced. I testified before Congress the next year when it passed the federal Surface Mining Control and Reclamation Act of 1977, which had a dramatic impact on coal operators.

I was also involved in several labor disputes during my twenty years in the coal industry. By 1960, the financial situation of the small coal operators in eastern Kentucky had become an issue. The UMWA's national contract set union wages at $3 or $4 an hour. This was far above the federal minimum wage of $1 an hour, which was what most of the small, locally owned mines were paying. The UMWA had established a welfare fund that provided health insurance and retirement benefits for coal miners who were union members. Every union coal operator was supposed to contribute 40 cents to that fund for every ton of coal their mines produced. The UMWA built hospitals in McDowell, Pikeville, South Williamson, Whitesburg, and West Liberty, Kentucky, as well as several others in Virginia and West Virginia, where it had members.

By the mid-1950s, many laid-off coal miners had started their own truck mining operations. Most of them had signed the UMWA contract, but they paid the miners the federal minimum wage or less, and they weren't contributing the full 40 cents a ton to the UMWA welfare fund. Some of these small mine operators started shaving their contributions to 20 cents a ton by reporting only half the coal they mined. The union didn't do anything about it. It knew that if it forced these small operators to pay the full amount, they would have to shut down their mining operations. Many of these miners were older men, and they didn't want to go to Detroit, Columbus, or Cincinnati to find work, so they felt like they had no choice but to work for less money. The miners told the UMWA, "Hell, you can't get me union wages, so I'll just work for what I can get." By 1962, many of these small mines had stopped making payments to the union's welfare fund altogether. However, the miners were still union members and had welfare cards that entitled them to free health care at UMWA hospitals and a pension. There were hundreds of these little contract truck mines all over eastern Kentucky, and eventually the UMWA got tired of providing hospital benefits for miners who weren't paying their fair share into the welfare fund. In 1962 the UMWA canceled their welfare cards.

After the UMWA canceled the miners' welfare cards, the mine operators in Pike County and several other counties said, "Well, we'll just cancel the whole union contract." The miners didn't want to do that, so they united and organized an area-wide strike against the coal companies. These bands of roving pickets, many of whom worked for larger companies and still had their welfare cards, traveled the coalfields and forced working miners to go home. However, after a couple of weeks, most of the coal operators and miners in Pike and some other counties said, "To hell with it. We're going back to work."

The Turner Elkhorn Coal Company was dominant in Floyd County. It loaned miners money and equipment that allowed them to open small truck mines. Turner Elkhorn built about a dozen railhead tipples around the county to handle the contract coal produced by these small mining operations. The company wanted to stay in the union because it was selling coal to steel companies. The steel companies were unionized, and their union contracts required them to buy coal only from unionized mines. The UMWA demanded that the small mine operators honor the 40 cents a ton contribution to the welfare fund. Turner Elkhorn wouldn't agree to guarantee the payments, but it also wouldn't cancel the union contract. Roving pickets continued the strike in Floyd County for two or three months, and they drove to other counties to try to stop coal production there. The striking miners sent daily patrols to each mine to make sure no one was working. When the pickets showed up, the mine operator would close the mine and send his miners home. However, the mine would open the next day, and the miners would come back to work. To prevent that from happening, the pickets would blow up an offending mine's coal hopper every week or so. It got so bad that some coal operators employed armed guards to protect their tipples.

On the first day of the strike, Walker Moore and I were loading a truck at Jake's equipment yard in McDowell in Floyd County. Jake's mine was a UMWA mine. I was standing on the back of the truck when I saw a large caravan of cars coming down the road. They came to a stop when they got to where we were, and about two hundred men piled out of those cars. They were very angry and threatened to kill us if we didn't stop working. Their livelihood was at stake, and they were desperate. After a standoff that probably lasted five minutes or less but seemed like an hour at the time, we said, "Okay, we'll quit," and we got in the truck and left. We went back to work the next day but in a less visible location.

I was still living in Floyd County and drove to Pike County almost every day to work at the tipple Nick and I operated there. The house where my wife and I lived with our children was very close to the main road. At night, some of these striking miners would drive up and down the road, shoot their guns in the air, and yell things at our house to disrupt our sleep and let me know they were watching me. Anticipating that there might be some real violence against my father-in-law and myself, I sent Carol and the children to stay at Jake's house, which was fairly secluded, located up a little knoll about a thousand feet away. I stayed at my own house to guard it. One night when the striking miners came down the road and shot into the air, I got mad, grabbed my shotgun, stood on my front porch, and shot into the air until the gun's magazine was empty. I guess the men in the car didn't know whether I was shooting at them or not, so they took off as fast as they could. I figured I had just become a marked man.

We learned that some of the mine operators had armed themselves with military surplus M-1 carbines, a small World War II semiautomatic rifle that was easy to handle and had fifteen- and thirty-round magazines. Nick decided we needed a few of these guns for ourselves, so he drove to a gun store in Lexington, but it was sold out of M-1s. However, the owner gave Nick the name of a gun store in Chicago that stocked them. He drove to Chicago and bought three M-1s—one for himself, one for Jake, and one for me. The salesclerk asked Nick, "What the hell is going on? We must have sold fifty of these things to people from eastern Kentucky!" Floyd County had become an armed camp.

I was still traveling to the tipple at Virgie three or four days a week to supervise the operation there. I purposely drove three different routes, and I always carried a .38-caliber revolver, a shotgun, and the M-1 carbine in the car with me during the strike. However, I don't recall being afraid. I guess I was too young to be scared. At twenty-five years old, I was itching for a fight. Fortunately, as you get older, you get a little smarter. I figured the roving pickets probably knew what routes I took to get to Virgie and would be waiting for me. I decided I wasn't going to let them beat the hell out of me. If they stopped me somewhere on the road, I planned to run into the hills and start shooting. This cat-and-mouse game between the strikers and me went on for six or seven weeks, but they never did catch me.

Turner Elkhorn management finally decided it had to go back to work. The company had a mine at Garth Hollow in Floyd County, about halfway between McDowell and Martin, and the owners said, "Okay, Monday, we're going to work." The governor had sent a heavy contingent of state police to Floyd County to try to keep the powder keg from blowing up. Turner Elkhorn managers informed the state police what they intended to do, and the police promised to be there because they knew a large number of striking miners would show up too.

Between five and six o'clock in the morning, the roving pickets started to gather, and by the time the mine opened, there were two hundred to three hundred of them. Turner Elkhorn had men with rifles on the hill overlooking the mine, positioned behind the leafless trees. The pickets knew they were up there. The company had erected a fence about two hundred feet up the hollow in front of the mine, and management had warned the state police, "Don't let the pickets cross that fence line because we're not going to allow it." It was a very tense situation. The police cleared a path through the pickets so the miners could get to work and the trucks could haul the mined coal. There was a lot of noise and a few rocks were thrown, but no other physical violence. I don't remember anyone being killed during that strike.

Opening that mine broke the strike, and Turner Elkhorn negotiated a "sweetheart" deal with the UMWA. The company would contribute to the welfare fund on only 50 percent of the tonnage mined. In return, the UMWA agreed to let the miners keep their welfare cards. Floyd County remained a UMWA stronghold for several years afterward. My father-in-law's Sizemore Mining Company at McDowell was a signatory to the UMWA contact. He negotiated the same deal as Turner Elkhorn but created a new company called the New Circle Coal Company. That deal lasted for several years.

Every three years during the 1960s, the UMWA contract would come up for renegotiation, there would usually be a nationwide strike, and the mines in Floyd County would shut down. The roving pickets would travel to the other nonunion mines in coal-producing counties and try to shut them down. The idea was that if they shut down every mine, the coal companies would be pressured to settle the strike on terms favorable to the miners' union. Sometimes we shut down our mines in Pike County for a week, but then my miners would tell me, "We've got bills to pay. We need to go back to work. We aren't going to get anything out of the strike anyhow! They're not going to give us our welfare benefit cards back." I provided hospitalization benefits for my workers, which cost me about $24 a month, but no retirement benefits at the time. Later on, when the market improved, we did establish a retirement plan for our employees. Today, there are no UMWA mines in Floyd County or Pike County and very few in eastern Kentucky. The UMWA decided to sell the five hospitals supported by the welfare fund in eastern Kentucky on July 1, 1963. That accelerated the process of small mines in the region going nonunion.

During one of the strikes, several picketing miners blocked the entrance to our Kentucky Elkhorn mine near Virgie in Pike County. Sheriff Bill Deskins, a coal operator himself, and some of his deputies showed up to make sure no trouble erupted. One evening as I was leaving the mine in my pickup truck, Sheriff Deskins and his deputies were trying to get the pickets to move back so I could get through. I was driving very slowly, inching my way through the crowd, when one of them thumped the fender of my truck with his hand and began to hobble around on one leg shouting, "He hit me! He hit me!" This got all the pickets stirred up. Sheriff Deskins, thinking all hell was going to break loose, told me to get into his marked car, which I did, and we drove away. Some of the pickets got in their vehicles and followed us to the town of Virgie, where Deskins drove us to the home of one of the county magistrates, Clarence "Coon" Newsome. Magistrates held court at that time and could issue warrants and impose fines for minor violations. Looking very serious, the magistrate told the pickets that he would file a complaint against me and see that justice was done. That satisfied the pickets, and they got back in their cars and left. Most of them were from out of the county and didn't know that Coon was a friend of mine and had no intention of following through with that complaint. After the pickets drove away, we had a nice laugh and Coon told me not to give it another thought. However, for years afterward those miners claimed I had "run over" one of their pickets with my pickup truck. This was patently untrue, but it became part of eastern Kentucky folklore.

In 1972 Nick and I bought a mine near Pikeville that we named the Chaparral Coal Corporation, and I managed it. It was a signatory to a contract with the Southern Labor Union, a UMWA competitor. The UMWA would have preferred a mine to be nonunion than Southern Labor Union. I increased production there, and we were shipping a fair amount of coal by the time the 1973 Arab oil embargo occurred. We had a contract to sell coal for $9 a ton. Then the market price shot through the roof at $40 a ton, and it later went as high as $55 a ton. Eastern Kentucky resembled California during the gold rush. Everybody wanted to mine coal, legally and illegally. People were stealing bulldozers and mining equipment from all over the Midwest and bringing it back to Kentucky. I remember going to see my doctor for something or other, and all he wanted to talk about was getting into the coal business.

Some people in eastern Kentucky were making millions of dollars, and financiers from New York bought many of these companies for millions more, thinking, "Well, if that dumb hillbilly can make that kind of money, I can certainly do better!" The McCoy Elkhorn Coal Company sold for more than $40 million, and Don Johnson, a coal operator from Elkhorn City, sold a few of his companies for more than that. Everybody was making money hand over fist. By 1975, Nick and I were making a lot of money too. We had invested $10 million, much of it borrowed, in new equipment. I was paying myself a salary of about $10,000 a month, and so was Nick. We were doing so well financially that we started a bonus program for our employees. We gave them end-of-the-month bonuses that were bigger than their paychecks. One man actually cried when he saw the amount of his bonus check. One year we made so much money that I bought all the miners' wives small diamond rings! We all prospered in the 1970s. Times were good.

Despite my financial success, I tried to stay true to my upbringing. I never bought expensive clothes. I had a nice car, but nothing extravagant. In the 1970s I bought a small boat for water skiing on Dewey Lake. However, I always considered myself a middle-class commoner. As far as I am concerned, I was born a commoner, I was raised a commoner, I have lived

When I was at the coal mine, I worked alongside my employees. I never asked them to do something I wouldn't do myself. (Author's collection)

like a commoner, and I will be buried a commoner. I have had a few elite jobs during my lifetime, but I never considered myself an elitist or better than anyone else. I'm just Paul Patton, an ordinary person.

My personal life has not always been as successful as my business career. In 1976 Carol and I divorced. We had married too young, and although we tried to make our marriage work, in the end, we wanted different things. That happens to many couples. In 1977 I married Judi Conway Johnson, whom I had known since college, and we combined our families. We each had two children from our previous marriages: my Nicki and Chris, and her Bambi and Jan.

In 1978 Nick and I decided to sell Chaparral Coal, in which I had a 40 percent interest. We received $7.5 million up front, with a continuing royalty of 3 percent of the sale price of all the coal mined from the property, guaranteed to be $500,000 a year for twenty years. I felt that was more than enough to live comfortably for the rest of my life. However, I was only forty-one years old, and after working twelve to fourteen hours a day, six days a week, for nearly twenty years, I wasn't ready to retire. I didn't envision myself golfing every day or watching television all day long, so I began to look for another challenge.

2

My Entrance into Politics

One day in late December 1993, when I was lieutenant governor, my staff and I were driving to Memphis to watch the University of Louisville football team play in the Liberty Bowl against Michigan State University. When we reached the end of the Bluegrass Parkway at Elizabethtown and began to merge onto I-65 South, one of them, Bill Beam, innocently asked me how I got involved in politics. By the time I stopped talking, we were on the outskirts of Memphis, and Bill said, "Boy! I'm never going to ask him *that* question again!" Well, it *is* a long story.

When I was a fledgling coal operator, I worked long days and had a wife and young children, so I didn't have time to get involved in politics. However, beginning in 1969, I started to make good money in the coal business, and I had more free time. That was when I got interested and involved in politics. Once I had accumulated a substantial amount of money, I also attracted the attention of politicians who were looking for people to contribute to their campaigns and raise additional money for them.

The first election I was actively involved in was the 1971 Democratic primary for governor of Kentucky. Lieutenant Governor Wendell H. Ford from Owensboro was running in the primary against former governor Bert T. Combs, who hailed from Prestonsburg. At the same time, Kelsey Friend Sr., an attorney in Pikeville who specialized in black lung cases, was running for the state senate against incumbent F. M. Burke, a prominent coal operator and Pikeville attorney. I supported Combs in the gubernatorial primary and contributed $1,000 to his campaign. I didn't know Friend at that time, so I supported Burke for state senator. As it turned out, both Combs and Burke lost. Even though I had supported his opponent, Friend apparently recognized me as someone who could be helpful to him and the Democratic ticket in the fall election. He invited me to play poker with him and some of his friends on Monday evenings in Pikeville, and our friendship grew. Our relationship might seem a little odd, since we were sometimes on opposite sides in the courtroom (him representing coal miners in lawsuits against my coal mines). Kelsey used to say that he would take my money at the poker table on Monday night and then sue me in court on Tuesday and take more of my money. However, our professional lives never interfered with our friendship.

In the summer of 1971 Kelsey asked me to raise money for Ford's fall campaign from among the small coal operators in eastern Kentucky, and I did. After he took office, Governor Ford arranged for me to be elected as a delegate to the 1972 Democratic National Convention in Miami. That really got me interested in politics.

My first foray into the legislative process occurred in 1972. During his campaign, Governor Ford had pledged to remove the sales tax on food. This would create a $40 million shortfall in the state budget, so Ford proposed a 5 percent severance tax on coal to make up the difference. At Ford's request, two University of Kentucky professors studied the tax's effect on coal production in eastern and western Kentucky. The state legislature engaged these same two professors to study the effect of overweight coal trucks on Kentucky's highways and roads in the two regions. The two studies came up with different conclusions. The first study found that because there was a fundamental difference between the types of coal produced in each region, the sale price of the coal should determine the amount of the severance tax, not the tons of coal produced. The second study found that there was fundamentally *no* difference between the coal in eastern and western Kentucky, and because overweight trucks were not transporting coal on the public roads in western Kentucky, there was no reason to allow overweight trucks in eastern Kentucky. I was more knowledgeable about this issue than most state legislators, who were just waiting for Governor Ford to tell them what to do. I had actually read the two reports and knew what they said.

During the committee hearing on the coal severance tax, I brought the discrepancies to the attention of Senator Friend, who got Senator Gibson Downing, a lawyer from Fayette County and one of the ablest legislators in the General Assembly, to push the issue. Downing interrogated the two professors about the differences in their conclusions, and he led the charge against the 5 percent coal severance tax. Governor Ford was forced to scale back the tax from 5 percent to 4 percent to get enough votes to pass the bill. That was my first attempt to influence legislation, and it pleased me that I had been at least partially successful.

Kelsey bought a house in Frankfort, and when the legislature was in session I would go to Frankfort and stay at Kelsey's. I introduced myself to other state legislators and mingled with them socially, just for fun. Over the remainder of the 1970s, I continued to travel to Frankfort to learn how the legislature worked. I became acquainted with almost all the legislators, both Democrats and Republicans. I also began to attend the pre–legislative session conferences held by the Democrats at Kentucky Dam Village in western Kentucky in late November. There, they elected leaders and discussed possible legislation prior to the start of the regular legislative sessions in January of even-numbered years.

I raised money for Julian Carroll's gubernatorial campaign in 1975, during which an article on political fund-raising in eastern Kentucky referred to me as a "neophyte." I didn't know what a neophyte was, but I knew it wasn't complimentary. That made me mad, but there was little I could about it. Once elected, one of Governor Carroll's initiatives was to propose an increase in the coal severance tax from 4 to 4½ percent and to extend that tax to the cost of hauling and preparing coal. That would amount to an almost 50 percent increase in the tax. Industry leaders promised to fight it as hard as they could. Because of my relationship with Senator Friend and the Carroll administration, I knew that the governor's proposal also included five new programs that would help the coal industry and the coal-producing regions of the state.

The coal operators from Pike County set up a meeting with Governor Carroll to voice their complaints. They met for lunch at the Frankfort Country Club beforehand to discuss their strategy. I was there, and I advised the group to be cautious because Carroll's proposal was not all bad. Despite my warning, they vowed to fight the governor's plan.

When we arrived at the governor's mansion, Carroll greeted us courteously and offered us drinks and snacks. Then he immediately began his presentation: "Now, guys, I'm going to pass my tax, and there's nothing you can do about it! But let me tell you what I'm going to do with the money." He had a green blackboard and some yellow chalk, and he listed his tax proposals and how much money they would generate. I think it amounted to something like $50 million. Then he listed his programs, which totaled considerably more than the new severance tax revenue. Because the market for coal was so good, it was clear that his tax proposal was not going to be a real problem for the industry.

At the end of Governor Carroll's presentation, F. M. Burke stood up and, in his most elegant voice (he was one of the best old-time orators in Kentucky), said, "Governor, that's the best proposal for the coal industry and our people that I have ever seen, and I move that we endorse it!" Bob Holcomb, president of the local coal association, stood up and said, "I second that motion!" Everyone present expressed their approval. When the measure came up for consideration in the legislative committee, no one from our part of the coal industry opposed it.

During Carroll's governorship, I became well acquainted with most members of his administration, and I learned how the state government really worked. I had the time and the money to devote to politics, and it was like a form of entertainment to me.

Everyone knew that Terry McBrayer would be Carroll's handpicked candidate to succeed him in the 1979 gubernatorial election. I supported Terry because Governor Carroll did and because McBrayer was from my part of the state—Greenup County in eastern Kentucky. Carroll and his brain trust had a plan to control the governor's office for the next twenty years: McBrayer would be Carroll's successor, Bill Cox would follow McBrayer, Jackson White would follow Cox, and Bill Curlin would follow White. McBrayer had been secretary of the Commerce Cabinet for about two years before leaving the Carroll administration to organize his own gubernatorial campaign. Cox had been Carroll's chief adviser in the governor's office, and White had been Carroll's cabinet secretary. It was supposed to be a twenty-year reign for the Carroll wing of the Kentucky Democratic Party.

State auditor George Atkins, who had made Carroll's life miserable during his term in the auditor's office, was also a candidate for governor. Melvin Wilson, a wealthy eastern Kentucky insurance adjuster, was supporting Atkins and raising a lot of money for him from the coal industry. Congressman Carroll Hubbard, who represented Kentucky's First Congressional District in Washington, wanted to run for governor, but first he had to run for reelection to Congress. Hubbard wasn't a member of the Carroll wing of the party, so to thwart his candidacy for governor in 1979, Carroll had the 1978 legislature pass the "Carroll Hubbard ripper bill," which stated that a candidate could not spend money raised to seek election to one office on a campaign for a different office. This prevented Hubbard from building up his congressional campaign war chest to use in his gubernatorial campaign, and he couldn't raise money to run for governor while he was also running for Congress.

In September Wayne Rutherford, the Pike County judge/executive and Hubbard's contact person there, telephoned me and said, "Paul, Carroll Hubbard wants to talk to you about the possibility of you running for governor. He said that if the Democrats want to hold on to the governor's office, they have to come up with a new face. The Julian Carroll bunch is crooked, and if we don't get a new face to run who can self-fund the race, we'll lose the gubernatorial election. Congressman Hubbard wants to talk to you about it." I told him I would have to think about it.

Initially, I didn't take the idea seriously and didn't call Rutherford back. However, he phoned again about a week later and said, "Paul, Congressman

Hubbard wants to talk to you this weekend in Louisville." I was flattered, of course: a US congressman wanted to meet with me, a rinky-dink coal operator, about becoming a candidate for the office of governor of the commonwealth of Kentucky! That prospect was good for my ego, so Judi and I drove to the Galt House in Louisville that weekend and met with Hubbard and a couple of his assistants. He reiterated what Rutherford had told me about the Democrats needing a fresh face to run for governor, free from the dark cloud hanging over Carroll, his administration, and his handpicked candidate McBrayer. Hubbard said, "Listen, Paul. Julian may be *in jail* by the time the election gets here. They might *all* be in jail, which will destroy the Democratic Party in the gubernatorial election unless we find someone fresh and new to run and raise the money it will take. I'll even be your campaign manager if you run for governor!"

Hubbard had come to our meeting prepared. He and his assistants had my campaign all planned out, including campaign posters personally selected by Hubbard. He said, "The only thing I'm asking is for you to commit to contribute $1 million to the campaign, and in four years, you support *me* for governor!" (This was fourteen years before the state legislature passed the gubernatorial campaign financing bill and voters approved an amendment to the Kentucky Constitution to allow governors to succeed themselves in office.) Then he asked, "What do you think?"

I responded, "Whoa! I'm flattered, but I'm going to have to think about it."

"Well," he said, "I have to have an answer soon. Can you give me an answer by next weekend?"

Thinking out loud, I said, "I have to go back to Pikeville and talk to Kelsey Friend and some other people about it. On Thursday I have to go to western Kentucky, and then I have to attend a Pikeville College board meeting on Saturday."

He said, "Oh, you'll be in western Kentucky on Thursday? Can you come down a day early and meet with some of my friends?"

"Well, yes, I guess I can do that," I agreed. So we planned for me to meet with some of his supporters at the Ramada Inn in Madisonville on Wednesday.

On Tuesday, on my way to Madisonville, I was driving on the Kentucky Parkway when the news came on the radio. As I approached the Beaver Dam rest stop, I heard the news anchor say, "A millionaire coal operator from Pike County, Paul Patton, is conducting a tour of western Kentucky while he considers making a run for governor." I immediately pulled off the parkway, found a pay phone, and called Hubbard's office. When I got him on the phone

I said, "Congressman, I thought my meeting with your friends was supposed to be confidential. This is embarrassing. It's all over the radio!" He said, "Is it? Well, I didn't tell the press. I guess one of my friends must have leaked it."

Eddie Ford, father of former University of Kentucky basketball player Travis Ford, was Carroll Hubbard's field representative. He met me at the Ramada Inn in Madisonville and we had dinner together. He told me that he had set up appointments for me to meet with Hubbard's supporters throughout the next day. Starting at eight o'clock the following morning, I met with different county delegations, each consisting of between five and eight people, every hour on the hour for nine hours. By lunchtime, I had memorized my rationale for running pretty well, and I thought I was doing a good job: "Julian Carroll and his gang are crooks. They'll all be in jail by Election Day. The Democratic Party needs a fresh face to avoid being humiliated in the election, and I'm out here to see what you think about my possible candidacy."

At noon, the door opened and Eddie Ford came into the room. "Paul," he said, "the television reporters are here with their cameras, and they want to come in and interview you." The television reporters were on Eddie's heels and already in the room, so I didn't have much choice but to agree. With the cameras rolling, I gave the reporters the same pitch I had been giving Hubbard's friends all morning, but I was concerned about how quickly everything was happening.

After the final meeting with the last delegation of Hubbard's supporters, I called Wendell Ford—now a US senator—in Washington, DC. "Senator, what would you say if an anonymous, articulate young coal operator from eastern Kentucky was willing to put a million dollars in a race for governor and would have Carroll Hubbard as his campaign manager?" I knew Ford didn't like Hubbard. In fact, Ford had made sure that his hometown of Owensboro was not in Hubbard's First Congressional District. Ford didn't want Hubbard to be *his* representative in Congress!

After a long pause, Ford said, "Well, I would suspect that this anonymous, articulate young coal operator from eastern Kentucky was being made to look like a fool by Carroll Hubbard."

I said, "I'm beginning to suspect you're right."

Ford said, "Let me call you back."

Twenty or thirty minutes later, he called me back and said, "I want you to drive to Henderson and meet with Shirley Prichett, Charlie Pryor, and J. R. Miller. They'll explain what's happening." I drove up to Henderson and met with those three people, who were influential, important political gurus in the Kentucky Democratic Party. In fact, they were Wendell Ford's political brain trust. They explained that George Atkins was making a lot of headway with the coal operators in eastern Kentucky—the very people Hubbard needed on his side if he hoped to win the next gubernatorial election—so Hubbard was trying to slow down Atkins's momentum. Hubbard couldn't get personally involved in the governor's race until after he was reelected to Congress in November. Ford's people told me, "What will happen after the election is, Hubbard will say, 'Paul, you're just not catching fire in this race, so *I'll* run this time and you help me raise the money for the race. I'll help *you* the next time.'" They made it clear that Hubbard was playing me. I thanked them and left the meeting.

As I drove back to Madisonville on the Pennyrile Parkway, I felt angrier and angrier. The madder I got, the faster I drove. I zipped right past the Madisonville exit, and the next thing I knew, I was almost in Tennessee! I turned around and headed back to Madisonville. My interview with the television reporters made the six and eleven o'clock news throughout Kentucky on Wednesday evening, and my interest in running for governor made headlines in some of the state's major newspapers on Thursday. My potential gubernatorial candidacy was big statewide news on four consecutive days, which surprised me.

I felt like I needed to mend some fences, and I decided to start with Governor Carroll. After my Thursday meetings were over, I called him and said, "Governor, I'm perturbed about this development. I need to talk to you." He invited me to stop by the governor's mansion on my way home. After I explained that I actually supported McBrayer's candidacy and how this all came about, the governor said, "Well, I'll tell you what we'll do. We'll just set up Mr. Carroll Hubbard." He then drafted a letter I had supposedly written to a friend explaining how Hubbard had used me and tried to take advantage of me, but with the recipient's name blacked out. Then he had one of his staff members leak the letter to the press.

On Friday, I was the subject of another newspaper headline: "Patton Backs out of Race for Governor." Hubbard had used me as a political pawn, and I didn't like it. However, my brief four-day run for governor had made me something of a statewide figure. In retrospect, and considering how it all turned out, that series of events actually led to me eventually becoming governor.

A few weeks later, Governor Carroll asked me to be one of the cochairs of Terry McBrayer's gubernatorial campaign. Charlotte Baldwin, the mayor of Madisonville, and Bobby Richardson from Glasgow, Carroll's hand-picked majority floor leader in the Kentucky House of Representatives, were the other cochairs.

McBrayer's campaign was going well until John Y. Brown Jr. suddenly entered the race just sixty days before the primary, not long after marrying former Miss America and CBS sportscaster Phyllis George. Brown won the primary election, and I started to travel with him as he campaigned in eastern Kentucky. Brown knew I had some money after selling my coal company and was looking for something to do, since I no longer had a real job. He was looking for businesspeople who wouldn't abuse the public's trust to make money. Brown didn't have a serious challenger from the Republican Party, so his election was assured. He said he wanted me to have a role in his administration and asked what position I would consider. I mentioned secretary of transportation, but Brown said he had already promised that job to Bill Cox from Madisonville in western Kentucky. I acknowledged that Bill was better qualified (he had been the federal highway administrator), but transportation secretary was the only job that could persuade me to move my family to Frankfort. Brown revisited the subject several times, and I always gave him the same answer. After the election, Brown's assistant Larry Townsend called and asked if I was still interested in the position of secretary of transportation. I said yes, and he invited me to come to Louisville and discuss it with Brown. When I got there, Brown said, "Well, Patton, what can we work out?" I replied that I was still interested in being secretary of transportation, and he replied that he still intended to appoint Bill Cox to that position. About that time, Cox called. "Bill," Brown said, "do you know Paul Patton?" He must have said yes, because Brown then explained the situation to Cox and suggested that he and I meet to see if we could work something out. At that meeting, Bill explained that he expected to be very involved in helping Brown run the governor's office and would be spending a lot of time over there. If I accepted the position of deputy secretary of transportation, I would be running the cabinet most of the time, as Cox was mainly interested in making decisions about western Kentucky. I decided to take the job, and a press conference was held to make the announcement.

Then, just a few days before the inauguration, Cox got mad about something and decided not to take any position in the Brown administration. My friends and I began an intensive lobbying campaign to get me the job, but Brown decided to give it to another close friend of his. Frank Metts was a wealthy real estate developer from Louisville who had very little experience in road maintenance or construction, and he realized that as deputy secretary I could cover a lot of his weaknesses. I wasn't hung up on titles. I just wanted to be in a position to influence road issues in eastern Kentucky, so I agreed to stay and work under Metts.

As it turned out, Brown took office just as the national economy entered a deep recession, and he faced a revenue shortfall. To shore up the state budget, he decided to rescind Governor Carroll's programs that used the coal severance tax revenue to improve roads in the coal-producing regions of the state, as well as other projects. I vehemently disagreed with this decision, so I resigned in March 1980.

After I resigned, I needed something to do. Kelsey Friend made a suggestion: "Now, Chief [which is a term politicians use so they don't have to remember everybody's name], why don't you stay here in Pike County and run for county judge/executive? You can build yourself a political base, get experience running part of the government on a smaller scale, and establish a record before you ask the people of Kentucky to elect you governor and let you run the entire state." I took Kelsey's advice and decided to run against incumbent Pike County judge/executive Wayne Rutherford, the person who got me involved with Hubbard's scheme. Kelsey had no way of knowing whether I would ever be governor, but he figured I would spend enough money to beat Rutherford, and that's what he wanted. Wayne was the leader of the other faction of the Democratic Party in Pike County and Kelsey's political rival.

Initially, I didn't know what my wife's reaction would be to the idea of me running for public office. When I brought up the possibility of running for county judge/executive (hereafter referred to as county judge, for simplicity's sake), I also outlined my overall plan: I would run for county judge in Pike County in 1981, and if I won, I would run for reelection in 1985. Then I would run for lieutenant governor in 1987, and if I won, I would run for governor in 1991. After hearing my plan, Judi said, "Then that's what we'll do!" I knew this scenario was a long shot, but I think it's healthy to have lofty goals. If you attain all your goals, maybe you didn't set your sights high enough.

If the people of Pike County elected me county judge, I was determined to do a good job, and if that was all I achieved, I wanted to be proud of it. If I ended up elected to a higher public office, that would be icing on the cake. Throughout my life, whenever I have decided to do something, I've always been all in, and my run for county judge in 1981 was no exception. I hired a national pollster, Peter D. Hart. Tommy Preston and Bill Wester from Lexington, two of Wendell Ford's top lieutenants, ran my campaign.

I traveled all over Pike County almost every day from April 1980 until the primary in May 1981, meeting people and trying to convince them to vote for me. In August, when campaigning began in earnest, I received a list of voters that included twenty-five thousand registered Democrats in

Pike County. By Election Day, we had registered an additional nine thousand Democrats. I think a lot of Republicans switched parties that year.

I won the race, and during my tenure as county judge, I stayed in close contact with the people of Pike County. I never established a political organization there because I wasn't interested in building one. I was interested in doing a good job and eventually convincing the people of Kentucky to elect me as their governor.

One of the lessons I learned as county judge was to give other people credit. They will appreciate it. You don't always have to take the credit yourself and say, "*I* got that done." A good example was my successful effort to get a major road improvement in Pike County *before* I became county judge. I took a group of leaders from the Peter Creek area of Pike County to meet with Frank Metts, secretary of the Transportation Cabinet. Even though I had quit as Frank's deputy, there were no ill feelings, and I maintained a good relationship with both him and Governor Brown. Frank had agreed to improve the road even before the meeting, but I gave all the credit to the Peter Creek people who accompanied me. I discovered this was just good politics.

I spent $250,000 on my 1981 campaign for county judge, a race that normally cost a candidate $20,000 to $30,000. Rutherford, my opponent, received more votes than in any of his three previous campaigns for county judge, but I still beat him two to one. When the election results came in, Kelsey told me, "Chief, we may have oversold you just a little bit!"

Not long after the November election and before I took the oath of office as county judge, I had a telephone conversation with Frank Metts about a situation in Pike County I wanted the state's help on. At the end of the conversation, he said, "Paul, you need to talk to the governor about this. Here's his telephone number, and you should call him now." It was a little after six o'clock in the evening, but I called the number anyway, and I was surprised when Governor Brown answered himself. It must have been his private number upstairs at the governor's mansion. I said, "Governor, this is Paul Patton. What are you doing?" This was a dumb thing to say, and I hate it when people ask *me* that. However, Brown was unfazed and replied, "You know, I was just sitting here thinking about appointing either you or Dale Sykes as chairman of the Kentucky Democratic Party." I chuckled and then steered the conversation to the project I had called him about. Suddenly he said, "Paul, wait! Phyllis is coming on television. Let me call you back." He hung up, and since I had already gotten what I wanted, I really didn't expect him to call me back.

At about two o'clock in the morning, my telephone rang and it was Governor Brown. He said, "Paul, Dale has more experience than you, so I'm going to appoint him chairman, but I want you to be the vice chairman." I sleepily agreed because I knew Sykes *was* more qualified. He had been a member of the Democratic National Committee and President Jimmy Carter's contact person in Kentucky. And as a newly elected county judge who would need the governor's help down the road, I wasn't going to tell him no. Brown said, "Come to Frankfort tomorrow. The Democratic Party's executive committee is meeting at two o'clock, and I'll announce the appointments then." Fortunately, I had planned to drive to Frankfort anyway for another meeting I had scheduled, so I said I'd be there.

I walked into Kentucky Democratic Party headquarters at 1:30 in the afternoon, and the outgoing party chairman, Tracy Farmer, said, "You know what the deal is, don't you?"

I replied, "Yes. The governor is going to make Dale Sykes chairman and me vice chairman."

He said, "No, no, no! That is *not* the deal! He's going to appoint *his dad* chairman and appoint you the vice chairman, but he will expect *you* to run the party. He wants to let his dad have the prestige of being the chair of the party while you do all the actual work. This is a *big* mistake. The press will crucify him, but I can't talk him out of it."

At that moment, Brown called Farmer to say that he would be late. Tracy pleaded, "Governor, let me ask you one more time, don't do this. The press is going to crucify you, your father, and the party. Your dad is already walking around the building introducing himself to the staff, telling them that he is going to be the new chair. The executive committee is waiting! The press is waiting!" Farmer listened for a couple of seconds as Brown replied, and then Tracy looked at me and said, "Here. He wants to talk to you."

He handed me the telephone and Brown said, "Paul, why don't you be the chairman?" I was a newly elected county judge! What was I going to say? I wanted to get into state politics, and I would have done anything to stay on good terms with the governor, so I accepted right then and there.

After the meeting was over, Brown's top aide Larry Townsend sidled up to me and said, "By the way, Skipper Martin will be your executive director." The executive director was a paid position at party headquarters, whereas I was a nonpaid figurehead. I didn't know Martin, and Townsend offered to arrange a meeting. Andrew "Skipper" Martin had served in Todd Hollenbeck's administration in Jefferson County in the 1970s, and he was the commissioner of local government in the Brown administration. At that particular moment, he was attending a meeting of the Appalachian Regional Commission in Washington, DC. No one had bothered to tell

I campaigned in the same clothes I wore as a coal operator. (Author's collection)

The race for reelection as county judge in 1985 required hard work and a more aggressive theme. (Author's collection)

Skipper that he had a new job. That evening when he called his wife, Hanna, she demanded to know why he had changed jobs without telling her. "What are you talking about?" Skipper asked. She was the first to inform him, "It's all over the news. You are going to be the new executive director of the Kentucky Democratic Party."

When Skipper got back to Louisville, he and I met at the Waffle House on Hurstbourne Lane and got acquainted. It soon became evident to me that Skipper knew ten times more about Kentucky politics than I did. But neither of us had any idea that our nascent association would eventually take us both to the governor's office.

Given the party's dire financial straits, Skipper and I decided to travel around the state to raise money and reenergize local party organizations. Governor Brown didn't have any interest in doing this, but he would make appearances at fund-raisers when we asked him to. Skipper and I ran Kentucky's Democratic Party headquarters without interference from the governor's office. I usually spent about two days a week attending to party business. I traveled to all 120 Kentucky counties and established personal relationships with party chairs, mayors, and county officials. When it came to grassroots organizing, I had a knack for relating to people regardless of their station in life. Networking is an undervalued commodity in politics today.

As chairman of the Kentucky Democratic Party, I met many prominent Democrats, including Senator Ted Kennedy, who spoke at a meeting in Lexington. (Author's collection)

The primaries for the next gubernatorial election were just around the corner, and the major Democratic candidates were Harvey Sloane from Louisville and Martha Layne Collins from Versailles. Sloane was the favorite. Even so, Grady Stumbo, secretary of the Cabinet for Human Resources in the Brown administration, decided to get into the race too. Stumbo's presence took votes away from Sloane, allowing Collins to win the primary. As was customary in Kentucky, the winner of the primary selected the new party chair. Collins recommended Joe Prather, a legislator from Elizabethtown, and the executive committee approved him. That ended my tenure as chair of the Kentucky Democratic Party, but it was a pivotal position that allowed me to build a statewide base of support.

This is an abbreviated version of how I got into politics, but you can probably understand why Bill Beam regretted asking me the question. In fact, I'm just getting started! I still had a lot to learn about governing.

3

Pike County Judge

Before taking office, I hosted a dinner for the four magistrates-elect, where we discussed how the fiscal court would operate. Kentucky had an open-meetings law, so the members of the fiscal court couldn't get together and discuss county business unless the session was open to the public and the press. I never held an illegal meeting as long as I was county judge.

I told the magistrates-elect that I wanted to be as cooperative as possible, but above all, I wanted things to be done legally. I encouraged them to come and ask me if they needed something done, and I would try to accommodate them. I may have boosted my standing with the magistrates when I informed them that one of my first recommendations was going to be to allocate money so that each magistrate could rent an office, furnish it, install a two-way radio, and have the use of a radio-equipped county vehicle, which I suggested should be a four-wheel-drive V-8 Jeep. I also supported the idea of hiring assistants to staff their offices and relay messages. (Most of the time, they hired their spouses.) I thought these recommendations were justified because Pike was the largest county in area in the state, it was doing well financially at the time, and the job of magistrate had evolved into a full-time position, paying the same salary as the county judge's.

I also established a policy of giving the magistrates an agenda prior to each fiscal court meeting, so they knew what issues would be discussed and why. I let them know that I was always available for one-on-one meetings if they had questions or problems. There were a few rocky moments during my first year in office, partly because I was still learning that I was not the *boss* of the fiscal court. I believe I had a good relationship with all the magistrates except one: Ken Damron. Ken initially wanted to be a little more independent and a little less cooperative. But after my first year in office, when Ken saw that I let the magistrates have their say and get their way sometimes, we got along just fine.

There was seldom a dissenting vote on the fiscal court during my first term as county judge. But in the next election, six to ten people filed to run for magistrate in each district, and almost all of them ran on a platform to counter "Paul Patton the Dictator." They assumed that because there was so little dissent, I must be some kind of bully and the sitting magistrates were afraid of me!

I changed the schedule for fiscal court meetings from once a month to twice a month, holding one in the afternoon and one in the evening. I scheduled the evening meetings so it would be more convenient for residents to attend. I rotated locations among the different magisterial districts so that more people could come to the meetings, giving them a better opportunity to be heard and to better understand how their county government worked.

I kept my home telephone number listed in the phone book. People would call me on weekday evenings and on weekends, and I would take their calls because I didn't want to hide from my constituents. They would generally start the conversation by saying, "Judge, I didn't want to call you in the office because I knew you would be busy."

I soon discovered that I didn't have to try very hard to get people upset with me. Larry Webster, a Republican attorney in Pikeville, wrote a regular column titled "Red Dog" in the local newspaper, the *Appalachian News-Express*. He liked to lampoon state and local politicians, most of whom were Democrats. Larry was also a bluegrass banjo player, and he and I were friends. After Judi and I got married, he hosted a little party at his house for us. He had even supported me in my campaign against Wayne Rutherford.

I had been county judge for just over a week when Larry came into my office and said, "Paul, I want you to sign this petition to call a wet or dry election."

I said, "Oh, Lord have mercy, Larry. I can't get into the wet or dry issue!"

He replied, "You don't have any choice. I've already got a petition approved by the county clerk. The law stipulates that when presented with a valid petition, the county judge 'shall' set a date for a vote on the referendum between sixty and ninety days from receipt of the petition. So all you have to do is select the date."

Being new at the job, I didn't have the presence of mind to call the county attorney for advice. Not knowing any better, I took Larry's word for it and signed the petition, which he promptly filed with the county clerk. About two hours later, the county attorney, Gary Johnson, came into my office and exclaimed, "Judge, what did you do?"

I explained, "Well, Larry came in and said I needed to sign that petition, that I had no choice."

Gary replied, "Judge, that petition was for a wet or dry election in a *magisterial district*, not the whole county, and you can't do that. That isn't legal anywhere except in Magoffin County, and it's only legal there because no one has challenged it in court."

"What am I going to do?" I asked.

He said, "You're going to have to revoke the petition." Gary wrote out the revocation order, which I signed, and he took it down to the county clerk's office and filed it.

A few days later, Larry returned to find out what had happened to his petition. I cursed him up and down for putting me on the spot and taking advantage of me. In so doing, I made a mortal enemy. I also made the pro-wet supporters mad, as well as some pro-dry supporters who got angry when I initially signed the petition. After that, Webster sued the county every chance he got.

Six years later, when I ran for lieutenant governor, Webster waited until the last possible moment before going to Frankfort and filing to run in the Republican primary for lieutenant governor. He thought I would win the Democratic primary, and although he knew he had no hope of beating me, he just wanted to be in a position to harass me. As it turned out, I lost my primary race, but Larry won the Republican nomination! Given my defeat, he didn't get the chance to crisscross the state and criticize me, as he had anticipated. Webster was a very liberal Republican. He later changed his registration to independent. He ran for Pike county clerk as an independent in 2018 but lost. He occasionally writes a satirical column for the *Lexington Herald-Leader*. We now manage to adopt a civil attitude toward each other when we meet on social occasions.

When I was a coal operator, I was the boss. I knew how to run a company and how to supervise people. I didn't have a board of directors telling me what to do. If my banker was willing to loan me the money, I could do whatever I wanted to do. I took that mentality into public office with me. I was a hands-on coal operator and a hands-on public official. I had no doubt that I could administer the county less selfishly and more efficiently than Wayne Rutherford because I actually had management skills. I believed the people of Pike County were entitled to good jobs, decent roads, clean water, fire protection, and recreational facilities. Therefore, economic development became my primary focus. My underlying belief was that Pike County needed to diversify economically. However, there was a steep learning curve.

Early in my first term as county judge, a fellow came in and raised Cain, claiming that a county road supervisor was not doing his job and demanding that I fire him. Having someone yell at me in front of my staff made me so irate that I told the fellow to get out of the office and never come back! It took me about six months to realize that I was operating in a different arena than I was accustomed to, and I needed to handle these situations differently. I changed my demeanor and made an effort to be civil to people, even when they were not civil to me. I learned that, as a public official, I had to listen to people's complaints respectfully and then calmly explain what I could and couldn't do.

When Henry Ward ran for governor in 1967 against Louie Nunn, people said Ward could tell people "yes" and still make them mad! I realized that the last thing people want to hear when they have a real or perceived problem is the word "no," and they certainly don't want to be told, "Hell no!" Therefore, I learned to say, "Now, I don't know whether I can or not, but I'll try." Even when I knew I probably couldn't do what the person was asking of me, I seldom gave them a flat-out negative answer. If I couldn't do what they requested, I knew they would eventually figure that out on their own.

There is no doubt that my experience as county judge made me a much better governor. It helped me realize that I was *not* the boss. The county judge primarily executes the orders of the fiscal court and has very few inherent powers. I learned to share authority with the magistrates for everything from hiring and firing people to spending the county's money.

Business executives elected to public office often mistakenly try to run government like a business. You can apply business principles to certain areas of government, but government is *not* a business. In government, the majority rules, and I had to work with the magistrates to reach agreement about what I wanted to do. Then I had to hire competent people and supervise them to ensure they did what they were supposed to be doing. I had to train the supervisors and much of the workforce, particularly the road crews. I took my job seriously. I arrived at the office early in the morning and left late in the evening. This is what made the office of county judge function properly. After a few months, it became obvious that we were making a real difference in the county.

Keep in mind that my goal was to run for governor, and being county judge was great preparation for that. The legislature decides what to do throughout the commonwealth because it controls the purse, and the governor executes that policy. The same basic principle applies to the office of county judge. Despite my higher political aspirations, I wanted to accomplish something as county judge because *even I* realized that my becoming governor was a long shot. I didn't want to waste my four or eight years in the county judge's office since, in all probability, I was never going to be governor.

When I took office, I quickly discovered that the Pike County government was not well organized. Rutherford had been skillful at promoting wild ideas that sounded good but produced few or no results over time. I organized the county government into four departments: Road, Finance, Public Works, and Social Services. After a solid waste ordinance was passed, we established the Department of Solid Waste.

I was a hands-on administrator. Most of the department heads and I would meet in my office by seven o'clock in the morning to have coffee and talk about what was going on in each department—and there was a lot to discuss. For example, the Public Works Department was responsible for county water lines, flood control, cable television, housing projects, civil defense, fire protection, the airport, the four remote county courthouses, and county planning. If there was a problem with a road or a bridge, I would meet with Forest Stanley, head of the Road Department, and we would drive out to the location, eyeball the situation, and tell the road crew how to make the repair.

One area I didn't want to get involved with was law enforcement. Rutherford had established a county police force separate from the sheriff's office. The sheriff is an elected official over whom the county judge has no oversight. The sheriff's office received no money from the fiscal court; it was funded by property taxes. Rutherford had created the county police force because he wanted to control it and increase his political power. I saw no need for two county law enforcement entities, so I dissolved the county police force and turned all the resources over to the sheriff's office. I had a good relationship with the Pike County sheriff's office during my ten years as county judge.

I learned that being a county judge was a more difficult and time-consuming job than running a coal company. If I wanted to purchase a piece of equipment for my coal company, I just bought it. As county judge, I had to consider public opinion and the possible reactions of the magistrates and their supporters, which took a lot of time and effort. I became engrossed in my job, and I did a lot of thinking at night, trying to figure out ways to get things done. I liked challenges and enjoyed seeing the results. We were making people's lives better.

One of my first hires as county judge was Sammi Chaney, who had done some political work for my mentor Kelsey Friend before transitioning to my campaign. She became my full-time administrative assistant and later accompanied me to the lieutenant governor's office and the governor's office. I hired Wade Justice, a former magistrate who was affiliated with Friend's wing of the Pike County Democratic Party, to be the deputy county judge. I also hired Jim C. Justice, another one of Friend's allies and a former state legislator, as commissioner of public works. When we adopted a solid waste ordinance, I hired Ernie Chaney, Sammi's husband, to be the commissioner of the new solid waste program.

The county judge's salary in 1982 was about $28,000 a year—not quite a middle-class income. Rutherford had been a state parole officer before being elected county judge, so he wasn't a wealthy man. Despite being flamboyant, he lived on his salary as county judge (I assume). Having made a lot of money as a coal operator, I had no financial worries. Therefore, I could concentrate on my job as county judge and not have to worry about my financial well-being if I didn't get reelected. That gave me the freedom to do what I thought was right, even if I sometimes didn't have much public support.

I realized that low wages for local government leadership, especially in larger counties, was an impediment to getting qualified people to run for office. As governor, I led the effort to increase the salaries of local public officials so they could make a living wage. I implemented a sliding scale based on county population. Prior to that, county judges in the largest (Jefferson) and smallest (Robertson) counties in the states received the same salary. Until 1948, the Kentucky Constitution set the maximum salary of most county officials at a meager $5,000. At that time, the courts determined that the $5,000 salary could be adjusted for inflation.

My first major proposal to the fiscal court was mandatory solid waste collection in rural Pike County. At that time, no Kentucky county had developed a successful program to collect rural garbage. Trash disposal was a tremendous problem in Pike County and many other parts of rural Kentucky. When I first raised the issue, it upset many people. For years, people had been throwing their garbage and trash into the creeks and hollows behind their homes. When rural people lived off the bounty from their own gardens, garbage disposal was not much of a problem because most of the waste was biodegradable. However, once people started purchasing most of their groceries and dry goods from supermarkets, including disposable diapers, plastic milk cartons, Styrofoam containers, and plastic bags, these things wound up in the creeks and hollows too. During the rainy season, when there were periodic floods, these items got hung up in trees and shrubs or washed downstream to other people's property, leading to complaints.

When I became county judge, Pike County had an ineffective garbage collection program. Private companies had been contracted to pick up garbage in certain parts of the county where people had signed up for this service, but it had only minimal success. The problem was that it was voluntary, and habits are hard to break. Many people wanted the county cleaned up, but they didn't think a mandatory program would work. They thought people who had been throwing their garbage in the creek cost-free for years would refuse to pay to have it picked up.

To implement a mandatory garbage collection program, I first had to get the fiscal court to pass an ordinance. Initially, I had to deal with four magistrates on the fiscal court—three Democrats and one Republican—but political affiliation was never an issue. Magisterial districts are generally small, so personal relationships and personality are often more relevant in those elections than party affiliation or political philosophy. However, I quickly realized that the political dynamics of Pike County demanded greater representation on the fiscal court, so I succeeded in increasing the number of magisterial districts to six. I also figured that, politically, it would be easier for me to get what I wanted if the court was divided six ways instead of four. The county judge is merely the chair of the fiscal court, and he has one vote, just like the magistrates.

During my first term in office, when there were still only four magistrates, I needed two of their votes to pass a solid waste ordinance. Fiscal court meetings were rather informal affairs. I did not enforce *Robert's Rules of Order*. Citizens who attended the fiscal court meetings spoke up when they wanted to, and my philosophy was that the meetings would last as long as people had something to say. I recall one meeting that went past midnight! While we were debating the solid waste program, one citizen in the audience called me a "communist, a dictator, and a bully." It took me until June to convince two of the magistrates to support my proposal.

One of the initial problems with garbage collection was that many of the roads in Pike County were not wide enough to accommodate a standard-sized garbage truck, so I designed a smaller one that we called the "Patton Packer." My design utilized a pickup truck. After removing the regular truck bed, we attached a metal container with a big back door to the truck's frame. The door of the metal container was operated by means of a hydraulic cylinder—the door was pulled back to allow garbage to be thrown in the container and then, when it was full, the door pushed the garbage out to empty the bin. A local metal shop built the Patton Packers for us. As soon as the container on the pickup truck was full, the driver radioed a standard-sized garbage truck, and they arranged to meet on a main road. The two trucks rendezvoused, and the garbage in the pickup truck was emptied into the large truck. Once the large garbage truck reached capacity, it transported the garbage to the landfill.

I divided Pike County into four regions, and each region had two or three Patton Packers and one full-sized garbage truck. Each region also had a supervisor who drove a regular pickup truck and picked up larger items such as furniture or appliances, which he transported to the landfill.

We designed the program so that no household paid more than 1 percent of its income for garbage pickup. I think the initial charge was $7 a month, which was 1 percent of a $700-a-month income. The bill for someone who was getting by on a $300-a-month Social Security check was only $3, and there was no charge for people making less than $200 a month. I thought the system was fair. However, as soon as we started to send residents bills for garbage pickup, there were problems. To say the program was unpopular would be an understatement. Angry people showed up at fiscal court meetings and called us all kinds of names! During my first two years in office, I made few friends among the people living in Pike County. Rutherford was already planning to run against me in the next election, and he used the unpopular mandatory garbage collection program to his advantage. I thought a majority of people would eventually support the program if we could demonstrate progress. By my third year in office, the program was working, and we were cleaning up the county. Before declaring that I would run for reelection in 1985, I took a poll and discovered that 80 percent of the people supported the mandatory garbage collection program. That was very gratifying. We were cleaning up garbage dumps all over the county, and people had noticed.

My second major proposal was not immediately popular either. State law mandated that each county operate an animal shelter for stray dogs and cats, but Pike County didn't have one. A group of concerned pet owners asked me to follow the law and build an animal shelter, and I agreed. Road supervisor Forest Stanley, an avid fox hunter, knew many people who owned hunting dogs and warned me, "Oh, Judge, don't do that! We're going to end up picking up someone's hunting dog and it will get euthanized and the hunting dog owners will go crazy."

I said, "It's the law, Forest. We have to have an animal shelter. It's the right thing to do."

He replied, "Oh, Judge, this will just *kill* you out in the county! It will get you *beat* in the next election! This issue will flat-out get you beat!"

I optimistically told him, "If we do it right, maybe it won't." So we built the animal shelter and operated it correctly. We didn't kill people's dogs without cause, and to my knowledge, nobody's hunting dog was accidentally euthanized. In fact, most people were happy to learn that animal control had picked up their dog and it wasn't lying dead on the side of the road. Building an animal shelter turned out to be a nonissue.

The third problem I tackled as county judge was the road issue. Pike County had 723 miles of county roads, but only 15 miles were blacktopped. Access to good roads was a huge issue for people living out in the country. During the wintertime, many roads were almost impassable. As county judge, Rutherford hadn't really addressed the road issue. He divided up the money allocated for roads among the four magistrates and let them do whatever they wanted with it. If someone complained to him about a road, Rutherford would say, "Tell your magistrate. I don't have anything to do with that." That was smart politics on his part because he avoided blame for the poor condition of the county's roads. And that was the way the magistrates wanted it because it gave them political power. Each magistrate had his own equipment, including a truck, a grader, and a backhoe, as well as a road crew consisting of four to six men. They controlled who received gravel or blacktop for their roads or driveways, where ditch lines and drainage pipes were located, and who got hired on the road crew. Nobody questioned the magistrates' decisions or stood in their way.

One of the first things I did was to take away the magistrates' authority to spend road money. I knew that to improve the county's road system, we needed a well-developed, centralized plan so we didn't waste money filling the same potholes every few months or giving away gravel or drainpipes to the magistrates' friends and political allies. They had been blatant about it, and nobody thought anything of it. That was just the way things operated, as I discovered once I had access to all the county records and invoices.

Being a former coal operator, I knew something about road construction. The first thing you have to do when building a road is make sure the water will drain off of it. You have to cut ditch lines, put in drainpipes, and make sure the road has a crown in the center to allow the water to run off. Then you have to lay down a solid gravel base before it can be blacktopped. Without that base, the blacktop will shift and crack and won't last very long. Rutherford and the magistrates had laid a lot of blacktop, but it was only an inch and a half deep and lacked a gravel base, so they wasted a lot of money. I insisted on three inches of blacktop that would eventually compress down to two and a half inches. We didn't lay much blacktop during my first two years in office because we concentrated on getting the roads solid enough to hold the blacktop. But by the next election, we had doubled the miles of blacktopped roads in the county, and they were holding up longer.

There were also many bridges in Pike County, some private (serving just one residence) and some public. Most of the bridges were made of steel beams with wood decking. The wood decking would eventually rot through, creating many unsafe bridges. I can recall at least one car falling through a rotted bridge. Rutherford and the magistrates didn't differentiate between public and private bridges. They commonly refloored private bridges using county funds, depending on who lived in the house the bridge served. When I became county judge, we built prestressed concrete bridges, which were permanent structures, and we built or rebuilt only public bridges.

Shortly after I took office in January 1982 we had a heavy snowstorm, and practically none of the county's road equipment was in working order. The road graders had no headlights, so they could be used only in the daytime. The county had no automated salt spreaders. Forest Stanley and I shoveled salt out of the back of a pickup truck on a hill on Ratliff's Creek to make it passable. At that time, snow removal on Pike County roads was "every man for himself."

One of the things I did during my first term was to establish five road maintenance garages: one at Marrowbone, responsible for 80 miles of county roads; one at Elkhorn City, responsible for 117 miles; one at Pond Creek, responsible for 143 miles; one at John's Creek, responsible for 163 miles; and one at Shelby Valley, responsible for 130 miles. When the county was redistricted into six magisterial districts instead of four, I added a maintenance garage at Peter Creek. I also bought trucks, a paver, and a roller so we could do our own blacktopping. Initially, we had one dedicated crew that did all the blacktopping, and they would move from one magisterial district to the next during the warm months. This turned out to be a mistake because the blacktop crew had nothing to do in the wintertime, but we still had to pay them. We ended up selling the paving equipment because it was more economical to bid out the paving jobs to private contractors, and they did a more professional job. We asked the magistrates to prioritize the road projects in their districts, and we considered each request based on merit. By the time I left the county judge's office in 1991, we had paved about 500 of Pike County's 723 miles of roads.

Certainly, my relationships with state administrators in Frankfort were very helpful in getting small sums of money for road projects and grants for various other things. I spent a lot of time in Frankfort, getting acquainted with the bureaucrats who ran the state government and earning their respect. However, a county judge can't ask the governor directly for every little thing he wants or needs. Instead, I learned to go to the commissioner for local government, the secretary of the Transportation

Cabinet, or the secretary of the Economic Development Cabinet for help, instead of bothering the governor. The governor has more important things to do than find money to fund a road project, an industrial park, or a baseball field in Pike County. On average, I would drive to the capital once a week to meet with various state officials about one project or another. I knew where the safe was and who had the combination. Kentucky had three governors during the ten years I was county judge, and I was on good terms with all of them. Every time a governor came to an event in Pike County, I told the audience that this was the best governor we had ever had!

In my second year as county judge, Pike County had a budget shortfall, and I learned a valuable lesson: once money was allocated for a particular project, *psychologically* that money belonged to the program's constituents. When I had to cut the budget, I was taking *their* money, and they got very upset. Therefore, I learned that it was better to underbudget rather than overbudget for the fiscal year. If I underbudgeted and then managed to find some extra money for a project at the end of the fiscal year, I was a hero! In the coal business, I never had to deal with a budget. I just tried to bring in more money than I spent. Being county judge taught me a lot about budgeting, which was very helpful when I became governor.

In August 1984 Hindman native Carl Perkins, the longtime US representative from Kentucky's Seventh District, passed away. Martha Layne Collins was the governor at the time, and her husband, Bill Collins, contacted me and asked me if I would be interested in running for Perkins's seat. Although that wasn't part of my ultimate plan to run for governor, I told him that I would consider it. I thought I probably had a better chance of winning a congressional district race than winning a statewide gubernatorial campaign. According to Bill, some influential people in the district had committed to backing my candidacy. I figured I could get the support of the Pike County delegation, which was the largest in the district, so I gave it some thought for a few days. However, I couldn't get any firm commitments from influential people in Floyd County, the second largest delegation, so I decided not to run. Instead, Carl Perkins's son Chris, who was a freshman state legislator at the time, was nominated to fill out his father's term, and he was elected to a full two-year term that fall.

Another issue that needed my immediate attention was the county jail and courthouse situation. To solve the courthouse problem, I signed an agreement with the Administrative Office of the Courts in Frankfort to build two new circuit courtrooms, two new district courtrooms, and an office for the circuit court clerk, all for $3 million. I also knew the jail facilities were antiquated and in poor condition, so I convinced the fiscal court

With campaign manager Gay Dwyer and Bobby Richardson at the Campbell House in Lexington, awaiting the results of the 1987 primary. (Author's collection)

to allocate $2 million to build a new jail. The new courtrooms and the new jail would be housed in one new four-story building—the jail on the first two floors, and the courtrooms on the upper two floors. The entire project would cost about $5 million, which we would raise by selling bonds.

We made the mistake of hiring contractors who were not required to abide by the prevailing wage scale (ensuring skilled workers), and the result was some shoddy workmanship. Before it even opened, a water line broke, flooded the jail, and then froze because it was wintertime. We discovered the plumbing hadn't been installed up to code. Therefore, when I undertook the remodeling of the old courthouse, I hired different contractors who were required to pay the minimum wage prevailing in the region, and they delivered better workmanship and professionalism.

I had a successful first term, but I wasn't a shoo-in for a second term. I realized that, as the incumbent, I had to run a different kind of campaign because the bull's-eye was now on *my* back. I spent another $250,000 and beat Wayne Rutherford again, this time by twelve percentage points. With my reelection victory, my quest for the governorship appeared to be on track.

I knew I wasn't going to win the lieutenant governor's race in 1987, but the primary election was held on my fiftieth birthday, so we turned it into a birthday party. (Author's collection)

4

First Campaign for Statewide Office, 1987

As I campaigned for reelection as county judge in 1985, I was up-front about my intention to run for statewide office in 1987. On January 5, 1986, the day I was sworn in for my second term, I officially announced my candidacy for lieutenant governor. I wanted to let the people of Pike County know that I would be out of the office a lot while I was campaigning.

For the most part, I made sure I was in Pikeville on Mondays for meetings of the fiscal court, and I sometimes worked in the office on Sundays. However, by Tuesday I was generally out on the campaign trail unless something needed my personal attention in Pike County, such as the twenty inches of snow that fell in early April 1987, causing power outages in more than half the county and blocking the roads.

My interest in running for lieutenant governor was based solely on using that office as a springboard to the governor's office. I had no other objective than to lay the foundation for a successful campaign for governor four years later. If elected, I intended to use my four years as lieutenant governor to build a statewide base of support for my gubernatorial campaign, as my official duties would be almost nonexistent. I had no desire to be part of the new governor's administration, whoever that turned out to be, and I didn't expect the new governor to offer me a policy-making role.

I knew that I would be running for lieutenant governor as a rural candidate, so I kicked off my campaign in the New Madrid bend of Fulton County at the Stepp residence. Fulton is the westernmost county in the state, and the Stepp home was the westernmost residence in Kentucky. At the press conference, I told the gathering that I was from Pike County, the *easternmost* part of Kentucky. I said that my home was as far away from the state capital as Fulton County was, which wasn't exactly accurate, but I made my point.

It was a crowded field in 1987, and I was good friends with most of the other candidates for lieutenant governor. They included state senator David Boswell from Owensboro, state superintendent of public instruction Alice

McDonald from Louisville, Kentucky attorney general David Armstrong from Louisville, Thoroughbred horseman Brereton Jones from Woodford County, and Wilton Cupp, a fringe candidate I didn't know. Initially, I didn't take Brereton Jones's candidacy very seriously. I knew he would be well financed and would get the support of the horse industry, but I didn't know how much money he would spend. I figured he was the only candidate who could possibly compete with me financially.

My campaign slogan was "Others Promise Progress. Patton *Is* Progress." I had a good record of honest government. I had paved hundreds of miles of rural roads in my county, laid miles of water lines, increased fire protection, and implemented a solid waste program. The Pike County government was working like never before, and people in Frankfort had noticed. My campaign pitch was simple: I wanted to create jobs. To help economically distressed counties, particularly in eastern Kentucky, I proposed the Kentucky Distressed Counties Development Act. My original idea was to use $100 million in state bonds to entice companies to build or relocate in specific counties where the unemployment rate had been above the state average for five consecutive years. The state would then direct the personal income taxes of these companies' employees and the companies' corporate income taxes to a special fund that would be used to pay off the bonds.

My rationale for the program was multifaceted. First, the state wasn't collecting personal income taxes from unemployed residents or corporate income taxes from nonexistent companies in counties with chronic high unemployment. In my mind, the state wouldn't miss the revenue used to pay off the bonds because the state wasn't collecting it in the first place. Second, the chronically unemployed were already receiving state benefits in the form of public education for their children, police and fire protection, highway maintenance, welfare checks, food stamps, and unemployment benefits, so the program wouldn't cost the state any additional funds. Instead, it would reduce the number of unemployed, get people back to work and off welfare, and *save* the state money.

In 1987 the candidates for lieutenant governor didn't hold individual campaign rallies. Very few people would have attended such a rally, as not many people cared who the lieutenant governor was. Instead, we held private fund-raisers around the state and attended the rallies organized by the candidates for governor. I didn't mind piggybacking my campaign on these events. For example, I went to a rally at the Kentucky Horse Park for John Y. Brown Jr. and worked the crowd there. I also attended a rally for Wallace Wilkinson in Montgomery County. As I went around pressing the flesh and working the crowd, I learned that an influential individual named David "Cornbread" Manley was present. David was a firefighter in Montgomery County and was active in the Kentucky Firefighters Association. After someone pointed him out to me, I went up to him and said, "I'm running for lieutenant governor, and I'd like to have your support."

He replied, "I'm sorry, son, but I can't help you. I'm for that Paul Patton fella from Pike County." He knew that, as county judge, I had built volunteer fire stations all over Pike County and had supported volunteer firefighters in many ways.

"Hell," I said, "*I am* Paul Patton!" We both had a good laugh, and I appointed Manley state fire marshal during my first gubernatorial administration.

There was little animosity among the candidates for lieutenant governor in 1987, and I don't recall any negative campaign ads either. It was a friendly rivalry. We often attended the same events, such as the County Judge Association's meeting, and we would reserve a room and hold a reception. Afterward, we might get together in someone's room to discuss things. I developed good relationships with David Armstrong and his brother Tom, as well as with David Boswell and Alice McDonald. Brereton Jones didn't engage in that kind of campaigning.

A couple of weeks before the primary, polls indicated that Armstrong was in the lead, but Jones and I were closing the gap. Jones spent a lot of money on television advertising during the last two weeks of the campaign and was able to win the primary. I knew heading into the last weekend that I would probably lose. Polls had Jones ahead with 21.1 percent, followed by me with 18.3 percent, Armstrong with 17.4 percent, Boswell with 7.1 percent, and McDonald with 6.9 percent.

On the night of the election, my family and campaign staff and a few supporters gathered at the Campbell House Hotel in Lexington, where we planned to hold our victory celebration. I told them we probably weren't going to win and not to get their hopes up. The only thing that really surprised me was that I came in third rather than second. After the election, reports showed that I had spent $1.4 million and Jones had spent $3 million on a race that probably shouldn't have cost more than $200,000, based on prior elections.

It wasn't until the next day that the reality of losing hit me. The loss was devastating because I believed that any chance of my being governor had gone down the drain. I had invested seven years of my life toward a goal that now seemed to have vanished. As expected, I had carried eastern Kentucky, but that wasn't nearly enough. I knew Jones had run a smart and effective campaign, and his television ads were superior to mine. After the primary, as county judge, I attended one of Jones's fall campaign fund-raisers held in Pikeville, and I contributed $500 to show my constituents that I was supporting Jones. I think he appreciated it. I held no animosity toward him for beating me, but that didn't lessen the sting of my defeat.

The 1987 election was such a debilitating loss because, in the end, politics is personal. If I am a car dealer and a prospective customer goes across the street and buys a car from my competitor, the customer didn't reject *me*; he rejected my *product*. But if you lose an election, you feel like the voters have rejected *you* because you were the product you were trying to sell them. That's how I felt after the 1987 primary, and it was a traumatic experience. For almost an entire month, I was as depressed as I have ever been.

There was a good side to the experience, however. Judi and I considered ourselves blessed to have been able to travel around the state and see its diversity firsthand. We met a lot of nice people and made many new friends. After the primary, she and I talked about it, and we decided that the $700,000 of our own money we had spent on the campaign was well worth it, even though the outcome wasn't what we had hoped for. We still had more than enough money to live comfortably. But, with my dream of being governor seemingly over, at the age of fifty I had to reevaluate what I was going to do with my life.

Of course, I was still Pike's county judge, and I was back in my office by noon the day after the election. But I knew my enthusiasm for that job would wane now that it wasn't going to be a stepping-stone to the governor's office. I also knew I didn't want to get back into the coal business. Frankly, I didn't know what I was going to do. I just knew that I was giving up politics for good. One beating was enough for me. What I really needed was something to occupy my mind.

I still wanted to create jobs in eastern Kentucky. Anticipating the 1988 session of the General Assembly, I talked to Senator Friend about trying to pass my distressed counties plan. He got the Legislative Research Commission to draft the legislation and then introduced it in the senate. Even with the backing of an influential legislator like Kelsey, there was no guarantee that SB 280 would pass in both chambers, but it passed in the senate with only one dissenting vote. Kelsey then arranged for us to meet with Governor Wallace Wilkinson so that we could explain the bill to him. The governor said, "Go talk to Roger Wells," the secretary of the Finance and Administration Cabinet, "and let's see what he thinks about it."

We discussed the proposal with Wells, and he suggested some changes to take the state off the hook in case the investment didn't work out. We ended up funding the program without using state bonds. Instead of directing personal and corporate income taxes into a special fund to retire the bonded debt, the companies would be permitted to keep the taxes and reimburse themselves for the capital investment. Each company would file its corporate income tax return and report the personal income tax deducted from employees' wages but would keep the money. Employees would file their state tax returns as usual and get credit for paying their personal income taxes. We also changed the deduction from employees' wages from a graduated scale of up to 6 percent of income to a flat 4 percent deduction across the board.

Afterward, we took the bill back to Governor Wilkinson, and he agreed to endorse it. However, the bill was still languishing in the Kentucky House of Representatives, so I personally lobbied for its passage. The problem was that some legislators wanted their counties included in the definition of "distressed." Pete Worthington, a Democrat from Ewing in Fleming County, proposed an amendment that would allow counties to participate if their unemployment rate was above the state average for four out of five consecutive years. Approval of this amendment meant that Fleming, Daviess, and Warren Counties now met the requirement. The watered-down version of the bill passed in both the house and the senate.

However, because the law included some changes in the tax system that might be unconstitutional, it was subject to review by the courts. In plain English, the Kentucky Constitution states that it is unconstitutional to give public money to private enterprises. In drafting SB 280, we had used a 1986 law devised to lure Toyota to Scott County as our constitutional precedent. The Kentucky Supreme Court had ruled in the Toyota case that reducing unemployment is a legitimate state expenditure, and the intent of SB 280 was to reduce unemployment. The issue of SB 280's constitutionality went first to the Franklin County Circuit Court and then to the Kentucky Court of Appeals, both of which ruled that the law was constitutional, even though, in my nonlawyerly opinion, it clearly was not. The Kentucky Supreme Court refused to hear the appeal, which meant that the appeals court's decision stood. The judicial process took almost two years, if I remember correctly. Someone didn't like the name Kentucky Distressed Counties Development Act, so it was changed to the Kentucky Rural Economic Development Act, or KREDA. I saw no need to argue over that minor detail.

When it came to plans for the future, my lack of direction didn't last very long. My rescuer turned out to be Wallace Wilkinson, the Democratic candidate for governor. Sometime in late June or early July 1987, he asked me to be the organizational chairperson of his fall campaign. Now *that* was something I could sink my teeth into, and I did! Wilkinson didn't have much competition. After the presumptive Republican candidate, Larry Forgy, withdrew from the race, it was a foregone conclusion that Wilkinson would easily defeat the substitute Republican candidate, John Harper, in November. However, we didn't take anything for granted and went through the motions of organizing a full-fledged campaign. I spent about two days a week at Kentucky Democratic Party headquarters in Frankfort, working with party chair Danny Briscoe and putting together a "Wilkinson for Governor" political organization in each county, including appointing chairpersons and committee members.

During that time, I reengaged with a number of politically active people. Some said to me, "Paul, why don't you run again? Don't give up." I've always believed that when it comes to politics, two people urging an individual to run constitutes a "movement," and three people constitutes a "draft," so by the time November rolled around, I had decided to run for lieutenant governor again. Judi and I made a plan: I would run for a third term as county judge, and then I would run for lieutenant governor again in 1991. Surely there wouldn't be another wealthy candidate like Brereton Jones willing to spend millions of dollars to win a minor office (besides me, of course).

In retrospect, losing the lieutenant governor's race in 1987 was the most fortuitous thing that could have happened to me. First, it allowed me to gain four more years of experience as county judge. Second, I doubt that I would have had any meaningful job as lieutenant governor in the Wilkinson administration. Being a businessperson himself, Wallace liked to do much of the economic development work on his own, and that was my primary interest. Third, if I had been elected lieutenant governor in 1987 and governor in 1991, I would have been a one-term governor because voters didn't approve the gubernatorial succession amendment until 1992. Of course, I didn't know this at the time.

Back in Pike County, one of the first issues I had to deal with was county employees' desire to join a union. Initially, I opposed the idea, not because public employees shouldn't be allowed to organize as a means of communicating with management but because public employees shouldn't be allowed to strike. I understood that in the private sector, the ability to strike is the union's hammer in bargaining with management because striking employees can cost the stockholders money. In my opinion, the ballot box is public employees' only hammer in bargaining with management, and unions can influence elections. A strike doesn't cost elected officials any money; it punishes the citizens. Once we worked through the strike issue, I reversed my position and county employees were allowed to unionize, with the clear understanding that we would talk and negotiate but strikes would not be part of the process.

I also persuaded the fiscal court to pass several necessary amendments to the county's administrative code, many of which are still in place today. One amendment prevented county supervisors from using coercion for political purposes. This protected county employees from being pressured to contribute to political campaigns in order to obtain or keep their jobs. Although it didn't apply to administrative employees, it covered at least 80 percent of all county employees. I never pressured county employees for political purposes, and I wanted to make sure my successors didn't either. It was fundamentally a simplified version of the state merit system.

In addition, I recognized that an undereducated population was holding back Pike County, and eastern Kentucky as a whole, economically. Therefore, I actively promoted the importance of education at every opportunity as county judge, lieutenant governor, and governor. The state's First Lady, Martha Wilkinson, was also interested in adult education. She established the Kentucky Graduate Equivalency Diploma (GED) Foundation and served as its chair. I worked with the foundation and the Kentucky Department of Education to create the Kentucky Workplace Literacy Project, utilizing federal funds to help private-sector employees earn their GED. Two coal companies, the Kentucky Carbon Company and the United Coal Company, were the first businesses to participate in the program in Pike County. I enrolled myself in a training course on how to teach people to read, and I tutored a man with a learning impediment. I encouraged people to volunteer to teach others how to read. Then I took it a step further and implemented a GED program for Pike County employees. I offered a $300 bonus to every county employee who earned a GED through the Pike County Business Council for Adult Education. I had discovered that of the 260 people employed by the county, 88 had not earned a high school diploma. Thirty of those 88 county employees agreed to enroll in the program. Given my statewide political aspirations, I wanted public employees all over Kentucky to be on my side. When Martha Wilkinson resigned from the foundation to run for governor, I took over as its chair and served until I took office as lieutenant governor.

I also wanted to refurbish the old county courthouse to make it a suitable location for the county's administrative offices. At the time, the county finance office was located in a rented room on the third floor of a building across the street from the courthouse, and the Road Department's office was in a mobile home on the new area created when the federal government relocated the river around Pikeville. It made sense to me to centralize

Election night, 1991. I gave my victory speech at the Galt House in Louisville.
(Author's collection)

the county's administrative offices. It was going to cost about $4 million to refurbish the county courthouse and add a brand-new wing.

I had to focus on my responsibilities as county judge if I hoped to win reelection in 1989. I had two opponents in the Democratic primary that year: Charles Cantrell and Don Branham. Branham was a political lightweight from Wayne Rutherford's wing of the Democratic Party. He often wore a clown suit to party rallies. Cantrell was a leader in the United Steel Workers union, a friend of Kelsey Friend, and a fishing buddy of mine.

I ended up winning the primary easily, getting 53 percent of the vote. My Republican opponent in the November election was Billy Hatfield. I took the election seriously and campaigned just as hard as I had in 1981, but I spent only about $100,000 this time. Hatfield ran a serious campaign, but the people of Pike County appreciated the fire stations, swimming pools, water lines, senior citizens' centers, water districts, baseball fields, paved roads, and garbage collection I had built or established as county judge. Hatfield couldn't compete with my popularity, and I won the election with 75 percent of the vote. I had no intention of serving out that four-year term, however. I immediately began to focus on my 1991 campaign for lieutenant governor. I had lost once, and I didn't intend to lose again.

5

Lieutenant Governor's Office, 1991–1995

My desire to run for lieutenant governor a second time was not a secret. Everyone in Pike County and Frankfort knew about it. As I formulated my campaign strategy, I tried to learn from the mistakes I'd made in 1987.

I had learned that I needed the support of organized labor, and I needed to run a viable campaign in Louisville and Jefferson County, where I had received just 6 percent of the vote in the 1987 Democratic primary. I knew I needed to do better in northern Kentucky as well, where I had received only 12.5 percent of the vote in Boone County, 9 percent in Campbell County, and 7 percent in Kenton County.

When I was chairperson of the Kentucky Democratic Party, I'd forged a close friendship with Andrew "Skipper" Martin, who worked for Harvey Sloane, the county judge of Jefferson County, from 1986 to 1990. In mid-1990, when my second candidacy for lieutenant governor was in its infancy, Skipper came to me and said, "I'm taking over as manager of your campaign. You don't have to pay me, but I'm going to run it." It was a command decision on his part, and I had no objection because Skipper was more familiar with Kentucky politics than anyone I knew. And he could afford not to collect a salary for a year or so. Once he decided to run my 1991 campaign, Skipper practically dedicated his life to it. His mission was to get me elected not just lieutenant governor but eventually governor.

Skipper also persuaded me to hire his friend Danny Ross and to pay him a salary. Danny had good connections with organized labor in Louisville and Jefferson County as well as the rest of the state. Skipper and Danny proved to be among the most consequential members of my inner circle during my twelve years in Frankfort: four years as lieutenant governor and eight years as governor.

The 1991 Democratic primary for lieutenant governor was just as crowded as the 1987 primary had been. By the filing deadline in late January, there were six other candidates. I knew all but two of them fairly well. Fred Cowan was the sitting attorney general of Kentucky. Bobby Richardson had been a cochair of Terry McBrayer's 1979 campaign for governor with me; he was a member of the Kentucky House of Representatives and its former speaker. Bobby was a friendly person, and I always liked him. Steve Collins was an attorney and the son of former governor Martha Layne Collins. Pete Worthington was the speaker pro tem in the Kentucky house. Judge Ray Corns had ruled in 1988 that the Kentucky school system was unconstitutional, which led to passage of the Kentucky Education Reform Act in 1990. I was acquainted with Corns but didn't know him well. John Stewart was a labor attorney in Louisville whom I didn't know at all. Although Cowan would come very close, Skipper and I had vowed that no one would outspend us.

I officially kicked off my campaign in mid-January at American Legion Post 220 in Shively, just after the First Gulf War started and at the end of a three-day barnstorming tour of western Kentucky. I deliberately chose that location because I wanted to demonstrate to retired military veterans that I supported them and the troops involved in Operation Desert Storm to free Kuwait from Iraqi occupation. More importantly, I chose Shively because it was a solidly blue-collar, pro-union suburb of Louisville. I wanted to build an identity as someone who was pro-union and would represent the middle class in Frankfort. During the campaign, I made the rounds of all the Democratic clubs in the Louisville metropolitan area with Skipper, Danny, and Larry Clark. Clark had been elected to the Kentucky House of Representatives in 1984 and was a strong presence in Local 369 of the International Brotherhood of Electrical Workers. I was determined to forge a good relationship with organized labor in Jefferson County.

As expected, Fred Cowan took the early lead in the polls and maintained that lead until the last three weeks of the primary campaign. I employed Washington-based pollster Peter Hart again, but I brought in a new media consultant. Many people thought my 1987 television ads weren't slick enough, so I hired a national consultant, Robert Squire from Washington, DC, for my 1991 campaign.

By mid-January 1991, I reported that I had raised a little over $700,000 for my campaign, which far exceeded the amounts raised by my opponents. Half of that money was actually mine, but I wanted the other candidates to know that money wouldn't be an issue for me, though it might be for them.

I figured Cowan would run strong in Louisville and Jefferson County, even though he wasn't very popular there, and I thought he would certainly receive the endorsement of the *Courier-Journal*, his hometown newspaper. Fred had a reputation for being a little arrogant and an elitist, and he rubbed some people the wrong way. He was not a hail-fellow-well-met backslapper like me! I didn't think I could actually win in Jefferson County, but my goal was to hold Fred's margin of victory down so that I could surpass him in other parts of the state where he was less popular and less well known.

In late February 1991 Ron Cyrus, a former state legislator who was head of the Kentucky AFL-CIO, announced that the union had endorsed Brereton Jones for governor. He also announced that none of the Democratic candidates for lieutenant governor had received enough votes to earn the union's endorsement. The top three vote-getters had been Fred Cowan, me, and John Stewart. I considered that a victory! During my time as a coal operator, the United Mine Workers had always accused me of being anti-union. However, as county judge I had supported the unionization of county employees. That was apparently enough to keep anyone else from winning the AFL-CIO's endorsement. Cowan had connections to organized labor in Louisville and Jefferson County, so Cyrus's announcement must have been a big disappointment to him.

My campaign centered on job creation, and my campaign slogan was "Fight for Jobs in Kentucky!" I emphasized my personal experience with economic development as county judge. I accentuated my role as the point man in convincing the Mountaintop Baking Company of McComb, Ohio, to expand its operations, which brought five hundred jobs to Pike County. I wasn't shy about underscoring my role in writing and persuading the legislature to pass the Kentucky Rural Economic Development Act (KREDA), which was instrumental in creating new jobs in many parts of the state.

When I went to Owensboro, I said, "You know, this factory you have out here, that's a direct result of the bill I wrote." I could give the same kind of speech in Somerset, Murray, Elizabethtown, and a dozen other towns all over Kentucky. Talking about job creation is always good politics. Every candidate, from president of the United States to local dogcatcher, promises to create jobs once they are in office. Good jobs are what people need and want, and they want a leader who at least acknowledges that having a good job is a necessity and that government can act as a catalyst. Job creation is a universal need, and good-paying jobs are a universal want. I played heavily on that theme throughout my second campaign for lieutenant governor.

Fred Cowan hired a political consultant from Chicago whose name might be familiar: David Axelrod. Axelrod later became Barack Obama's chief political consultant during the 2008 and 2012 presidential campaigns. I heard that Axelrod practically chained Cowan to his desk and told him to

"Raise money!" because he knew I would spend a lot to win the race. While Cowan spent most of the last month of the campaign on the telephone raising money, I crisscrossed the state, making speeches and meeting with influential people in all 120 counties. The fact that I didn't need to raise as much private money was a great advantage. Still, two weeks before the primary, polls showed me trailing Cowan by five percentage points.

On the Saturday two weeks before the election, we held a phone meeting that included my family, Skipper, the pollster, and the media consultant. The pollster said we had two choices: go negative or lose the race. None of the family wanted to run negative ads, and besides, we didn't have much of an issue to go negative on. After an hour or two, we decided to adjourn until 2:00 p.m. on Sunday.

That night, I was home in bed in Pikeville when the telephone rang just after 1:00 a.m. State treasurer Robert Meade, who was running for state auditor, said, "Paul, I'm on the loading dock of the *Courier-Journal*. The Sunday paper just came out, and they've endorsed *you!*" I couldn't believe it, but Meade assured me it was true. I knew we were still in an uphill battle, but obtaining the newspaper's endorsement was definitely a plus.

In the meeting on Sunday, we agreed to go negative. The media people didn't have much to work with, but they agreed to come up with something. In the meantime, they developed a television commercial that went something like this: "In the race for lieutenant governor, who did the *Louisville Courier-Journal* endorse? The hometown boy Fred Cowan? [An unflattering picture of Fred fades into the background.] No! They endorsed Paul Patton! [A nice picture of me appears.] What does the *Courier-Journal* know that we don't know? Stay tuned!"

We had no idea what the follow-up would be, but the gods were on our side. On Tuesday, the *Courier-Journal* ran a scathing story about a highway contractor who had accused Cowan of trying to coerce a campaign contribution from him because the attorney general's office had subpoenaed him to testify before a grand jury. There was probably no truth to the charge, but the *Courier-Journal* made it seem like the biggest sin since the creation. The pollsters said they had never seen a candidate fall so far in such a short time.

The Cowan campaign came roaring back with negative ads about me. Who knew how this race was going to end? The 1991 primary campaign for lieutenant governor was the only race I've run where I wasn't sure of the outcome ahead of time.

On the day of the primary election, I was at peace. I felt we had done a good job, and I had resigned myself to accept the outcome, whatever it was.

After voting in Pikeville in the morning, Judi and I drove up to the Galt House in Louisville to await the results. Immediately after the polls closed in western Kentucky, I told my family that if we won, we would be gracious winners, and if we lost, we would accept defeat with dignity. I knew that if I lost, my political career was over and I would have to find something else to do, and I was okay with that.

However, by nine o'clock that evening, I knew I had won. It was very exciting and gratifying for Judi and me because it put us one giant step closer to the governor's office. I beat Fred Cowan by forty-two thousand votes. Steve Collins came in third, Bobby Richardson was fourth, Pete Worthington came in fifth, and Ray Corns finished last. I think John Stewart had dropped out. The outcome was just about what I had predicted early in the campaign when I first sized up my competition. I don't remember whether my opponents called to congratulate me because that night was somewhat of a blur.

At some point in the evening, Brereton Jones, who had won the Democratic gubernatorial primary, called and invited me to join him the next morning at the entrance to General Electric's Appliance Park to greet employees as they arrived for work, which I did. When Judi and I drove back to Pikeville the next day, we were surprised to find a celebratory caravan awaiting our arrival at Betsy Lane, as if I were a big hero. We all drove to the courthouse in Pikeville, where I gave a short speech. I thanked everyone for putting their trust in me, first by electing me county judge and then for their support in the race for lieutenant governor. It was a big day for Pike County and for all of eastern Kentucky. The Republicans had elected Eugene Goss from Laurel County as their candidate for lieutenant governor, which meant that regardless of the outcome of the November election, someone from eastern Kentucky would occupy the lieutenant governor's office. Not since Bert Combs was elected governor in 1959 had an individual from eastern Kentucky served in such a high statewide office.

I knew the governor's race would be dominant in November, and it was likely that whoever won that race would pull the entire party ticket over the finish line with him. At the time, the candidates for governor and lieutenant governor ran separately, not as part of a slate, as they do now. The Republicans' gubernatorial candidate was Congressman Larry Hopkins of the Sixth District. He had barely squeaked by Larry Forgy in the Republican primary, even though Hopkins had the backing of the Republican establishment and a lot more money. Forgy had exposed some major weaknesses in Hopkins, not the least of which was his unfamiliarity with Kentucky issues after serving in Washington for fourteen years. Having been politically wounded during the primary contest, Hopkins had already spent a lot of his campaign money fending off Forgy. Most political pundits and prognosticators considered the fall election a mere formality, confident that Jones and the entire Democratic slate would win a resounding victory. When Hopkins's name surfaced in the congressional banking scandal in mid-September, it all but sealed the election for us Democrats. Hopkins was eventually cleared of any wrongdoing in the banking scandal, but it had damaged him politically. In reality, Hopkins never had much of a chance, thanks to Forgy cutting his political legs out from under him, and he was soon out of politics for good. That was a shame because Hopkins was a good man and represented the Sixth Congressional District tenaciously and honorably.

Jones defeated Hopkins by 246,000 votes, and I defeated Goss by 263,000 votes. Our wide margins of victory weren't necessarily because we were such great candidates. The fact is, the Republicans just imploded that year. For me, election as lieutenant governor was only a means to an end. Historically, I knew that I would be in a very favorable position going into the next gubernatorial election. Four of the last six lieutenant governors had gone on to occupy the governor's office, so under normal circumstances, I would be the favorite in 1995. However, that was four years away, and I was determined to roll up my sleeves and work hard to make it happen.

Sixteen days after the election, I was pleasantly shocked when Governor-elect Jones asked me to serve as secretary of the Cabinet for Economic Development. It was unprecedented for a Kentucky governor to ask the lieutenant governor to be a member of the administrative team. I readily accepted because the lieutenant governor had no constitutional duties other than presiding over the state senate when the General Assembly was in session (and staying alive in case something happened to the governor). When the legislature wasn't in session, lieutenant governors typically planned their campaigns for governor in the next election. That's what Skipper and I had planned to do: travel all over Kentucky, meet with key people in every county, and build a statewide campaign organization second to none. My appointment as secretary totally changed the dynamics of that strategy because I now had a *real* job to do!

There is no doubt that Brereton Jones did me a great favor when he asked me to assume that cabinet position, and as a result, I was 100 percent loyal to him. I think he made a wise choice. I had great credentials, including authoring KREDA and getting it passed in the General Assembly in 1988; it was a very successful program. I had also made job creation a central part of my efforts as county judge.

Taking the oath of office as lieutenant governor at midnight on December 10, 1991, in the living room of the lieutenant governor's mansion was exhilarating for Judi and me. For a small-time coal operator from Pike County, it was a heady moment, and I was really pumped up! Standing on the inaugural dais later that day, I realized that in four years I had a good chance of being the next governor of Kentucky. However, I also realized that a lot can happen in four years. Even so, history indicated that I was in a good position to succeed Brereton Jones.

The speeches Brereton and I gave that day were very similar. I never employed a speechwriter as lieutenant governor or governor, but I'm sure I wrote that speech in consultation with Jones's people. The entire day was very exciting, interesting, and enjoyable, and I was ready to begin this new adventure. One of the thrills of the day was seeing a pickup truck with a dozen of my friends from Louisa High School drive by the inaugural booth. Judi and I beamed with pride.

I brought several members of my campaign staff to Frankfort to work in the lieutenant governor's office. Skipper agreed to be my chief of staff, and Danny Ross served as my liaison with organized labor. Sammi Chaney was my administrative assistant, and Vivian Johnson was my receptionist. Both Sammi and Vivian had worked for me when I was county judge. As finance director I hired Bill Beam Jr., who had volunteered to work on my campaign with no compensation. Every member of my staff was loyal to me, and I was loyal to them. I treated them with respect, fairness, and dignity, and I didn't hesitate to show my appreciation. I would have trusted any one of them with my life. Their mission was to get me elected governor, and they knew it was a long-term commitment.

Being the secretary of the Cabinet for Economic Development was one of the best posts in state government because there was little downside to the job. The secretary could celebrate and publicize the successes of the cabinet in a high-profile manner while burying the failures— and there were a lot more failures than successes. My campaign for lieutenant governor had been based on my record of creating jobs as county judge, and now Governor Jones had given me a huge job-creating platform on which to base my 1995 gubernatorial campaign. Jones had let me know that the appointment would be temporary. He planned to restructure the cabinet and turn it into a quasi-independent agency called the Kentucky Economic Development Partnership to make it less political. That fit with my plan to get out into the state and start plowing the ground for my gubernatorial campaign. I couldn't wait to get started on both fronts!

Governor Jones did me another huge favor by appointing Gene Strong as deputy secretary. Gene and the governor were friends, and I understood that Jones had chosen him not only for his economic development expertise but also to keep an eye on me. When Jones's office contacted our office, the caller usually asked for Gene, not me. However, Gene was a professional and was not at all political, and we bonded quickly. He was a great asset to me and was very good at his job. He had a lot of experience and was much more knowledgeable about the intricacies of economic development than I was, but I knew much more about the legislature than he did, so we made a good team. In fact, after the legislature passed Governor Jones's bill creating the Economic Development Partnership, the agency's board conducted a nationwide search and hired Gene to lead it.

The Cabinet for Economic Development was a very small operation with no more than 120 employees. Jones allowed us to make all personnel decisions, and Strong recommended that we hire James Navolio to lead the most important department in the cabinet: new business recruitment. Navolio had worked for the Grey Construction Company based in Glasgow, Kentucky, which was doing business worldwide and had built the Toyota plant in Georgetown. Jim turned out to be a good hire. He was a true professional without a political agenda, and because of his contacts we met with Canadian, European, and Japanese companies. The three of us made a good team. Denis Fleming served as the cabinet's legal counsel, and I thought so highly of him that I brought him to the governor's office as general counsel after my election in 1995. Donna Moloney also worked in the cabinet, and she became my major events coordinator when I became governor.

While I worked on economic development, my staff in the lieutenant governor's office was planning my forthcoming gubernatorial campaign. Judi and I moved into the lieutenant governor's mansion, which was totally furnished. Living there wasn't mandatory, but we saw it as an advantage because we had to move to Frankfort anyway, and the lieutenant governor's work is 99 percent political. My staff was busy inviting local officials and influential people around the state to meetings and events held at the mansion. I think we wore out the kitchen staff with all the luncheons, garden parties, and evening receptions we held there. Judi played an integral role in arranging those events, and she enjoyed doing that. We entertained in grand style. When I became governor, I allocated money to renovate the lieutenant governor's mansion and the gardens behind it. I put Judi in charge of overseeing the renovation, so she definitely left her mark on that property.

My staff made sure I attended as many political events as I could. If the local Democratic Party in Boyle County was hosting a picnic on Saturday, they got me there if it was at all possible. My staff was devoted to promoting my candidacy for governor and ensured that the sixteen months I spent as secretary of the Cabinet for Economic Development weren't wasted politically.

Strong and I developed our own economic development plan. We advertised Kentucky in all the trade publications, including *Site Selection Magazine,* and emphasized Kentucky's strategic midwestern location, available workforce, and access to airports and interstate highways.

When dealing with economic development prospects, confidentiality is paramount. Companies looking to relocate generally don't want their current communities to know about it until the final negotiations are under way, so they hire consultants to do all the preliminary legwork. The company may instruct the consultant to look for two relocation sites in Indiana, two in Kentucky, and two in Tennessee. The consultant contacts the appropriate department in each state, explains that an anonymous company is looking to build a new plant or relocate, and presents the company's criteria. Each state's economic development staff then conducts research and recommends suitable locations. With or without a company representative, the consultant makes unannounced visits to the recommended communities. If they like what they see, the consultant informs the economic development staff, and they arrange a meeting among the consultant, a company representative, and a few influential members of the community, such as the mayor, the county judge, and a member of the Chamber of Commerce or the Rotary Club. (Today, I understand that a lot of this work is done on the internet.)

During the sixteen months I was secretary, we brought between fifty and seventy-five companies to Kentucky. Some of the negotiations took more than a year, and some took a little less. Most of them were small companies with twenty-five employees or so, but they were big enough that the state was willing to offer incentives. Twenty-five jobs might not sound like a lot, but I guarantee it meant everything to those twenty-five people who now had jobs. Many of the companies started small, just to see how they liked the community; most of them increased in size over time if they did well. It wasn't uncommon for a company to quadruple its employees, especially those located in small communities in rural Kentucky. I always thought that coming to a rural Kentucky county, especially one with a farming ethic, was a good choice for almost any company.

During the 1992 legislative session, Strong, Navolio, and I brainstormed about how to enhance Kentucky's image as a good place for companies to build or relocate. There were career bureaucrats in the cabinet who really knew what they were doing, and they were tremendously helpful to us. The result was that we presented three economic development proposals to the legislature, and they all passed. One bill established the Kentucky Job Development Authority (KJDA), which attracted service industries to the state and contained some of the same incentives as KREDA. The second bill created the Kentucky Industrial Development Authority (KIDA), which lured manufacturers to counties that did not qualify for the KREDA program. The third piece of legislation, the Kentucky Industrial Revitalization Act (KIRA), focused on keeping existing manufacturing businesses in Kentucky. All these programs allowed companies to keep their corporate income taxes and perhaps their employees' personal income taxes to help retire their capital investment. These four programs (some renamed and modified in recent legislative sessions) continue to be the backbone of the state's economic development efforts.

The beauty of our approach to economic development was that a company wouldn't benefit from the economic incentives if it didn't deliver on its promises. If the company failed to hire the number of people it promised, it couldn't keep the personal income taxes those nonexistent employees would have paid. If the company didn't generate the income it promised, it couldn't keep the corporate income tax it would have owed the state. It was a self-policing program. On the flip side, the state hadn't been collecting taxes on businesses that didn't exist yet, so by allowing companies to keep those taxes as an incentive to build or relocate in Kentucky, the state wasn't losing any money, and more Kentuckians would have jobs. It was a win-win situation.

New jobs bring new money into the state. New employees spend their money at retail establishments and create more jobs for employees who pay income taxes and work at enterprises that pay corporate taxes. Our research indicated that each "original" job—that is, one that produced goods or services that were exported from Kentucky and brought new money into the state—created two additional jobs in other businesses, such as bowling alleys, theaters, restaurants, hair salons, hardware stores, and other retailers. It was a great concept that worked very well. However, many surrounding states enacted similar legislation that eventually reduced our competitive advantage.

Kentucky's great advantage is its central geographic location. It has five interstate highways and nine limited-access turnpikes that serve industries and residents. The problem is that the population is undereducated compared with most competitor states. Companies looking to build or relocate need a healthy and well-educated workforce, a solid infrastructure, and a sound economic base. In the modern global economy, businesses are mercenary, and management will do what is in the company's best interests. Competition is the basis of a capitalistic society, so I can't argue with that.

There are always circumstances that you can't plan for and can't do anything about. The North American Free Trade Agreement (NAFTA), passed by Congress in 1994 during President Bill Clinton's first term, had a negative impact on Kentucky's economy. NAFTA wiped out Kentucky's garment industry, which had employed close to twenty-four thousand people. The industry shut its Kentucky facilities and moved its manufacturing plants to Mexico and Central America, where labor costs were cheaper. There was nothing we could do to prevent the companies from leaving.

Going into big and small communities all over Kentucky to talk about economic development was a good excuse to meet with people who could help my upcoming gubernatorial campaign. I used my job as lieutenant governor to good advantage for the people of Kentucky, but it was also good for my future political prospects. I wanted to establish a reputation as a jobs creator in every Kentucky community I visited. Whenever we attracted another company to the state, I made sure I was standing next to Governor Jones when he made the announcement and later during the ribbon-cutting ceremony. I wanted to make sure I received credit for landing that company. I'm convinced this played a major role in my win in 1995. I was for jobs, jobs, and more jobs! That's what many people were looking for in a governor—someone who could bring more good-paying jobs to Kentucky—and I had a proven track record of doing just that.

One of my duties as lieutenant governor was to preside over the state senate. Although I wielded the gavel, I did so under the direction of president pro tem John "Eck" Rose and Democratic majority leader Joe Wright. I never received any parliamentary training, and they probably preferred it that way. Before the 1992 legislative session began, Rose and Wright informed me that they could remove me from the president's chair any time they wanted to, but they wouldn't as long as I did what I was told. At the start of each day, I got a copy of the day's agenda and a script of what I was supposed to do and say. That was fine with me. They never asked for my advice, and it wasn't my job to interfere with what the senate was doing.

I made more than one mistake. Part of my job was to recognize individual senators who wished to speak during debates on the senate floor. The protocol was to introduce each speaker as "the senator from [his or her home county]." If there was more than one senator from a county, it was protocol to add the number of the district he or she represented. One day I recognized Susan Johns from Jefferson County. I said, "The chair recognizes the lady from Jefferson 42." The problem was that there were only thirty-eight senate districts (and therefore thirty-eight senators). After my gaffe, whenever she wanted to speak, she would smile and wave a little sign at me with her district number on it. On another occasion, I angered David Williams from Cumberland County because I didn't recognize him and let him speak. It was a complete oversight on my part. Still, I considered David a friend at the time, and his reaction to my error revealed a side of his character I hadn't seen before.

I knew my position in the state senate was mostly ceremonial. Even that role ended when the voters approved the gubernatorial succession amendment in November 1992, which also gave the senate the authority to elect its own presiding officer. I wasn't really interested in what the senate was doing anyway, but I did listen to the floor debates, which was good training for when I became governor. However, as lieutenant governor, I wasn't interested in making policy. As part of the executive branch of government, I wasn't invited to the senate's Democratic caucus, and I didn't really belong there. The legislative branch had established coequality with the executive branch by 1992, and the lawmakers didn't tolerate any intrusion on their independence.

Jones had come to the governor's office with a broad legislative agenda. Health insurance reform was his number-one priority, but he also wanted to reform campaign financing, the selection of universities' boards of trustees, and executive branch ethics, as well as obtain financial help for the Thoroughbred horse industry. Some of these agenda items didn't require heavy lifting, but others were very controversial and required a lot of work on Jones's part. I always believed a governor ought to concentrate on two or three major issues, but I knew there were many smaller issues a governor had to address.

I wanted Brereton to succeed. I liked him personally, but I also had political reasons for wanting him to be a successful governor. A gubernatorial term rarely goes smoothly, no matter who is governor. No governor is perfect. I know I wasn't. However, I knew that if the Jones administration wasn't viewed as successful, the Republicans would have a better chance of beating me in 1995. But if Jones had a successful four-year term, his accomplishments would rub off on me. I thought I would be better off following a successful Democratic administration than an unsuccessful one.

In 1992 Democrats outnumbered Republicans in the Kentucky Senate twenty-seven to eleven and in the Kentucky House of Representatives sixty-eight to thirty-two. Even though Governor Jones had some Republican support on every major piece of legislation he initiated, I never gave the possibility of Republican control of the legislature much thought, which was a mistake. I should have paid more attention when the Republicans began to pick up seats in the state senate as Kentucky became more conservative and the national Democratic Party became more liberal. We Democrats thought our losses were aberrations or that we hadn't chosen the right candidates and would win those seats back in the next election. We never gave the Republicans the credit they deserved, and we never thought they would take control of the state senate in 2000, let alone the state house of representatives in 2016. It is fair to say that this was a failure on my part.

When I was lieutenant governor, I invited the legislature's minority Republican leadership to the lieutenant governor's mansion for dinner, hoping to get better acquainted. At one point I asked John Rogers, the senate minority floor leader, why his party tried to obstruct legislation on hot-button issues that everyone knew needed to pass? He replied, "Paul, if they let us in and let us be involved and have input, we'd work with the senate Democrats. But as long as they keep us outside the process, we're going to keep throwing [rhetorical and procedural] grenades from the floor of the senate." The only thing the Republican caucus could do to influence legislation and gain attention was to oppose the Democrats. The party in charge—in this case, the Democrats—is responsible for the outcome. The party in the minority position—in this case, the Republicans—doesn't have to be fair and look at all sides of an issue. It can cherry-pick the controversial issues and demagogue them to death. I didn't understand this at the time, but it wouldn't have mattered because I had no influence with either Eck Rose or Joe Wright.

Even before Governor Jones took office, he told state agencies to prepare for $85 million in budget cuts because of a projected $155 million budget shortfall. Most governors cry "poor mouth" during their first legislative session, claiming the previous governor spent it all. And that is usually true! Those same governors then spend as much money as they can find so that they get credit for building projects, pay raises for state employees, and funding increases for state agencies. If they want to spend even more money, they just inflate the estimate of new state revenue and don't worry about the budget implications for the next governor.

Much of this guesstimating by governors stopped after Jones created the Consensus Forecasting Group (CFG), a nonpartisan group of seven economists from across the state who forecast state revenue. The governor and the legislature then use those revenue projections to develop the state budget and for long-range budget planning. Normally, the state budget has been within 1 or 2 percent of the CFG's revenue projection. If the governor and legislature draft a conservative budget, the budget will probably end up with a surplus. The creation of the CFG added stability to state government, and it took some of the pressure off the governor and the legislature. In my opinion, this was one of the most important public policy successes of the Jones administration, along with the gubernatorial succession amendment.

As lieutenant governor, for the first time in my life I found myself working with people who were more highly trained, more highly educated, and more knowledgeable about certain subjects than I was. I discovered that most of the time I had to depend on their advice rather than my own knowledge, which was a new experience for me. The vast majority of the time I found their advice to be valuable, sincere, and right on the money. To demonstrate my appreciation and gratitude, every year I held a reception at the lieutenant governor's mansion and later at the governor's mansion for state employees, and as governor, I made sure they got time off from work to attend.

Governor Jones also established the Rainy-Day Fund, a surplus account to use as a hedge against lower-than-expected state income or higher-than-expected state expenditures. He left the state treasury with a substantial balance; however, the legislature passed several tax cuts, including one for retirement income, during the last year of his administration that drastically affected income in the next biennium. I had to deal with this situation when I became governor.

One legislative initiative that Governor Jones promoted and I strongly supported was campaign finance reform. I thought this was one of his most important accomplishments as governor. Even though it would reduce my ability to self-fund my upcoming gubernatorial campaign and perhaps reduce my chances of winning in 1995, I thought it was the right thing to do. I think Jones made it part of his legislative agenda because he was fundamentally in favor of good government. As lieutenant governor, I already had a built-in advantage that none of my potential opponents would have, and if I couldn't win the governorship based on that advantage, I didn't deserve to sit in the governor's office. Three of the four previous governors had been multimillionaires who used their personal wealth to win election. I could have done the same if campaign finance reform hadn't passed.

John Y. Brown Jr. spent more than $1 million of his personal wealth on his whirlwind run for office in 1979. Wallace Wilkinson spent close to

$10 million of his own money in 1987, and Brereton Jones spent more than $7 million to defeat Larry Hopkins in 1991. The limit on individual campaign contributions at the time was $4,000, and Jones wanted to reduce that amount to $100 to lessen the influence of special-interest groups on the governor's office. The final bill reduced the amount an individual could contribute to gubernatorial and legislative campaigns to $500.

I strongly supported Jones's initiative on campaign finance reform. I played a small part in shaping the language of the bill, but my most important contribution was persuading members in both chambers to vote for it. Those who supported my candidacy for governor realized that it would take away one of my advantages in that election—namely, money. I was in a position to raise more money than anyone, and I was wealthy enough to finance as much of my gubernatorial campaign as necessary. I never liked asking people for money, and I had pretty much financed my own campaigns in the past. I think accepting money in the form of campaign contributions can be a corrupting influence in the governing process. At the very least, it gives the impression of impropriety, particularly with regard to the state bidding process and the awarding of state contracts. I agreed with Governor Jones that campaign finance reform was just good government.

In the senate, I worked with Mike Moloney, the bill's chief architect, to shape some of the bill's language. In the house, I worked with Greg Stumbo, Mike Bowling, Rocky Adkins, Clayton Little, Martin Sheehan, and Herbie Deskins to round up the votes to pass it. It didn't take much to convince Eck Rose to support the bill because, unbeknownst to me, he had gubernatorial aspirations himself and wanted to prevent wealthy people like me from "buying" the 1995 election. Rose wanted a level playing field when it came to campaign financing. I don't blame him.

Once Governor Jones took the position that the gubernatorial succession provision would not apply to him but would take effect after the next gubernatorial election, most state legislators fell in line and supported the whole package. The exception was the Republicans, who were more interested in grandstanding than in good government. The bill that passed during the 1992 regular session of the General Assembly set the maximum amount that gubernatorial candidates could raise privately at $600,000, which would then be matched two to one by the state. Any candidate who accepted the state's matching money could not spend more than $1.8 million on the election. However, candidates were not required to participate in the public financing plan. If any gubernatorial candidate decided not to participate, the other candidates who had agreed to abide by the law could exceed the $1.8 million spending limit, and they would still receive the two-to-one state matching funds for any additional money they raised. Therefore, the law contained built-in provisions that put candidates who spurned the campaign finance law at a disadvantage. Although the Republican Party did not support the bill, its 1995 gubernatorial candidate, Larry Forgy, abided by the new campaign finance law, and I defeated him!

Campaign finance reform (Senate Bill 226) became part of a more comprehensive reform package that included the constitutional amendment that allowed a governor to serve two consecutive terms, which I fully supported. This made campaign finance reform even more vital: with no limit on the amount of money an incumbent governor could raise, it would be practically impossible to defeat the incumbent, no matter how incompetent or corrupt. The constitutional amendment also eliminated the antiquated provision under which the lieutenant governor became the acting governor when the governor left the state for any reason, a practice lieutenant governors had abused in the past. And it required each political party's candidates for governor and lieutenant governor to run as a slate, rather than separately.

The amendment also uncoupled the legislative election cycle from the gubernatorial election cycle. This allowed a member of the General Assembly to run for governor or lieutenant governor without first giving up his or her legislative seat. An added benefit of this provision was that it allowed the leadership a full year to get newly elected legislators up to speed on important issues. In addition, it made newly elected lawmakers less dependent on the governor for leadership on legislation.

I supported the succession amendment because four years is not enough time for governors to pass and implement their programs. Governors' first terms should be used to pass their legislative agendas, and their second terms should be used to implement those agendas and make sure the reforms do what they were intended to do. When I ran for governor, I fully intended to serve two four-year terms. I viewed my reelection in 1999 as the people's evaluation of my first term, sort of like a college midterm examination.

I also fully supported the provision that required the governor and lieutenant governor to run as a slate. That eliminated the possibility of having a governor from one political party and a lieutenant governor from the other party, such as when Republican Louie Nunn was the governor and Democrat Wendell Ford was the lieutenant governor. It also meant the lieutenant governor's office was no longer an automatic stepping-stone to the governor's office. I once told my lieutenant governor, Steve Henry, "You can't be the lieutenant governor for eight years and expect to get elected

The lieutenant governor's mansion was a great place to entertain. Judi and I enjoyed hosting people from all over the state. (Courtesy of Kentucky Department for Libraries and Archives, Archives and Records Management Division)

Dr. Steve Henry, my lieutenant governor running mate. He helped us get additional votes in Louisville, Owensboro, and Bowling Green. (Courtesy of Kentucky Department for Libraries and Archives, Archives and Records Management Division)

Even as lieutenant governor, there was no shortage of people, especially young people, who wanted their photograph taken in my office. (Courtesy of Kentucky Department for Libraries and Archives, Archives and Records Management Division)

governor because you'll get all of the blame for what I did wrong and none of the credit for what I did right!" He didn't take my advice.

I believe Governor Jones thought his health insurance reform law and his gubernatorial succession and campaign finance law would be his last-ing legacies. But the insurance companies torpedoed the health insurance reform law, and the Republicans eventually sank the campaign finance law. Even so, there was a lot of good in that legislation that survived. I think Jones still deserves an A for effort. The Republicans, both in Kentucky and nationally, were dead-set against any campaign finance law because their party catered to the moneyed class. But there weren't many Republicans in the state legislature in 1992, so nobody paid much attention to them or their "welfare for politicians" slogan. Little did I know that this issue would rise from the ashes like a phoenix during my second term as governor.

6

The 1995 Campaign and My March to the Governor's Office

After serving as Governor Jones's secretary of the Cabinet for Economic Development for sixteen months, I began my unofficial campaign for governor. Thus, nobody was surprised when I officially announced my candidacy after the November 1994 election. Going into the campaign, my strategy was to win in eastern Kentucky, win big in Louisville and Jefferson County, and do well enough in western Kentucky to offset the support for Larry Forgy, the probable Republican nominee, in central Kentucky and in the Fifth Congressional District.

Official announcements by candidates for governor occurred later than usual because the voters had approved the gubernatorial succession amendment in 1992, which required each gubernatorial candidate to select a running mate for lieutenant governor before raising any money for the campaign. Over the past sixteen months, Skipper, Bill Beam, Judi, and I had discussed several possible running mates. But we were hindered by the fact that some of the people under consideration were still deciding whether to jump in the gubernatorial race themselves or run for some other state or local office. We narrowed it down to six or eight people who might be interested in being lieutenant governor and could bring in additional votes on Election Day. I had personal discussions with all of them.

After much deliberation, we finally settled on Louisville orthopedic surgeon Dr. Steve Henry, who seemed like an ideal candidate. As our self-imposed deadline for naming a running mate approached in the fall of 1994, Judi was the one who tipped the scale in Steve's favor when she said, "Well, *I* think it ought to be him." I have always trusted Judi's political instincts, and her endorsement was good enough for me. Steve and I were friends but not particularly close political allies. Steve was originally from Owensboro, which was trending Republican, and he still had family there. He had been a starter on the Owensboro High School basketball team in 1972, when it won the state championship. He earned a bachelor's degree from Western Kentucky University (WKU), where he served as president of the student body and was a voting member on the WKU Board of Regents. His fraternity brothers included future WKU president Gary Ransdell and future Kentucky Supreme Court chief justice John Minton Jr., so his personal connections would be helpful politically. After graduating from WKU, Steve earned his medical degree from the University of Louisville. During the first Persian Gulf War, he gained international attention for his innovative technique of utilizing antibiotic beads to treat musculoskeletal infections. Steve had also achieved a high political profile in Jefferson County, serving as a county commissioner on the fiscal court and being involved in several good-government initiatives. Steve's selection certainly helped me get votes in Jefferson County that I otherwise might not have received. I truly believe that if my running mate had been someone from eastern or far western Kentucky, I would have lost the 1995 gubernatorial race.

When I asked Steve to be my running mate, I told him there were two stipulations: First, he had to agree not to run against me in 1999 because I fully intended to run for a second term. Second, he had to agree not to publicly oppose any of my policies or legislative initiatives. I assured him that I would never pressure him to publicly advocate any policy or initiative with which he disagreed, particularly regarding health care issues. He agreed to both stipulations.

During both the primary and the fall campaigns, we relied mostly on volunteer labor, including Skipper, Beam, Mary Ray Oaken, Melissa Forsythe, George Helton, my children, my sisters, my brother-in-law, and scads of local people all over Kentucky. They were not paid a dime out of campaign funds; nor did we pay them under the table. We also didn't promise any of the volunteers a job in my administration. Some of them ended up being hired simply because they believed in my policies and were competent people, but there was never any quid pro quo. We decided to use $1.6 million of the $1.8 million spending limit to pay outside campaign consultants and pollsters, so we essentially ran a person-to-person campaign on just $200,000.

Immediately after I officially announced my candidacy for governor, we were off and running! We hit the campaign trail and made stops in Louisville, Frankfort, Owensboro, Paducah, Bowling Green, and Pikeville on the first day. I didn't stop campaigning for the next twelve months. Despite the advantages of being lieutenant governor, I anticipated stiff competition in the Democratic primary in May 1995. I certainly didn't want to put the cart before the horse, so we concentrated on winning the primary before focusing on the November election.

Senate president John "Eck" Rose expressed his intention to run for governor. He selected Denise Harper Angel, the Jefferson County property valuation administrator (and, as of 2022, a state senator), as his running mate, and I thought that was an astute choice. She was a proven vote-getter in southern and western Jefferson County, and she had some union support. She would likely add as many Jefferson County votes to Rose's campaign as Steve Henry did to mine. However, I thought Rose lacked the name recognition, the people skills, and the fund-raising ability to truly challenge me in the Democratic primary.

The one candidate I took seriously was Kentucky secretary of state Bob Babbage. He was the scion of a prominent political family and had served as state auditor during Wallace Wilkinson's administration. He believed those two state posts would help get him elected governor in 1995, an office he had sought his entire adult life. Whereas I didn't envision Rose as governor material, I thought Babbage was, plus he had statewide name recognition and political contacts. He was certainly a more polished speaker than I was at the outset of the campaign, and he probably presented a better overall image as well.

Babbage, who hailed from Lexington, in the heart of the Bluegrass, officially kicked off his gubernatorial campaign on the same day I did. Tommy Thompson from Owensboro, president of the National Association of Homebuilders, was his running mate. Babbage claimed that he and Thompson were running as "New Democrats" in response to the Republican electoral tidal wave that had taken place nationwide in 1994. In Kentucky, Ed Whitfield had defeated Democratic incumbent Tom Barlow in the First Congressional District, and Republican Ron Lewis had defeated Joe Prather to fill the late William Natcher's Second Congressional District seat. By running as a so-called New Democrat, Babbage was trying to put some distance between him and the old-style Democratic Party, which was rapidly losing its grip on power in Kentucky, and the more liberal national Democratic Party headed by Bill and Hillary Clinton.

Babbage identified me as one of the "Old Guard" Democrats in Kentucky, and he vowed to take the Kentucky Democratic Party and the commonwealth in a new direction with a unique campaign platform. That platform included a proposal to amend the Kentucky Constitution so that any major tax increase equal to 1 percent or more of the General Fund would have to be approved by referendum. This was probably a good political position, but it was not good policy. Voters in Kentucky approve only amendments to the state constitution by referendum, and I think that is the right approach. There are generally two sides to any important public policy issue, particularly if it involves a tax increase. The General Assembly is better able to weigh both sides of an issue and do what is best for the entire state over the long run. Another plank in Babbage's platform offered free college tuition to high school graduates with A and B averages and a free vocational school education to any high school graduate, paid for by proceeds from the state lottery. (My administration secured adoption of a law that allocated all lottery money to college scholarships using a different and, in my opinion, much better system.) Because of these ideas and others, I viewed Babbage as my main opposition in the Democratic primary.

Bob Babbage was an honorable man, and he and I were and are friends. He was the grandson of former Kentucky governor Keen Johnson, and I considered him a good Democrat. However, at just forty-six years old, he lacked the life experience to be governor. After I won the election in 1995, I thought enough of his political acumen to appoint him chair of the Kentucky Democratic Party, the same position I had held from November 1981 until June 1983. Babbage's selection of Thompson as his running mate was a good one, and they ended up beating me and Henry in Daviess County by 757 votes. I didn't know Thompson all that well, but I heard he was a good family man, and he and his wife were always friendly toward Judi and me.

Rumors were that Ben Chandler, the state auditor, was wavering between getting into the governor's race and running for attorney general. He certainly had the charisma to be a formidable opponent and ample name recognition around the state, being the grandson of former governor Albert B. "Happy" Chandler. He had already run a successful statewide campaign for state auditor in 1991.

Lexington lawyer Gatewood Galbraith also ran in the Democratic primary. Everybody knew he had no chance to win, and my campaign staff thought he would pull more votes away from Babbage than from me, as they were both from central Kentucky. Therefore, we never considered him a real threat.

I had a fatalistic attitude about the gubernatorial campaign. If I lost, it would definitely spell the end of my political career, but I was okay with that. I would go home to Pikeville and find something else to do. I paid attention to who my opponents were, but I didn't obsess over any of them. My attitude was very matter-of-fact: "It doesn't matter who decides to get in the race. I'm running, and I'm running to win!" After the field for the Democratic primary was set, I had no serious doubts about finishing first. But with multiple candidates in the race, the question was, could I get 40 percent of the vote, as required by law, to avoid a runoff election?

Two years prior to my official announcement that I was running for governor, Skipper and I had divided the state into eighteen campaign regions and appointed a campaign chair for each region. These folks were county judges, state legislators, and businesspeople. We called them our "board of directors" during the campaign. These people then carved up their regions of responsibility into smaller areas and recruited individuals to manage the campaign there. Once the November 1994 election was over and I made my official announcement, the campaign hit the ground running in all eighteen regions of the state. Mine was probably the last gubernatorial campaign in Kentucky to employ such an extensive volunteer grassroots organization, and it really made a difference, both in the primary and in the November election. Our campaign organization went all the way down to the precinct level, especially in the urban areas. This was "old school" politics, and those precinct captains were instrumental in getting out the vote.

During the primary campaign, I presented a plan to reform the juvenile justice system in Kentucky that I estimated would cost between $30 million and $50 million a year, including $8 million to shift the cost of jailing juveniles from the counties to the state. As a county judge, I had seen firsthand what happened to incarcerated juveniles. County detention facilities for juveniles were wholly inadequate. Young people were housed in jail cells with adults, where they were subjected to sexual or physical abuse and exposed to hardened criminals. The state's juvenile justice system was so bad that during the Jones administration, the US Department of Justice had ordered the Kentucky Justice Cabinet to straighten it out or face the loss of federal funding, which was substantial.

My reform plan included opening most juvenile court proceedings to the public and instituting random drug tests for juveniles convicted of drug offenses, local curfews, home incarceration, day treatment, work programs, and military-style boot camps for juveniles convicted of nonviolent crimes. I thought violent juvenile offenders ought to be tried and punished as adults. Under my plan, the penalty for adults who used children to sell drugs would be ten years in prison without parole.

In early March 1995 I received the endorsement of the Kentucky Educators Political Action Committee, which was the political arm of the Kentucky Education Association. I didn't take any monetary donations from political action committees (PACs), mainly because I didn't need to in order to reach the $600,000 limit set by the public financing law. In addition, in the wake of the FBI's 1992 investigation of corruption within the Business, Organization, and Professions Committees in the Kentucky General

Assembly (commonly referred to as the BOPTROT scandal), I didn't want there to be any hint of quid pro quo deals with special interests.

Polls in early May indicated I was the front-runner heading into the last three weeks of the primary campaign. I led Bob Babbage by thirteen percentage points, and I was ahead of Eck Rose by twenty-two percentage points. However, 35 percent of those polled were still undecided, which was too many for me to feel comfortable heading into the primary. I knew I was going to come in first, but it was unclear whether I would get to the 40 percent threshold to avoid a runoff election.

A runoff election would be dicey. If the losing candidate threw his support to my opponent in the runoff, I might not be able to overcome that. Therefore, late in the primary campaign, we decided to run a negative television ad against Babbage, where I accused him of flip-flopping on abortion, the death penalty, the lottery, and lowering the voting age to sixteen. This went against my preference to run a positive campaign, but I really needed to avoid a runoff.

My grassroots organization on the ground, combined with a modern television ad campaign, proved to be enough to win the primary outright. I received 45 percent of the vote—the largest margin of victory in a Democratic primary in twenty years. Babbage came in a distant second with 24 percent, and Rose came in third with 21 percent. Galbraith, who ran solely on the issue of legalizing marijuana, did better than I expected, receiving 9 percent of the vote. As excited as we were about winning the primary, we knew we would be swimming upstream in November.

As expected, Larry Forgy easily defeated his opponent in the Republican primary, Bob Gable. Beating Forgy in November would be difficult because the Democratic Party had been ensconced in the governor's office for twenty-four years, and I anticipated that some negative aspects of previous Democratic administrations would be pinned on me. Therefore, I didn't rest after winning the primary. I knew it was going to be a tough fight, so I wasted no time getting back to the grind of campaigning. Political campaigns are endurance races, not sprints.

As anticipated, Forgy's pitch was straightforward: "It's time for a change." And after twenty-four years of Democratic governors, there was no effective counterargument. Forgy said the election was not just about him and me; it was about Kentucky and its people. He stuck to his main theme of taking back government from the Democrats in Frankfort, who had been taxing and spending Kentuckians to death for twenty-four years.

I viewed Larry as a formidable opponent. He appeared to be the perfect candidate. He didn't have a lot of weaknesses. He was well known, a great orator, and knowledgeable about the state. He had been Governor Louie Nunn's budget director, so he was familiar with state government. The Republican establishment had been grooming him to run for governor for many years. He had some influential support among the Democratic establishment as well, such as former state senator and Kentucky Democratic Party chair Howard "Sonny" Hunt; Jack Hall, who had been Governor Julian Carroll's right-hand man; and former congressman Bill Curlin. Some Democrats believed it was inevitable that the next governor would be a Republican, and they wanted to be on good terms with him. Forgy had also been a member of the prestigious Louisville law firm Wyatt Tarrant & Combs, and he was highly regarded by former governor Bert Combs and Combs's lieutenant governor, Wilson Wyatt. Therefore, defeating Forgy would not be easy.

The day after the primary election, Skipper and I talked about the fall campaign. Our biggest, most immediate challenge was deciding who to recruit to chair the Kentucky Democratic Party. Because we were adhering to the new campaign finance law, the amount of money the campaign needed to raise was limited; however, the political parties themselves did not have such restrictions. Each political party could contribute only $500 to their respective gubernatorial campaigns, but there was no limit on how much they could spend on behalf of the entire ticket, as long as there was no coordination between the party and the individual campaigns.

We first considered attorney Pat Mulloy, who had run unsuccessfully for Congress in 1984, chaired John Y. Brown Jr.'s unsuccessful campaign for governor in 1987, and been secretary of the Finance and Administration Cabinet in the Jones administration. However, Pat couldn't commit to the three days a week the job required. Then one day, a couple of weeks after the primary, I received a phone call from my friend Brent Rice, a Lexington attorney and law partner of Terry McBrayer. Brent said, "Paul, I think if you ask him, Terry would be willing to be chair of the party." So I asked Terry, and I was relieved when he accepted, even though he agreed to serve only until the November election. I can honestly say, without hesitation, that the two people who can claim credit for getting me elected governor are Skipper Martin and Terry McBrayer. If not for them, I never would have had a chance. They made all the difference in my campaign, and I sure didn't make it easy for them.

I knew at the time that McBrayer's appointment as chair of the party was important, but I didn't realize until later *how* important it was. Terry was a fund-raising heavyweight and had national contacts. During my campaign, he raised money for the Kentucky Democratic Party at the national level, and he got the Democratic National Committee and the Democratic Governors Association to help. He knew how to raise money, and it didn't bother him in the least to ask people for it. Under Terry's direction, the party raised close to $2 million! He passed away in 2020, and his death hit me hard. He was a dedicated and loyal friend.

Given Forgy's argument that twenty-four years of Democratic domination of the governor's office was long enough, we couldn't promise four more years of the same. So we tried to divert voters' attention to other issues that weren't necessarily relevant to Kentucky state government. Fortunately, most voters didn't catch on. The Kentucky Democratic Party used the $2 million it raised to attack Newt Gingrich and his so-called Contract with America by calling it his Contract *on* America. Terry tried to tie Forgy to every radical idea advocated by Republicans, such as auctioning off the Tennessee Valley Authority, which included some of Kentucky's public lakes. That idea didn't sit well with many of Kentucky's outdoor enthusiasts, and we milked that issue for all it was worth. We engaged Forgy in arguments about school prayer and abortion, even though there wasn't anything either of us could do about those issues, which had already been decided by the US Supreme Court. At that time, Kentuckians were about evenly split on the abortion issue, and we were on the side of women's right to choose.

As a candidate in the summer of 1995, I was like a deer caught in headlights. I was not a good stump speaker, which became painfully obvious early on. Forgy was a trained lawyer who was accustomed to arguing cases in court and speaking publicly. In contrast, I was a small eastern Kentucky coal operator who felt like a fish out of water in front of large gatherings, despite my four years as lieutenant governor. I had a terrible inferiority complex when it came to being on the same stage as Forgy. Some political pundits described the gubernatorial race as "the engineer versus the silver-tongued orator," and I think that was a fair characterization. Larry was one of the best old-style stump speakers anywhere in Kentucky. He had a homespun charm, he could quote the Bible without hesitation, and he could spontaneously come up with stinging retorts. I would have enjoyed listening to him if I hadn't been his opponent!

The first time Forgy and I appeared together was at a Leadership Kentucky meeting in Louisville. I read a speech I had composed. I was very nervous and did a poor job of delivering it. Forgy was completely at ease and delivered an extemporaneous speech that blew me away. Later, in early fall, Forgy and I met again at a conference in Lexington on postsecondary education. I gave what I would classify as a very focused, detailed, and well-prepared speech, only to have Forgy outdo me again with his witty and folksy oratory. His funny phrases and biblical quotes had audiences eating out of his hand. I couldn't match him.

Because the new campaign finance law limited each campaign to $1.8 million, Forgy and I could spend only so much money on television advertising, and it didn't take either of us long to raise our $600,000. So we were both looking for invitations to speak to large groups of people to get our respective messages out. As a result, we made dozens of joint appearances all over the state. I noticed that the more appearances I made, the more comfortable and adept I was at public speaking. I was never as good as Larry, but by the end of the campaign, I was a hell of a lot better than I had been at the beginning. Later in the campaign, when we both spoke at a Kentucky Real Estate Investors Association meeting in Lexington, I actually thought I bested him. That event made me confident that I could at least hold my own.

After a while, I realized that Forgy was not as intellectually sharp as he appeared to be. He spoke well, but what he said sometimes didn't have much substance. I went into the summer thinking, "I'd *like* to be governor, but gosh, this guy is so well prepared, he would make a good governor too." By August, I knew that wasn't true. First of all, I thought Larry showed poor political judgment when he selected Tom Handy, an attorney in London, to be his running mate. Not that Handy wasn't a good man; I'm sure he was. However, London is located in the very Republican Fifth Congressional District, which Forgy was going to win anyway. He didn't need to shore up his support there. If Larry had been politically astute, he would have selected a running mate from northern or western Kentucky. If he had done that, I think he probably would have been elected governor. I thought his selection of an attorney as his running mate was another mistake. In our joint appearances, I would ask the crowd, "Do you want to elect an engineer and a doctor, or do you want to elect two lawyers?" This would always elicit nods and a few chuckles.

By September, the campaign had taken on greater meaning that went beyond my personal ambition to be governor. Some people just want the *title*, but I actually wanted the job of *governing*. I wanted the job because I was prepared to do it. I became more passionate about what I believed in and more knowledgeable about the issues that concerned Kentuckians, and in the process, I became a better public speaker. I began to believe that if Forgy were elected, it would be detrimental to Kentucky's future.

Nationally, there were only three gubernatorial campaigns in 1995: Mississippi, Louisiana, and Kentucky. The national focus was on Kentucky because it was seen as the first real referendum on the Republican "revolution" that had occurred in Congress and in state legislatures around the country in 1994. Our decision to nationalize the race and attack Newt Gingrich and the Republicans was thought to have implications for President Bill Clinton's 1996 reelection.

After the primary election, McBrayer and I publicly suggested to Forgy that we refrain from raising money for our parties. Not surprisingly, he rejected that proposal because, generally speaking, wealthy people are more likely to support the Republican Party than the Democratic Party. Under the new campaign finance law, we were plowing new ground as to what could and couldn't be done. We thought we knew what the law allowed and prohibited, and we believed we honored both the letter and the spirit of the law. We never felt we violated the law as it pertained to the relationship between the governor's campaign and the Kentucky Democratic Party. The Republicans did the same thing. They just didn't do it as well as we did. The Kentucky Republican Party raised money, but not quite as much as the Kentucky Democratic Party.

One special interest I wanted to court was organized labor because I truly believe that unions need a voice in the marketplace of politics. Plus, I knew I needed organized labor's support if I hoped to have any chance of winning the election. Danny Ross had worked for me in the lieutenant governor's office as my liaison to organized labor, which was a political job. His specific job had been to stay in contact with labor unions around the state. He left that position before the 1995 primary and went to work for the International Brotherhood of Teamsters in Louisville to help them get their members out to vote.

Throughout the summer, both Forgy and I composed position papers and tried to stamp out small fires, some of which were beyond our control. For example, in late June I sent a strongly worded letter to President Clinton urging him to stop the federal government's efforts to classify tobacco as a drug because of the nicotine content. That letter was pure theater; it wouldn't influence the Clinton administration, but it offered me some political cover with tobacco farmers. My letter short-circuited Forgy's attempt to use the tobacco issue against me, and it allowed me to distance myself from President Clinton.

In mid-July Forgy came out in favor of term limits for county officials, state legislators, and members of Congress. Forgy proposed limiting all legislators to twelve-year terms, which would be six terms for state representatives and members of the US House of Representatives, three terms for state senators, and two terms for US senators. I responded by saying that I was in favor of term limits for presidents and governors but not for the legislatures in either Washington or Frankfort. I believe the legislative branch of government needs continuity and slow, evolutionary change. The legislature requires institutional memory. Many newly elected members of Congress and the General Assembly are full of piss and vinegar when they arrive and believe they can change the world. They provide much-needed energy and enthusiasm, but that passion needs to be tempered by older heads who have been around a while and can say, "Yes, we've heard of that or we tried that, but here's why it didn't pass or here's why it didn't work as planned." Experienced legislators who have been in office a while at the national or state level know how to steer clear of the pitfalls. That institutional memory is needed to avoid repeating the same mistakes. To me, the real issue is gerrymandering. Most legislative districts are noncompetitive due to partisan gerrymandering. This leads candidates to take extreme positions instead of seeking the middle ground, which is where I think government ought to be.

In July former governor Wallace Wilkinson appeared on a Lexington television show and said that because of my endorsement of collective bargaining for state employees and teachers, he hadn't decided whether to support me or Forgy. To me, this indicated that members of the Democratic establishment thought Forgy had a good chance of winning, so many of them were hedging their bets. By October, however, I was a much better candidate than many people had anticipated, and the polls indicated that it would be an extremely competitive race. Wilkinson ended up endorsing me that month, and that is when I realized some of the so-called establishment Democrats were going to come home and support me.

In early August, at the annual Fancy Farm picnic, we may have stooped to a new low. Former Republican governor Louie Nunn had turned against Forgy at some point, and Phil Patton, a supporter of mine from Nunn's hometown of Glasgow (but no relation to me), had purloined a copy of Nunn's recorded interview on that subject, which my staff hooked up to the event's sound system. When it was my turn to speak that afternoon, I started talking, but as planned, campaign intern Adam Edelen walked over to the podium carrying a telephone and said, "Governor, I've got a phone call for you." I acted surprised and said, "Not now, Adam! Can't you see I'm making a speech here? I can't take a phone call!" Adam replied, "Well, it's Governor Louie Nunn calling." I raised my eyebrows in mock surprise and said, "Oh, Governor Nunn is calling? Well, let me take that!" I took the phone and said, "Hello, Governor. How are you doing?" Then my staff played an excerpt from Nunn's radio interview over the sound system, such as Louie's statement to the effect that "Forgy's lust for power, Forgy's financial greed, Forgy's social ambition has taken its toll on a good mother's son. Obviously, he has deceived many of us, and he's attempting to deceive the voters of Kentucky." I said into the phone, "Is that right? Oh, well, I didn't know that!" Then my staff played another of Nunn's derogatory remarks about Forgy. All this was happening while an uncomfortable Forgy sat four feet behind me in plain view.

Next we brought the "Pander Bear" onstage to make fun of Forgy's pandering to every special-interest group he came in contact with. I admit this stunt was my idea. It must have been one hundred degrees that day, but we had a staffer wearing a heavy panda suit throwing "pander dollars" to the crowd as we sang to the tune of "Happy Days Are Here Again." It went something like this: "The Pander Bear is back again, oh the Pander Bear is back again, he will pander here, he will pander there, he'll pander everywhere!" My supporters roared with delight. The only retort the Forgy supporters had was loud yells and air horns, which made it impossible for me to be heard.

After I ended my speech and sat down, Edelen, who had moved into the crowd in front of the stage, held up one of my campaign signs. It blocked the view of Ted Jackson, Forgy's campaign manager, who reached up and grabbed the sign. Adam turned around and was getting ready to haul off and punch him in the nose when I grabbed Adam by the collar and pulled him back before he landed the punch. The crowd went wild, and we almost incited a full-scale donnybrook! I turned around and saw that everyone on the stage, including Forgy, was laughing.

The mood didn't get much better as the day progressed. When the Republican candidate for secretary of state, Steve Crabtree, started to speak, he went overboard in criticizing former governor John Y. Brown Jr., who was the father of his opponent, John Y. Brown III. Brown III jumped from his seat with blood in his eyes and headed straight for Crabtree. I grabbed young Brown around the waist as he passed me and stopped him just short of his target, or it would have been an event for the ages!

Because of what we and the Republicans instigated that day, there are now rules about what a candidate can do, and barriers are erected to keep the crowd away from the stage. Many people think the Fancy Farm political event is crude theater, but I think it's useful. It puts the candidates under pressure and allows voters to observe how they react. We felt like we came out ahead at Fancy Farm, and it built enthusiasm and momentum in the Democratic base heading into the fall campaign.

In late August I did what just about every successful Kentucky politician has to do: I "kissed the ring" of the National Rifle Association (NRA) when I came out against banning assault-style military weapons. Once again, this was a strictly political decision on my part. If I had supported a ban on assault-style weapons, it probably would have doomed my chances of winning. In actuality, I am in favor of banning assault weapons, and I say this as a life member of the NRA and a gun collector who owns more than seventy-five weapons of various makes, models, and calibers. I don't think the average citizen needs an atomic bomb, 155mm howitzer, tank, flamethrower, hand grenade, or military-style assault rifle.

Today, we hear a lot of talk from Republicans about sticking to the original meaning of the US Constitution at the time of its composition. People on the political right call themselves "originalists." I'm an originalist myself, but I have a different interpretation of the Second Amendment than they do. When the framers wrote the Constitution, the nation did not have much of a standing army. In fact, there was a strong sentiment against a standing army. At that time, the individual state militias, which had played a major role in winning the Revolutionary War, were the nation's only effective defense. Most militiamen were armed with smoothbore, single-shot muskets or Kentucky single-shot long rifles—the same weapons they used to hunt wild game and for personal protection. Today's weapons designed to kill masses of human beings as quickly as possible, such as machine guns and automatic weapons, didn't exist. I'm fine with people owning hunting and sporting rifles, but I don't know a single hunter who shoots game with a military assault rifle. They are impractical for that purpose. However, during the 1995 governor's race, I pandered to the NRA for the sake of my campaign. Besides, that issue had nothing to do with the governor's office. The NRA did not endorse me.

In late summer I borrowed an idea from Bob Babbage's primary campaign against me. I began to advertise myself as a "different kind of Democrat" to distinguish myself from the more liberal national Democratic Party. Kentucky Democrats are more conservative than East Coast and West Coast Democrats. Democratic candidates in Kentucky have to acknowledge that fact if they hope to succeed. I didn't want Forgy to brand me a liberal Democrat, so I decided to get out in front of that issue early in the fall campaign. My strategy was to emphasize my employment and education agenda, which are always popular issues among voters, while at the same time putting Forgy on the defensive. At every opportunity, I tried to tie him to Newt Gingrich and the Republicans' idea of privatizing the Tennessee Valley Authority, including all its power plants and lakes. That was an important issue in rural Kentucky, and we exploited it.

In a joint appearance with Forgy before the Kentucky Bankers Association in mid-September, I came out in favor of annual sessions of the

Kentucky General Assembly. In my opinion, it is the governor's job to lead the public discussion on issues such as higher education, criminal justice reform, and protecting the environment, but it is up to the people, through their representatives in the General Assembly, to enact any changes to existing public policy. The fact is, the legislature should develop public policy—including the state budget, which determines policy priorities—and it should oversee the administration of that policy. Legislators cannot effectively oversee public policy administration if they meet only once every two years, as they did when I first took office. A governor's job is to implement and administer, through the cabinet secretaries, the public policy enacted by the legislature, whether the governor agrees with it or not, and to convince the public to change public policy, through the legislature, if the governor thinks it should be changed.

In a perfect world, public policy would be decided on merit alone, but as a practical matter, public policy issues usually have political implications. Governors spend most of their time trying to provide leadership on issues that they believe are important to the state as a whole.

Forgy took the position that annual sessions of the General Assembly would further erode the balance of power between the executive and legislative branches. Larry did not endear himself to influential members of the General Assembly, which worked to my advantage.

I also made a big issue of Forgy's tax returns because he was reluctant to release them. Steve Henry and I had released all our tax returns early in the campaign because I thought it was the right thing to do, whether someone is running for governor of a state or president of the United States. Tax returns can inform the public about a candidate's motivations, ethics, and sense of fair play. There might be legitimate reasons to redact some information, but I never did. I put my tax returns in a file and said, "If you're a legitimate member of the media, you are welcome to come in and look at them." Because Forgy was slow in releasing his tax returns, I sent a letter to the IRS and asked it to investigate whether Forgy had paid taxes on a 1994 South-East Coal land deal in Hancock County. He finally released his tax returns in early October, but even then, he withheld information on his capital assets, indicating there was something he didn't want anyone to see. Most of the shots I was throwing at Forgy were landing, and just like in a boxing match, they all added up. Larry played defense more than he should have and more than he needed to, but our attacks were very aggressive.

Our first debate on Kentucky Educational Television (KET) didn't help Forgy either. I felt very confident going into it, and Forgy was clearly off his game that evening. Both my staff and I thought I won the debate, and the media agreed, stating that I could now go toe to toe with my opponent. Forgy had a sweating problem that night, and afterward he claimed to be suffering from the flu. But according to some people on my staff, they had convinced Forgy's former girlfriend to attend the debate and sit in the front row, which put Forgy into a tizzy because he had no idea what she might do. Whatever the reason, he didn't give a good performance.

Later that fall, Forgy attacked me with the old eastern Kentucky "hillbilly" stereotype. He insinuated that, if elected, I would bring "Pike County–style politics" to the governor's office, which he described as consisting of "rougher elements" and a "hobnailed boot" kind of governance, evoking memories of Nazi Germany. I didn't appreciate that and asked him to apologize, but he said that would happen only if "hell froze over." That was a smart strategy on his part because voters in certain parts of the state had the impression that politics in eastern Kentucky was less than ethical. And unfortunately, there were many examples of that. I tried to diffuse the attack as quickly as I could because those stereotypes are difficult to shed. Larry reinforced an image of eastern Kentucky that many Kentuckians shared, and his attack was effective.

One of our advantages over Forgy was support from women voters. Larry's comments about women's role in society and his embrace, late in the campaign, of Dr. Frank Simon, a right-wing antiabortion, antigay activist from Louisville (and later head of the Kentucky Tea Party), helped us in that regard. I knew Dr. Simon by reputation, but I don't believe I ever met him. Forgy also had the support of out-of-state evangelical groups such as the Virginia-based Christian Coalition, which distributed voter guides and sponsored ads throughout the state. We worked very aggressively to get Black voters to the polls, whereas Forgy realized that this demographic was not going to support him, so he didn't court those voters.

Late in October, the media pointed out that when Forgy's campaign distributed his weekly itinerary, it failed to include events tied to the evangelical Christian right. The media accused him of trying to hide that association to avoid offending more socially moderate voters. They also attacked his inexplicable embrace of Dr. Simon. These issues were like manna from heaven for our campaign, and we capitalized on them to depict Forgy as an evangelical Christian extremist. It hurt him with independent voters as well as pro-choice women, particularly in urban areas.

We made defense of the Kentucky Education Reform Act (KERA) another pillar of our campaign strategy. Forgy had gone so far as to call the election a referendum on KERA, which he described as a boondoggle and a failure that should be repealed. I was happy to exploit that issue. I predicted that a Forgy victory would lead to a stampede to repeal KERA, and it was a shame that he was so cavalier about our children's future. I was not an authority on educational issues, but I trusted the experts who told me that KERA was cutting-edge legislation and a model for the entire country. I also hammered Forgy for supporting school vouchers—a dog whistle for racists—so parents could send their children to private schools that had fewer Black students and fewer students from poor families. I think he was appealing to parents who didn't want their kids going to inner-city schools. I said I wanted to *fix* KERA, not re-create a segregated school system.

Very late in the campaign, a group from the business community led by David Jones of Humana, Oz Nelson of UPS, and John Hall of Ashland Oil paid for television ads in support of KERA. Although these efforts were independent of my campaign, they greatly benefited me. A poll indicated that I was on the right side of this issue, as the majority of Kentuckians liked the reforms initiated by KERA. I think KERA was a visionary piece of legislation, and the General Assembly demonstrated a lot of courage in passing it, along with the largest tax increase in the state's history to support it. The Kentucky Supreme Court gave the lawmakers the political cover to do this by ruling that the old system of funding education was unconstitutional, so the legislature *had* to come up with a different funding plan. One of the most important accomplishments of my governorship was preserving the essence of KERA.

At the end of September, one poll indicated that I enjoyed an eleven-point lead among people who said they would definitely or probably vote and a five-point lead among people who said they would most likely vote. However, by the end of October, those figures had shifted significantly. The new poll indicated that my lead had shrunk to two percentage points among people who said they would definitely or probably vote, and it gave Forgy a seven-point lead among people who were likely to vote—a swing of twelve percentage points! The poll's margin for error among definite or probable voters was four percentage points, and among likely voters the margin for error was just over six percentage points.

At the end of October, both the *Lexington Herald-Leader* and the *Louisville Courier-Journal* endorsed me, as did the *Owensboro Messenger Inquirer*, the *Kentucky Post* in northern Kentucky, the *Glasgow Daily Times*, and the *Ashland Daily Independent*. Forgy got endorsements from the *Kentucky New Era* in Hopkinsville, the *Kentucky Enquirer* in northern Kentucky, and the *Gleaner* in Henderson. Although newspaper endorsements were less important than in previous elections, they still meant a whole lot more than they do today. I think the *Courier-Journal* and *Herald-Leader* endorsements were decisive because those two papers had the largest circulations in Kentucky. Had they endorsed Forgy, I believe I would have lost the election. Those endorsements probably gave me an additional twenty thousand to thirty thousand votes.

The KERA ads funded by the business community in late October and Forgy's embrace of Dr. Simon seemed to turn the election around in my favor. Before the airing of the pro-KERA television ads and before Forgy allied himself with Simon, our internal polls indicated I was trailing by several percentage points. After the KERA ads and after the newspapers attacked Forgy for his embrace of Simon, our internal polls had me ahead by two percentage points.

We used every available tactic to ensure a large Democratic turnout on Election Day. We used the media to great effect and had a strong organizational network. We had the support of organized labor, including the teachers' union, which could turn out the vote. We had the support of many county judges who knew how to encourage voters to go to the polls. We organized an extensive ground campaign consisting of volunteers who went door-to-door and who drove people to polling locations on Election Day.

Heading into Election Day, I thought I was in a good position and had a good chance to pull off the upset. I believed my campaign staff and I had done all we could to win. However, our outside political consultants told McBrayer and Skipper that Democrats across the country who had been ahead by only two or three percentage points were losing. Among voters who made up their minds at the last minute, the trend was to vote for Republicans—a statistic not reflected in the polls. Fortunately, no one bothered to tell me that.

There was no doubt in my mind that Forgy and his people thought they had the election won. Forgy felt so confident that he played golf instead of campaigning the Sunday before Election Day. And I heard that he sent staff members to Frankfort on Monday to meet individually with Jones's cabinet secretaries to begin the transition process. That is how sure they were of victory.

Forgy had reserved the Marriott Hotel in Lexington for what he assumed would be his victory celebration, and I had rented the Farnham Dudgeon Civic Center in Frankfort for mine. Shortly after 6:00 p.m. on Election Day, I went down to the Civic Center and found fewer than fifty people there. I thought, "Golly, this isn't a good sign!" The fact was, the polls didn't close in western Kentucky until seven o'clock, and almost everyone associated with my campaign was still on the telephone making "get out the vote" calls. To my relief, the place began to fill up shortly thereafter.

I understand that Forgy's people began to arrive at the Marriott before noon, and by six o'clock, they were in full party mode. I noticed that several establishment Democrats filtered into the Farnham Dudgeon Civic Center just before nine o'clock, and we heard that many of them had made a hasty retreat from the Marriott. Just after nine o'clock, Forgy called me to concede the election, and I'll never forget Terry McBrayer smiling from ear to ear as he lit up a victory cigar. I had a list of people I wanted onstage when I gave my victory speech, but by the time I got there, the stage was so full of people that even Judi and the rest of our family had trouble finding room. It was wild, it was delirious, and it was so much fun!

Truthfully, the 1995 gubernatorial election was Forgy's to lose, and he lost it. He had a compelling argument and a built-in campaign advantage: after twenty-four years of Democratic rule in Frankfort, it was time for a change. In my opinion, arrogance and a sense of entitlement lost the election for him. He spent too much money on staff and overhead. As a result, we spent 30 to 40 percent more on television ads than he did, and that was decisive. In my view, Larry and his people had a lackadaisical attitude during the campaign and just assumed that victory was theirs after winning the primary election in May.

In contrast, we ran an extremely energetic and focused campaign. I worked hard for fifteen long years to achieve my personal goal. Judi and I spent a lot of money on my previous campaigns. Winning the 1995 gubernatorial election was the pinnacle of my political career; it was what we had hoped for against some daunting odds. We could not have been more gratified. The people had elected me governor of Kentucky, and there was no better feeling! However, I knew that winning the election was only the beginning. I was eager to start leading and governing the commonwealth. I won the election as a middle-of-the-road Democrat on the political spectrum. That is what I have always been and will always be. I am also a champion of the middle class. I believe I governed that way from the day I assumed the office of Pike County judge in 1982 until the day I left the governor's office in 2003.

After the November election, Forgy alleged, without proof, that my campaign had bought votes all over eastern Kentucky. I knew we hadn't done that, so after taking office, I instructed the Kentucky State Police to investigate the allegation. When they questioned Forgy to determine the source of his information, he admitted he had no evidence of actual vote buying. The allegation was just his opinion. The state police made a report to that effect.

That didn't satisfy Forgy or his supporters. He continued to complain, insisting that the state police worked for me and weren't going to find anything that wasn't in my best interest. Knowing that we had done nothing wrong, and to put these allegations to rest, I asked the newly elected attorney general, Ben Chandler, to investigate the vote-buying issue, and I instructed the commissioner of the state police to provide two or three detectives to assist him.

Asking Chandler to investigate Forgy's allegations turned out to be a mistake. Chandler took the investigation in a wholly different direction after he discovered no evidence of vote buying in eastern Kentucky. The campaign finance law clearly gave the Kentucky Registry of Campaign Finance, a nonpartisan organization, the responsibility and the authority to administer the law and to investigate and prosecute any alleged violations. Chandler expanded the investigation to include charges that, by hiring Danny Ross, the teamsters' union had made a campaign contribution that sent us over the $1.8 million spending limit. The penalty for exceeding the limit was forfeiture of the governorship. The registry initially resisted Chandler's overreach but soon relented and decided not to contest the attorney general's intrusion into its area of responsibility. My team did not object because we believed the allegations had no merit.

In retrospect, we should have contested Chandler's actions, but we were confident we had done nothing wrong. Because of the numerous phone calls between the teamsters' office and our headquarters, Chandler charged that Danny was taking campaign directions from Skipper, which constituted a contribution to my campaign. Skipper and Danny denied the allegation both privately and publicly, and I had no reason not to believe them.

Forgy also claimed that we had bought votes in predominantly Black precincts. However, the newspapers reported that turnout in the Black precincts in Louisville, Hopkinsville, Franklin, and Paducah was not much different in 1995 than it had been in 1991; in fact, turnout in Lexington's Black precincts declined in 1995. As a result, at the end of March, the Registry of Campaign Finance reported that its preliminary investigation had uncovered no startling irregularities.

Denis Fleming, counsel to the governor's office, kept me informed whenever something of substance came up regarding Chandler's investigation, but I certainly didn't dwell on it. I voluntarily testified before the Franklin County grand jury and told them everything I knew because I had nothing to hide.

Chandler's investigation elicited a lot of media coverage, but I never thought the media treated me unfairly. I never felt the press was against me or out to get me. I understood that the reporters were just doing their job, and it was never personal. I don't believe the investigation adversely

The 1995 gubernatorial campaign was the first to operate under the new public campaign financing law, so money was not a problem. Meeting people and getting free media coverage were the real challenges. (Courtesy of Kentucky Department for Libraries and Archives, Archives and Records Management Division)

My inauguration as the governor of Kentucky was the highlight of my public life. (Courtesy of Kentucky Department for Libraries and Archives, Archives and Records Management Division)

affected the administration of state government in any way, and it certainly didn't influence or alter my legislative agenda.

Chandler pursued this investigation almost until the end of my second term. In my head and heart, I believe his objective was to put me in jail to further his own political career. He certainly used all the power of the attorney general's office to try to accomplish that. He indicted Skipper, Danny, and two teamsters' union executives and threatened to put them on trial in the fall of 2003, while he was running for governor. I was determined not to let him sacrifice those four good men in his pursuit of the governorship—an election I thought he couldn't win, given the circumstances. I pardoned all four in the summer of 2003. After almost eight long years, that ended the controversy surrounding the 1995 gubernatorial election.

Despite our personal history, I voted for Chandler in 2003. Admittedly, it wasn't easy pulling the lever for him in the voting booth, but my vote was more of a reflection on me than on him. I was showing my appreciation for what the Democrats had done for me and supporting the party based on its historical record of advocating for the vast middle class in this country. Whenever I look in the mirror, I want to be comfortable with who I see looking back. I've made mistakes, but I'm at peace with who I am.

7

Forming an Administration

Shortly after my election as governor, Brereton and Libby Jones invited Judi and me to the governor's mansion for dinner. During the meal, Brereton told me, "Paul, you are so much better prepared to be governor than I was." I think that was true. I had been in business for twenty years. I knew what it meant to meet a payroll and pay bills. I had been a county judge for ten years, where I learned that my permission to act came from a legislative body, the fiscal court. I learned that an elected official has to listen to the people. You can't always do what they want, but at least you can listen. I had been the deputy secretary of the Transportation Cabinet and the secretary of the Cabinet for Economic Development. I knew more about how the state bureaucracy actually worked than any governor in my memory. I had hung around the legislature for more than twenty years and presided over the state senate as lieutenant governor. I personally knew many of the legislators and understood the legislative process.

Although Judi and I were physically exhausted from the campaign, we were still running on leftover adrenaline from Election Day, so we kept going full bore during the transition period. As the election night celebration wound down, I told Skipper to meet me in the basement of the lieutenant governor's mansion at seven the next morning. When Skipper arrived, I asked him, "Okay, now what?" and we both laughed. We were like the dog that caught the car. During the campaign, we hadn't devoted any time to thinking about putting together an administration. Now what, indeed!

During a change in administration, important dates on the calendar dictate when some governmental processes and procedures have to be accomplished, such as planning for Inauguration Day, preparing the state budget, hiring staff for the governor's office, and appointing cabinet secretaries. Additionally, newly elected governors have to prepare the most important speech of their lives, and they have just thirty-five days to do all that.

The most pressing issues we faced were staffing the governor's office and hiring the cabinet secretaries. Skipper, Jim Ramsey, Sammi Chaney, and Danny Ross were the only people I knew I wanted to hire before I actually took office. The chief of staff and the secretary of the governor's executive cabinet are the two most important jobs in state government. Without question, Skipper was going to be my chief of staff, which is a very powerful and essential position in any gubernatorial administration. When the chief of staff speaks, he is speaking *for* the governor. The governor must have complete and total confidence in the chief of staff, and I had that in Skipper. He not only spoke for me but also ran the governor's office, which is essentially the political arm of state government. Skipper stayed for the entire eight years I served as governor and is still my best friend today.

The secretary of the cabinet is an equally important member of any gubernatorial administration and is critical to its success. That person essentially oversees the governing arm of state government and supervises the individual cabinet secretaries to make sure they are carrying out the governor's and the legislature's policies. The secretary of the cabinet must have very strong administrative skills and know how to run a large organization. My first secretary of the cabinet was Margaret Greene, who left a lucrative position at Bell South to take the job. She was succeeded by her deputy, Crit Luallen, and later by Ed Ford.

My job as governor was to convince or cajole members of both legislative chambers to support my legislative priorities, to sell my top two or three legislative priorities to the people, and to be a cheerleader for the state when I was representing Kentucky nationally or internationally. A governor is the face of state government, and the job requires different skills at different times, depending on the circumstances. A governor needs to lead the public in the direction he wants the state to go and convince the people that this is the right direction. A governor needs to listen and respond to the public's concerns, even if he can't do anything about those concerns. A governor has to be the "consoler in chief" in times of human tragedy and natural disaster, showing the people that he shares their grief and sense of loss. My experience as county judge and lieutenant governor prepared me for each of these roles. Newly elected governors who lack this kind of prior experience sometimes struggle to understand and master such tasks.

As chief of staff, Skipper was also the gatekeeper in the governor's office. If a governor met or talked on the telephone with every legislator, special-interest representative, and private citizen who wanted an audience, he wouldn't have time to do anything else. The chief of staff has to decide who needs to see or talk to the governor personally and who should speak to a cabinet secretary or department head instead. Skipper was superb at his job, and he was great at smoothing things over when people got upset. Skipper's personality is such that it's hard not to like him. As a result, I was able to get things done. A governor needs to stay popular among the citizenry to get the public's support for his legislative agenda, so the governor needs to be visible and travel around the state, not be ensconced in the governor's office in Frankfort.

Of course, one of the most important responsibilities of an incoming governor is to prepare a state budget proposal, and with less than sixty days to draft one, time is of the essence. I had already decided to ask Jim Ramsey to be the state budget director. Skipper and I agreed that the first telephone call I would make as governor-elect would be to Ramsey, a vice president at Western Kentucky University. I had become acquainted with Ramsey's reputation during the Wilkinson administration, and although I didn't know him personally, I knew he understood government finance. In fact, the day before the November election, during our barnstorming tour of the state by airplane, we landed at the Bowling Green airport and Jim came out to greet us as a representative for WKU. I optimistically told him, "On Wednesday [the day after the election], I'm going to call you because I'm going to need you to come to Frankfort and help me." He laughed and said, without much commitment, "Okay!" I don't know whether he thought I was going to lose or assumed I was just "gripping and grinning" and wouldn't follow through. When I actually called Jim the day after the election, he sounded a little surprised, but he accepted my invitation to come to Frankfort to talk about the job I had in mind for him.

At that meeting, I convinced Ramsey that I really did need his help, and he agreed to come to Frankfort as state budget director, particularly after I offered to arrange for WKU to continue paying him his current salary (which was more than what the state government could pay). He would be working for us as an independent contractor "on loan" from the university. He agreed to take the job at least long enough to help us hit the ground running. Jim's real love was higher education, and after I told him my first priority was to tackle higher education reform, he got more enthusiastic about the job. After we passed the postsecondary education law, he left to take a job with the University of North Carolina at Chapel Hill. We convinced him to come back about a year later, and he eventually ended up as president of the University of Louisville shortly before I left the governor's office.

We had to build an administrative team from scratch. I intended to staff my office with people I knew personally. I wanted individuals who were loyal, honest, hardworking, congenial, and dedicated to being part of a team. Skipper and I worked on hiring staff for the governor's office, but the process of filling cabinet positions was a little more complicated. I wanted my cabinet secretaries to be the best administrators I could find, which meant they would most likely have to be willing to accept a lower salary than they were currently earning. I got Ashland Oil and Humana to donate the services of their chief executive headhunters, Chuck Whitehead and Robert Harrar, respectively, to help us evaluate executive talent. We set up a "war room" in the basement of the lieutenant governor's mansion and spent a week interviewing forty candidates; some of them were referrals, and others had personally applied for cabinet positions. I didn't know most of the candidates. We ended up with an administrative team of twenty people that included six women, three African Americans, five Republicans, and people from all regions of Kentucky. My cabinet was truly a cross section of the state.

Nearly every new administration, whether at the gubernatorial or the presidential level, enjoys a brief Camelot-type atmosphere, when people can be convinced to make sacrifices to get in on the ground floor of a new experience. This was true of my first administration. We got some amazing, high-powered people to drop what they were doing, join my team, and set my administration on the right course. The day after taking the oath of office as Kentucky's fifty-ninth governor, the rest of my cabinet appointees took their oaths of office.

In my opinion, my cabinet selection process turned out just fine politically, although some Democrats—those who believed in the maxim "to the victor belong the spoils"—may have disagreed. Apparently, the media and the Democratic Party assumed that I would populate the state government with party loyalists. However, I wanted to send a message that I was going to run government the right way, in a nonpartisan fashion, as much as possible. Although I admired Bert Combs, Wendell Ford, and Julian Carroll in many ways, I didn't want to be portrayed as another good-old-boy politician, which would have been easy for the media and Republicans to do if I had filled my administration with Democratic activists, regardless of their qualifications. What we didn't publicize was that we installed experienced Democratic loyalists as deputy secretaries to make sure the cabinet secretaries were sensitive to the political aspects of their jobs. I made it difficult for the Republicans to criticize me, and they didn't—at least early on.

As far as public policy and political ideology went, we laid down the law to the cabinet secretaries from the start: "You always have the right to object and have your opinions considered, but once the policy is decided, you must implement the governor's policies, or you quit. Those are your choices." I had only one problem in that regard. I fired one cabinet secretary (not one of the original secretaries) because of a letter he wrote to the *Lexington Herald-Leader* in which he was critical of me and my administration.

As long as I have been a student of state government, I have observed power struggles between people at the top of various gubernatorial administrations. It's natural for conflicts to develop among such strong personalities. Too often, cabinet secretaries and other high-level people in the governor's office try to ensure that their opinions are reflected in the administration's policies. However, I don't recall any serious power struggles in my two administrations. I wasn't aware of them if they occurred, which meant that my secretaries of the executive cabinet did their job exceedingly well.

We had a four-person "executive committee" in the governor's office. I was the CEO, and the other three were cabinet secretary Margaret Greene (later Crit Luallen and Ed Ford), chief of staff Skipper Martin, and budget director Jim Ramsey. I often said, only partly in jest, that Margaret (and later Crit and Ed) ran the government, Skipper ran me, and Jim had to figure out how to pay for everything!

I was a hands-on governor, and although the secretary of the cabinet was the immediate superior of each cabinet secretary, I never hesitated to call a cabinet secretary directly. I wasn't much of a respecter of the chain of command. I'm sure Margaret, Crit, and Ed—and sometimes the individual cabinet secretaries—resented this, but that was just my way. I interacted most often with the secretary of the Transportation Cabinet because there were always issues about getting stoplights installed in some community or having dangerous curves straightened out on some rural road. I had an abiding interest in roads, having been a county judge myself.

Patronage is a term I don't like. I don't think state jobs or contracts should be given to an individual or a company in return for political support. Those decisions should be based purely on what is best for the citizens of Kentucky. However, *somebody* in state government has to make hiring decisions, and it's the governor's responsibility to ensure that these decisions are based largely on merit. No system is perfect, and some people are bound to be unhappy.

The procedure for hiring people not covered by the state merit system was administered through the Office of Constituent Services. As governor, I wanted to know what was going on in the state, and I certainly wanted to hire people who would be loyal to my administration. It would be foolhardy to hire individuals who would try to undermine my policies. The Office of Constituent Services kept the governor's office informed about what was going on in Kentucky, ascertained that state bureaucrats implemented administration policies, and ensured the hiring of competent, loyal employees. Every administration I know of, Democratic and Republican, had a similar operation. I think ours was among the best.

State government jobs covered by the merit system were handled differently. By law, the state had to test all applicants and could only choose among the candidates with the five highest test scores. This gave the hiring agency a little wiggle room when filling its positions. During my administration, when a job covered by the merit system became available in a particular county, it was posted on the internet and the Office of Constituent Services alerted our contact person in that county. If the county contact person knew of a qualified individual who supported my administration and needed a job, the contact person informed the potential applicant, who then signed up to take the merit system test. If that applicant earned one of the top five scores, the Office of Constituent Services would contact the agency and ask it to *consider* hiring that person. Not all my supporters were automatically hired. Some agencies deemed this an infringement on their right and responsibility to make hiring decisions. Sometimes a call from the governor's office on behalf of a political supporter was actually a deciding factor in that person's rejection. During my two terms, Hank Lindsay, Jerry Johnson, and Jody Lassiter did an excellent job as director of the Office of Constituent Services. Although I replaced all of Brereton Jones's cabinet secretaries, I didn't fire the thousands of people he had hired or appointed in nonmerit positions during his four years in office. For the most part, they were qualified people and friends of my administration too. Besides, we filled hundreds of other merit and nonmerit positions on an ongoing basis.

Another important responsibility of the governor's office is to appoint members of the many boards and commissions that administer or regulate vital government functions. Every governor makes upward of three thousand such appointments over a four-year term. My director of the Office of Boards and Commissions for eight years, Bill Beam, took his responsibilities very seriously. I'd walk into Bill's office and he would have stacks of files all over the place pertaining to people who wanted to serve on some board or commission. These appointments could be double-edged swords: although you wanted to appoint friends and supporters, they also had to be qualified, take the appointment seriously, and do a good job. I told Bill not to recommend any friend or supporter of mine who simply wasn't qualified, and if he made a few people unhappy, I'd be glad to take the heat. I had more than a few conversations with people who didn't get an appointment they sought. I would say, "Well now, I understand you're disappointed. But there are only so many openings on that particular board or commission, and I just *had* to put so-and-so on it. Rest assured that when there's another opening, I'll *try* to put your name at the top of the list to fill it." That would generally satisfy the individual. The word *try* is a handy one. Sometimes I didn't try too hard! I was careful not to tell anyone flat-out that they weren't qualified or were less qualified than the person I appointed because that would have made them angry. Beam did a good job filling those boards and commissions, and he didn't create many problems for me.

My hard-and-fast rule for cabinet secretaries was: "Do what's right. Don't ever do anything that's not right just because I or somebody from the governor's office suggests you do it. If you do the right thing, I'll back you up."

No secretary in my cabinet told me no as often as my second secretary of the Transportation Cabinet, Jim Codell. Jim replaced Fred Mudge about a year into my first term. I didn't hesitate to call him if someone asked me to speak on their behalf about a road issue. I appreciated Jim's willingness to tell me diplomatically, "Governor, I don't think you want to do that." When Jim told me no, that was the end of the conversation because I knew he was only trying to keep me out of trouble.

On the evening of December 11, 1995, the day before my inauguration, I gave a speech to hundreds of Democrats at party headquarters. I spoke about the state of the Democratic Party in Kentucky, which I described as crippled, lame, and sickly. I pledged to help rebuild the party at the grass-roots level and elect more Democrats to state and national offices. I knew the job would be difficult, if not impossible. The Democratic Party as an organization had practically disappeared in Kentucky, and although I had managed to pull off an upset win against Larry Forgy, I knew my success wasn't likely to be repeated in future elections. For Kentucky to remain a Democratic-leaning state, I knew that, as titular head of the Democratic Party, I needed to reestablish the principles on which it was founded.

Much of the Democratic Party in Kentucky had devolved into old-line, New Deal Democrats who were interested only in patronage. Many Democratic county officials cared only about their own political survival and were unwilling to put their reputations on the line by campaigning for statewide Democratic candidates. The health of the Kentucky Democratic Party was not high on their list of priorities. Since the election of John Y. Brown Jr., who didn't have strong connections among Kentucky Democrats, the party had withered during a succession of Democratic governors. That void coincided with the growing influence of Mitch McConnell in the Kentucky Republican Party and his strategy for remaking his party's image. Under McConnell's leadership, the Kentucky Republican Party had recruited many smart, energetic people from the business community who either ran for office themselves or supported other Republican candidates monetarily. The Kentucky Republican Party encouraged people to get involved and help get Republicans elected at the local, state, and national levels.

Kentucky was still a largely rural, agricultural state, with a mostly white and aging population. McConnell made the Kentucky Republican Party all about abortion, guns, and same-sex marriage, issues that resonated with Kentuckians. It was hard to understand how the Republicans convinced people who needed the most help from government and paid the least in taxes to vote against the Democratic Party, which had always advocated on their behalf. On the eve of Inauguration Day, I knew I had work to do if I hoped to rebuild the image of the Democratic Party in Kentucky.

Before I could prepare for the upcoming legislative session scheduled to start in early January 1996, I had to call a special session in December to deal with redistricting. The General Assembly needed to accomplish redistricting before the end of January, which was the deadline for candidates to file their official paperwork with the secretary of state if they wanted to run for office in 1996. Therefore, redistricting couldn't wait until the regular legislative session. I wanted to dispense with it immediately, before the holidays.

Redistricting takes place every ten years, as it is based on the federal census. Kentucky lost one of its seven congressional seats after the 1990 census, and fewer seats in Congress meant less influence for Kentucky. The state legislature had gone through the redistricting process in 1992, but the courts declared that redistricting plan unconstitutional. Redistricting can cause a lot of angst during normal times, but it can be especially acute when a congressional seat is in play. Normally, the Kentucky Senate and Kentucky House of Representatives draw up their own respective redistricting plans. Then each chamber approves the other's plan. However, in 1992 the redistricting process didn't go smoothly during the special legislative session called by Governor Jones.

That year, the senate's plan carved up Hal Rogers's Fifth Congressional District among the other five districts. Under the leadership of speaker Don Blandford, the house drew up its own redistricting plan. The special session lasted a week, and the result was that Hal Rogers and Chris Perkins ended up in the same congressional district. Greg Stumbo, majority leader in the house, and Grady Stumbo, chair of the Kentucky Democratic Party, fought to keep the two mountain districts separate. They contended that they needed two congressional seats to get more federal dollars for eastern Kentucky.

Chris Perkins called me one evening during the 1992 special session, when I was lieutenant governor, and asked me to convince Governor Jones to intervene on the house Democrats' behalf. Being a fellow eastern Kentuckian, I told him I'd try. It was about nine o'clock in the evening when I called the governor's mansion and told Jones about the telephone call I had received from Perkins. When I asked if he would consider going to bat for Chris with the legislature, Jones flatly replied, "No, I don't want to get involved with that." Perkins's district was absorbed by Rogers's Fifth Congressional District and Scotty Baesler's Sixth Congressional District.

Had Governor Jones intervened, it probably wouldn't have done any good. The legislature wouldn't have taken kindly to interference from the executive branch. Rocky Adkins called it a "dark day" for eastern Kentucky, and Herbie Deskins criticized "influential people" from central Kentucky for not supporting eastern Kentucky. I believe Herbie was right. I think state senators Eck Rose and Mike Moloney wanted a compact district around Lexington that was served by only one television market. Campaigns can get very expensive when you have to run television ads in multiple markets.

Following my predecessor's lead, I decided not to get involved in the redistricting issue during the special session I called in December 1995. Redistricting was the legislature's responsibility, and Rose in particular would not have welcomed my input. Besides, I had enough on my plate preparing for the regular legislative session. I wasn't about to make any new enemies over an issue that wasn't within the governor's purview. In the end, congressional redistricting went just about like it had in 1992.

My first priority was preparing the biennial state budget. State budgets are as much political documents as financial blueprints. "Run government like a business" is a tried-and-true campaign slogan, but it isn't a sound governing philosophy. A state budget is the most important public policy document of any gubernatorial administration, and there are no hard-and-fast formulas for drafting one. The decision-making process for formulating a government budget is different from that used to create a budget for a business. In business, you are trying to optimize the return on your investment. At the end of the year, your accountant will tell you if you've been successful. Businesses have two constituents: owners and customers. You have to please your customers to stay in business, but you *really* have to please your owners, or they will fire you. If there are several options to invest an owner's money, you can feed the risks and rewards into a computer and get an answer. In government, it's not that simple. In government, customers and owners are the same people, but they can want drastically different things.

In government, you start with the bottom line. You have only the revenue the people are willing to pay in taxes. And no matter how much tax revenue you have, it's never enough to do what needs to be done and certainly not enough to do everything the people want. You have to figure out where to "invest" the state's money to produce the best return for the majority of the people. For example, funding education is the state's most important responsibility, and it is the largest portion of the state budget. However, the entire budget can't be spent on education. The justice system, the transportation system, the health care system, the state park system, and many other entities need to be funded as well. And most citizens expect the government to provide basic social services.

You can't enter data into a computer and get a budget. Making state budget allocations is a "seat-of-the-pants" political judgment. Politicians care about budgetary priorities that will be popular, but budgets also make a statement about political priorities. In politics, perception is reality. If people *think* they are getting good government, they are probably getting the government they *want.*

Frankly, I didn't operate my business based on a budget. I got revenue from the products I sold, and I spent what it took to produce them. Some months I made money, and some months I lost money. Happily, I made more money than I lost. I learned about the budget process from my experience as county judge. I had prepared ten county budgets, so I was familiar with the theory of public budgeting and wasn't intimidated by the process. Plus, I had good people working on my first state budget, particularly budget director Jim Ramsey and his assistant, Beth Hilliard. I had a lot of confidence in them and in people such as Ron Carson and Bill Hintze in the Office of Policy and Management (OPM), who knew a great deal about state government. Fortunately, Governor Jones had created the Consensus Forecasting Group (CFG) to come up with two-year state revenue estimates. The Kentucky Constitution mandates a balanced state budget, so estimated expenditures cannot exceed estimated revenue.

To prepare the budget for the 1996 legislative session, we began by examining the existing budget and then adjusted it to meet our priorities. The budget document includes a lot of boilerplate that usually doesn't need to be changed, so that's where we started. Then we went through the existing budget line by line and decided whether we wanted each expenditure to increase, decrease, or stay the same, depending on our priorities. Governor Jones's budget priorities had been health insurance and the horse industry. My priorities were education followed by job creation.

Ramsey already knew the professionals at OPM, so it was a smooth transition between the Jones administration and mine. My first budget was a continuation of Jones's because it looked like there wasn't going to be any surplus money. Jones liked to say that he left me with a $100 million surplus, which was true regarding the amount in the Rainy-Day Fund. But what he failed to say was that he left me with a structurally imbalanced budget—that is, ongoing expenses exceeded ongoing revenue.

Governor Jones had called a special legislative session in 1995 to exempt private pensions from taxation by the state. Someone had filed a lawsuit challenging the state's practice of exempting state pensions while taxing federal and private pensions, and the state courts had ruled this unconstitutional. Rather than passing a law to tax state pensions and then increasing those pensions to make up for the new tax, the legislature passed a law that exempted private pensions from taxation, which amounted to a tax cut for many people. Thus, with a stroke of the pen, the legislature blew a $77 million hole in the state budget and did not adjust expenditures to compensate for the lost revenue. I studied the budget line by line to try to understand it. I probably knew more about the state budget than any governor since Julian Carroll, who could rattle numbers off the top of his head. As we prepared the new budget, we brought in each cabinet secretary individually and basically told them, "Sorry guys, there isn't any new money here."

Many laws appropriate money for certain activities that do not survive the budget process. The legislature can nullify any law passed by a previous legislature by temporarily suspending the existing law. "Notwithstanding Kentucky Revised Statute (KRS) [fill in the blank]" is standard language used in every budget to suspend existing laws. This is simpler and more politically palatable than repealing a law that purports to appropriate money for a specific purpose. The mandatory 5 percent pay increase for state employees was routinely suspended so the money could be used for other things. Similarly, the law requiring that 50 percent of coal severance tax revenue be returned to the coal-producing counties was routinely suspended.

One thing I tried to do as governor was to honor the 5 percent annual pay increase for state employees. I was able to do this my first six years, but the last two years included a recession, so we couldn't afford the full 5 percent. I think we raised state employees' pay 2 or 3 percent instead. We might not have had the money to hire additional state employees, but we made most of the existing employees happy. To this day, I still hear from state employees who say I was the last governor to honor that annual 5 percent pay increase, and they tell me how grateful they were. There were many underpaid state workers, and I tried to get their wages closer to that of their counterparts in surrounding states and in the private sector. Having skilled workers is the best policy for any enterprise, and state government is no exception. Even so, I think it is wrong for the legislature to mandate a specific increase; each budget should reflect existing conditions. The fact is, inflation had exceeded 5 percent for several years, resulting in underpaid state workers. A study conducted during my administration demonstrated that most state employees earned below-market-value salaries. I believed it was time to play catch-up for those employees.

During the Jones administration, the state workforce decreased from more than thirty-seven thousand employees to around thirty-five thousand. As governor, I found some of that effort to be penny-wise and pound-foolish. For example, the legislature enacted a law that required the inspection of new commercial heating and air conditioning facilities before the building could be occupied. The law included an inspection fee charged to those facilities to fund the salaries of four inspectors. Although there was money in the state budget for four inspectors, only one had been hired. After I was elected governor, I had building contractors tell me that their new buildings weren't occupied because they hadn't been inspected. We promptly hired three more building inspectors.

Likewise, I had commercial trucking company officials complain that they couldn't hire more truck drivers because there weren't enough state testers to certify them, so I hired more. The state may have saved a little money by not hiring these people, but we were shooting ourselves in the foot in the long run. We were depriving the state of the revenue those businesses could have added to the state treasury. Near the end of his administration, Jones was trying to reduce the number of state employees, but in some situations, it wasn't in the best interests of the state or its citizens. In my opinion, when the state regulates an industry such as construction, trucking, coal mining, restaurants, and the like, it has an obligation to live up to its end of the bargain.

A review of other states' tax structures may seem to indicate that Kentucky has a higher overall tax than some of its competitors. But in Kentucky, the state government provides a higher percentage of services than in many other states where local governments provide such services. Reducing the state workforce can negatively impact the delivery of necessary services all over the state.

When I became governor, one of my ideas was to modernize state government. So when Margaret Greene accepted the job of secretary of the cabinet, she looked seriously at the state government's business practices to determine what areas would benefit from modernization. For example, one of the state's computers was a converted IBM punch-card model that had been in use when I enrolled at the University of Kentucky in 1955! We created a new government efficiency program called EMPOWER Kentucky (EMPower Our Workers With Effective Resources).

As we got further into the legislative session, it became apparent that the state's revenue would exceed the CFG's estimate. We agreed with the legislature's leadership that we would split any revenue surplus fifty-fifty: 50 percent to EMPOWER Kentucky, and 50 percent to a list of projects submitted by the legislators.

I always thought of my relationship with the legislature as a partnership. I respected the lawmakers and recognized that they made most of the decisions regarding public policy. I can't remember ever refusing to see a legislator of either political party, even those with whom I disagreed. Senator David Williams and I had some real disagreements that sometimes turned personal, but I never refused to see him.

I had learned as a county judge that if I let the magistrates have some input into creating the county budget, they were a lot more likely to support it once we presented it publicly. I carried that idea with me into the governor's office. During state budget preparations, I would invite members of the legislative leadership down to my office on the first floor of the capitol and ask for their ideas and input, hoping to secure their support once I presented the budget to the entire legislature. In general, once a governor presents a budget proposal, the legislators can only tinker at the edges. Any money they shift around generally amounts to no more than 2 or 3 percent of the budget. During my eight years as governor, none of my budgets was significantly altered by the legislature, and my budgets were passed almost intact.

Most governors want it to be big news when they announce new or increased expenditures in their budget address, so they try to keep their proposals secret until then. I didn't worry about that. I wanted legislative buy-in. The budget starts in the Kentucky House of Representatives. Harry Moberly from Madison County was chair of its Appropriations and Revenue (A&R) Committee and an expert on budgetary matters. Harry held that position all eight years I was governor. We consulted him and used his expertise to our advantage. That also made us popular with the Democratic house leadership. We also consulted Mike Moloney, chair of the Kentucky

Senate's A&R Committee during my first legislative session. Mike retired after that session, and the chair of that committee changed a couple of times, so my relationship with the senate and house leadership differed.

Even those good relations didn't prevent legislators from tinkering with the budget to fund some of their pet projects. The legislature is particularly good at inventing money out of thin air. For instance, it would include language in the budget along the lines of, "The governor shall effect twenty million dollars in efficiencies," without specifying where I was supposed to find those "efficiencies." Then the lawmakers would go ahead and spend the $20 million on whatever projects they wanted. Moberly was very good at "inventing" money in this manner. When Earle Clements was governor, a legislator who did that would have wound up with two black eyes courtesy of Earle himself! However, those days were long gone, particularly after the legislature asserted its independence during John Y. Brown Jr.'s administration.

I honestly do not remember ever using the "stick" on the legislature as a whole or on individual legislators to get what I wanted. I did use the "carrot" quite a bit, though. If they tried to help me, I tried to help them. I learned that technique as a county judge. In my second and third terms as county judge, two of the six magistrates opposed me to the very end—and I mean to my last day in office! If I had some discretionary money left over at the end of the fiscal year, it didn't go to their districts. I didn't mistreat the people in their districts, but I had no desire to give those magistrates credit for anything either. I had influence in Frankfort when I was county judge, so when I went to Frankfort to obtain money for a road, that road would be located in the district of a magistrate who had been cooperative. I think it is fair to say that I didn't bend over backward to help those other two guys. I took that philosophy to the governor's office. I operated on the premise of making an effort to get along with everyone. I didn't try to punish people. I'm just not good at that. Also, I tried to be as frank as I could be with legislators. I always did my best to level with them. A lot of them never asked me for anything. I guess they knew they weren't going to get it. But many of them *did* get what they asked for, and many of them were Republicans.

After the special session on redistricting concluded, and after the respite provided by the holidays, I was ready to begin the 1996 legislative session. I postponed my budget address to the General Assembly by one day so I could go to Louisville to greet and meet President Bill Clinton. In my opinion, when the president of the United States visits Kentucky, the governor ought to be there to greet him, regardless of political party. In the five years our terms overlapped, I believe President Clinton came to

Kentucky eight times, and each time I was there to greet him. I took every opportunity to build a relationship with him in the hope that it would benefit Kentucky. I remember President George W. Bush coming to Kentucky only once in the three years we served at the same time. He had flown to Fort Campbell for some reason, and I was there to greet him.

By the way, I never had any presidential aspirations whatsoever, although I can understand why speculation circulated in the media. The week after the 1995 election, I accepted an invitation to fly to St. Louis to attend a meeting of the executive committee of the Democratic National Committee (DNC). The national chair at the time was Don Fowler, and the general chair was Senator Chris Dodd from Connecticut. They treated me like a hero! They were interested in learning how I had won my election just a year after Newt Gingrich's Contract with America swept the Republicans into power in Washington, particularly when I was the underdog. In fact, I subsequently learned that Clinton changed his reelection strategy in 1996 when he realized a Democrat could take on the Republican agenda in a conservative state like Kentucky and win. Clinton won in Kentucky both times he ran.

While at the DNC meeting in St. Louis, I accepted an invitation to appear at a midday news conference. I also appeared on a thirty-minute program broadcast on C-SPAN the next day, so I was getting some early national exposure. After I was reelected to my second term, some of my consultants thought I might be vice-presidential material. A *Newsweek* article mentioned me as one of the rising stars in the Democratic Party. However, I never wanted to be Al Gore's running mate in 2000, and to my knowledge, I was not considered. I think that, as governor, I had reached my political potential.

The two Democratic governors I most wanted to emulate were Bert Combs and Wendell Ford, for a couple of reasons: Combs because I admired his vision and commitment to education and his association with eastern Kentucky, and Ford because of his tenacity and his down-to-earth commitment to the ordinary person. There was no pomp and circumstance with Ford—what you saw was what you got. I had photographs of Combs and Ford hanging in the governor's office to remind myself that I had big shoes to fill. I still have those pictures in my office at the University of Pikeville.

8

The 1996 Legislative Session

Contrary to Larry Forgy's warnings during the campaign, the media noted that there wasn't a "hobnail boot" in sight on Inauguration Day, December 12, 1995, despite the attendance of many of my friends and supporters from eastern Kentucky. In my inaugural speech, which I wrote myself, I noted that I was the governor of all of Kentucky, but I was also a governor *from* eastern Kentucky. I vowed to be the governor who reformed higher education, much as Bert Combs was revered for supporting primary and secondary education in Kentucky.

Although Judi and I enjoyed the inaugural festivities, the truth was, I was eager to get to work. Despite getting only about three hours of sleep, I was at my desk early the next morning. After watching my cabinet secretaries take their oaths of office, I held a three-hour orientation session with them, my staff, and the budget team to address everything from dealing with media questions to finding office supplies.

As a county judge, I had learned that when the press attacked me, I had to suck it up and take it. As governor, I realized that although I had the bully pulpit, newspapers still bought ink by the barrel. I didn't place any restrictions on my cabinet secretaries when they dealt with the media, and I didn't require them to clear everything they said to the media with my office first. My cabinet secretaries were experienced professionals, and they knew what my policies were. As a result, I had a good relationship with the media for the entire eight years I was in office. The press knew I was not trying to filter the news that came out of my administration.

That evening, Judi and I hosted a dinner for my cabinet secretaries and staff at the governor's mansion. My first two days as governor had gone well. I had no idea what the future had in store, but I was ready to get down to the business of governing.

A week after the inauguration, Judi and I, along with several cabinet members, staff members, and state government officials, flew to Washington for a series of meetings with President Clinton and other federal officials. I met in the Oval Office with the president and vice president, and we discussed their proposal to have the federal Food and Drug Administration

(FDA) regulate cigarettes as drug delivery devices, as well as the federal budget's effect on health care programs in Kentucky. I was so awestruck that I don't remember much about the meeting, but I do know I was unsuccessful in getting the president to back off his position regarding the FDA's regulation of cigarettes. Any time you get to meet the president, it's a rare and special occasion. Bill Clinton can make you feel like you're the most important person in the world and that he's really focused on what you're saying.

The day before my meeting in the Oval Office, Judi and I spent the night in the White House. It was almost like checking into a hotel. We arrived on Sunday afternoon between three and four o'clock and had to go through a number of security clearances before we were taken to the Lincoln Bedroom. Judi and I both smoked back then, and after we were settled I wanted to have a cigarette. Judi said, "You can't smoke in here!" I proposed that I go into the bathroom for a smoke, but Judi nixed that idea. About five minutes later, there was a knock on the door. When I answered it, there stood a casually dressed President Clinton, who had just come in from a round of golf. He shook my hand like he'd known me forever and said, "I just wanted to welcome y'all! Do you have everything you need? Is there anything I can get you?" Then he came in and started telling us all about the history of the Lincoln Bedroom and its furnishings. Judi and I were stunned that the president of the United States would take the time to visit with us. When he left, she said, "Now, aren't you glad you didn't go in the bathroom and smoke that cigarette?"

This was heady stuff for a boy from Fallsburg! Judi and I later spent another night in the Lincoln Bedroom when I was chair of the Democratic Governors Association. I recall some controversy about President Clinton supposedly renting out the Lincoln Bedroom in exchange for a $10,000 campaign contribution, but Judi and I never paid a dime on either occasion, although I did contribute to both his campaigns.

In my many years of hobnobbing and campaigning with state legislators, I became much closer to members of the house than the senate, especially the leadership. I had many natural allies in the house, including majority floor leader Greg Stumbo, speaker Jody Richards, speaker pro tem Larry Clark, and representatives Rocky Adkins, Mike Boling, and Harry Moberly. As I prepared my legislative agenda for 1996, I began with the premise that I needed the support of house Democrats more so than senate Democrats if I hoped to get my agenda passed. But that didn't mean I could ignore the senate, especially the senate leadership.

To begin the process of courting the legislature, I invited the leadership of both chambers to lunch at the governor's mansion—first the house

Democratic leadership, and the next day the senate Democratic leadership. I also consulted the Republican leadership. I wanted the Republicans to feel that they had some input into the formulation of the budget and some other issues and that I was receptive to their ideas, which I was. I never missed an opportunity to invite members of both chambers to the governor's mansion whenever we hosted an event, especially while the General Assembly was in session.

I understood that just because Democrats controlled both the house and the senate, they wouldn't necessarily rubber-stamp everything I wanted. The house and senate leadership had their own respective agendas, and any correlation with my agenda was sheer coincidence. I knew the legislators would not allow themselves to be dictated to by me, but I believed they would give my ideas fair consideration. The Republicans didn't present a significant obstacle in 1996, as they were not a united caucus, especially in the senate. However, there were several Republicans in both chambers with whom we could work on certain issues.

Senate president Eck Rose and I were not on the best of terms at the beginning of the 1996 legislative session. After all, I had defeated him in the primary for governor. Rose was not overtly hostile toward me. He just wanted me to understand that the senate was an independent body and he intended to keep it that way. The two chambers of the legislature had their own professional staffs, and they had steadily gained confidence in their new role as a coequal branch of government. By December 1995, the legislature had matured, and the house and senate were two wholly independent bodies.

Over my two terms as governor, I found that the house leadership was generally easier to work with than the senate leadership. For the most part, the attitude of house Democrats was, "We're with you unless we just absolutely can't be." As a result, my staff and I often worked hand in hand with house leaders to draft legislation and round up support for my initiatives. Unlike the 1960s and 1970s, when Louie Nunn, Wendell Ford, and Julian Carroll were governor, by 1996, the governor lacked the power to control either chamber by threatening individual legislators. I preferred persuasion anyway.

Although I found the house leadership easier to work with, I discovered that state senators were generally more reliable when it came to keeping their commitments. If a state senator agreed to do something, I could generally take their word to the bank. However, a couple of senators were untrustworthy. One would always chuckle and say, "Well, I guess I lied." And I would reply, "There's no guessing about it!" I would say that, with the exception of Eck Rose, I had great relationships with house and senate leaders going into the 1996 legislative session. After he lost to me in the primary, Rose told the media that the senate had run the state for the previous four years and would continue to do so. I was able to work with Eck, but he certainly didn't owe me anything.

I wanted to get some legislators on my side before I went too far out on a limb with some important legislation. Too many governors want to make a speech, lay out a plan, and then expect the legislature to pass the laws necessary to implement that plan. I had enough sense to know that getting all the credit isn't important, so I always spread the credit around and included the legislature by calling my legislative agenda "*our* plan." I understood that when something happened on my watch as governor, I'd get *some* of the credit or *most* of the blame. That comes with the territory. I never gave a speech that contained any great surprises because I always discussed my intentions with key members of both legislative bodies and both parties.

I was an establishment Democrat, and I think the legislative leaders welcomed that kind of individual back to the governor's office after the independent, business-oriented administrations of Brown, Wilkinson, and Jones. However, they thought I needed to understand some of the "rules of the road." I remember a meeting in the governor's office with the senate Democratic leadership just before the start of the 1996 legislative session. Rose said, "Now, Governor, we expect you to run everything through *us*." I said, "Well now, Eck, I want to work with you all, I really do, but I reserve the right to talk to individual legislators on different subjects as they arise." Eck's message was that they expected me to play by *their* rules, and I was not to attempt any end runs around their five-man leadership group: senate president Rose, president pro tem Charlie Berger, majority leader David Karem, majority caucus chair Nick Kafoglis, and majority whip Fred Bradley. I heard what Eck said, but I didn't take it personally. He was only defending the senate as a coequal institution, and I respected that. As a county judge, I quickly learned that it doesn't pay to hold grudges. I had enough sense to know that your biggest enemy on one issue might be your strongest ally on the next one. It's okay to fight hard for or against an issue, but successful people don't make it personal because that's just not smart politics.

When the 1996 session of the General Assembly got under way, I didn't have an expansive legislative agenda. I wanted to move rather quickly on higher education reform because I knew that issue would be a rough row to hoe, but I preferred to do it in a special session, where the distractions of a dozen other issues wouldn't get in the way.

In my inaugural address I had said that my main goal was to improve higher education in Kentucky. To be honest, even though I had been on the Pikeville College Board of Trustees for a number of years, I knew very little about higher education administration, and I certainly had no idea what a higher education reform plan would look like. The job of a Pikeville College board member was to raise money for the college, and we trusted the president of the college to run the institution. However, experience had taught me that in the late twentieth century, postsecondary education was vital to the people's welfare and the state's economy. The Kentucky Education Reform Act, passed in 1990, was an important first step, laying the foundation for Kentucky's move forward. However, we couldn't make do with merely a foundation; we had to build a house—that is, modern and responsive colleges and universities accessible to every Kentuckian. In 1996 I believed it was time to take the next step and tackle higher education reform. I introduced the concept in my inaugural speech and made it clear that higher education reform would be my legislative priority. I knew it would be a difficult issue, but my philosophy as a public official had always been to do the hard things first, while you still have the goodwill of the people behind you.

In January I asked to appear before the Council on Higher Education to talk about my timetable for postsecondary education reform. I didn't have a *plan* at the time, just a timetable. I was the first sitting governor since Martha Layne Collins to appear before the council, and I told the members that I was going to appoint a task force to study the issues facing postsecondary education. Then I expected to call a special session of the legislature in January 1997 to address the issue. I laid down a few early markers to guide the council's future discussions. For example, if university presidents wanted more money from the state—which they *always* did—they would have to reform themselves and the system. I told the council members not to worry about upsetting the various university presidents. I wanted them to think outside the box. I wanted to implement reforms that transformed the system, not ones that merely trimmed around the edges, and I wanted to give the experts time to think about what those reforms should look like. I told the council I was well aware that reforming higher education would be difficult. If reform was easy, the legislature would have accomplished it already.

I knew I would encounter resistance to higher education reform. I just didn't realize how much resistance there would be and from which direction it would come. I figured I would cross that bridge when I came to it. The only action taken in the 1996 regular legislative session was to authorize the formation of a committee consisting of six members from the senate, six members from the house, and six members appointed by me to study the subject and issue a report for the General Assembly by the spring of 1997.

According to the *Courier-Journal*'s John Ed Pearce, my 1996 budget address to the legislature was about as "exciting and inspiring as Bob Dole reading the phonebook." I can understand his reasoning. I delivered the bad news to members of both chambers and told them the budget I was submitting was more or less a continuation of the last budget because of the $77 million hole created by the previous year's tax cut.

We were also facing a revamped Medicaid program that was expected to blow another huge hole in the state budget. Initially, the state's federal Medicaid allotment would decline by $64 million in 1996, after which Kentucky's federal allotment would grow from $1.5 billion in 1996 to $2.23 billion by 2002, which meant that the state's portion would grow a proportional amount. The estimate was that Medicaid reform would cost Kentucky $2 billion to $3 billion over the next seven years.

During the campaign, I had promised not to raise taxes. In addition, at Steve Henry's insistence, I had vowed to eliminate the provider tax on doctors' services, which would cost the state treasury $40 million a year. Then the legislature proposed increasing the rates the state paid doctors who treated Medicaid patients, which would cost another $50 million a year. Democrat Ernesto Scorsone, who served on the house budget committee, said the state couldn't eliminate the tax on doctors' services *and* increase doctors' Medicaid fees. I agreed: we could do one or the other, but not both.

In my budget address, I told the legislature that the first two years of my administration were not going to be much fun. Even though I was submitting a continuation budget, I promised to consider calling a special session to revisit the budget in January 1997 if the state's finances improved.

With the turn of the century just a few years away, I told the legislature that we had an opportunity to set the state on a new trajectory to propel Kentucky into the twenty-first century. If we aggressively improved our system of postsecondary education, our strategic geographic location would attract industries with good-paying jobs that would enhance the quality of life and standard of living for all Kentuckians.

Although I wanted to redouble efforts to attract manufacturing jobs to Kentucky, I also wanted to maintain as much of rural Kentucky as possible. I understood that, statistically, Kentucky was never going to be an economic powerhouse like California or New York, and I valued our country lifestyle. I think having a good-paying manufacturing or high-tech job while still having the privilege of raising a family on a small farm with a couple of cows, a pig, and some corn and other crops is a great way of life. We could be a progressive and prosperous state entering the twenty-first century.

The legislature passed the majority of my original budget proposal intact, including funds for my EMPOWER Kentucky initiative designed to create efficiencies, streamline processes, and bring the state government into the modern computer age. But the budget shortfall meant that I had to be realistic and temporarily postpone a few of my campaign promises. For example, instead of asking for an immediate repeal of the provider tax on doctors, I proposed phasing in that $43 million tax cut over four years, which the legislature approved in late March. I also had to backpedal a bit on my promise to cut income taxes by increasing allowable deductions to $1,700. I decided to phase in that tax cut over four years as well.

Spreading some of my legislative initiatives over my first four-year term was reasonable, in my view. In my budget address to the legislature, I pointed out that people wouldn't notice any benefit from the tax cut until 1998, and it would average only about $63 per taxpayer. During my two terms as governor, we implemented twenty-eight tax cuts, some legislatively, some by executive order, and some imposed by the courts. I never got much credit for cutting taxes. Taxpayers only notice when you increase their taxes because their take-home pay decreases. If their take-home pay increases, they think they deserve the extra money.

I also had to postpone my campaign promise to cut car taxes by assessing vehicles at the Blue Book trade-in value rather than the retail price. Before he left the governor's office, Brereton Jones settled a lawsuit that ameliorated the tax to some degree, so when I took office, I thought that settlement might be an acceptable substitute for cutting the car tax, which would have blown an $8 million hole in the Road Fund. Because I couldn't convince the legislature to pass a law to implement this initiative, I instructed the Revenue Cabinet to use the trade-in value to value cars. I think that was a reasonable thing to do. Before this, many people had been unable to sell their cars for anything close to the retail price in the Blue Book.

After Newt Gingrich's Contract with America swept Republicans into power in the US House and Senate in 1994, the pervasive attitude among voters everywhere, including Kentucky, was an unwillingness to pay for government services. Any time a governor takes the lead in promising to cut taxes, that state legislature is sure to follow. I didn't get much resistance from the Kentucky General Assembly when I presented my tax-cut programs, particularly since all one hundred representatives in the house and half of the thirty-eight senators were facing reelection in the fall of 1996. They wanted to be able to tell their constituents that they had voted to cut taxes.

I also had to defer my campaign pledge to return 50 percent of the coal severance tax revenue to the coal counties, instead of the 25 percent they were receiving at the time. When Martha Layne Collins was governor, the budget allocated 13 percent of the coal severance tax revenue to the Local Government Economic Assistance (LGEA) Fund. That money was then divided up and refunded to the coal-producing counties. County officials spent the money on a variety of programs, such as roads and jails, that they were obligated to fund. In 1982 I had urged Senator Friend to slip in an amendment so that the amount allocated to the LGEA Fund could not fall below 13 percent in future budgets. It didn't affect the Collins administration's budget, so there was no reason for her to object to it, and it passed. Brereton Jones had pledged to return 50 percent of the coal severance tax to the coal-producing counties, but the legislature reduced that amount to 25 percent, which included the 13 percent guaranteed under the Collins administration. They achieved that last 12 percent by increasing the amount 3 percent a year for the four years of the Jones administration. During my two terms as governor, I increased the percentage incrementally by 3 percent a year for eight years, or 24 percent. We also increased the 13 percent minimum to 14 percent. By the end of my second term, the coal-producing counties received the full 50 percent of the coal severance tax.

Voters should hold candidates to their campaign promises, but they shouldn't expect the impossible. To win an election today, candidates have to promise to give the voters what they want *without* increasing their taxes. In other words, candidates have to promise the impossible to get elected. Those who tell the truth generally lose. Of course, when elected officials fail to keep their promises, people call them liars and corrupt and claim that government doesn't work, which fuels antigovernment resentment. The truth of the matter is the problem is *not* the government! The problem lies in people's unrealistic expectations and a lack of personal responsibility. People *demand* government services, but they don't want to *pay* for them. It's that simple.

Early in the legislative session, I got involved in a dispute between Murray State University (MSU) and influential citizens in Paducah over the establishment of an engineering program in western Kentucky. The Paducah Gaseous Diffusion Plant needed engineers, and a group of influential citizens led by David Denton, a local attorney, wanted to establish an engineering degree program in Paducah. MSU didn't offer an engineering degree, but the University of Kentucky did, and UK was willing to operate an extension campus in Paducah if someone provided the funds to support it. Some businesspeople in Murray (home of MSU), particularly a few bankers, had a lot of influence at the university, and they wanted the engineering program located at MSU so that the businesses in Murray could reap the economic benefits. My view was that the MSU administration was being very parochial. I figured that by establishing an extension campus in Paducah, more people would earn engineering degrees in an area that needed engineers. Therefore, I brokered an agreement whereby the extension campus would be located in Paducah, and UK would partner with MSU to provide courses for an engineering degree. MSU would provide the nonengineering courses, UK would provide the engineering courses, and the degree would come with a UK imprimatur. I promised to commit $200,000 of state money over the first two years for the extension campus, followed by $800,000 in the third year. Over the course of my two administrations, we worked hard to appoint more open-minded members to MSU's Board of Trustees.

Any excess revenue in the state budget I put toward education. We fully funded the SEEK (Support Education Excellence in Kentucky) formula for elementary and secondary schools with a cost-of-living adjustment. I made sure that every public university received a funding increase of at least 3.2 percent. The community college system received an increase of 9.5 percent, and the Kentucky vocational schools received an increase of 7 percent.

My 1996 budget proposal included funding only for university construction projects that were already under way or that were considered essential. For example, I allocated $12.5 million for UK to convert Pin Oak Farm into an agricultural research center. Since UK was a land-grant university and had agricultural extension service agents in all 120 Kentucky counties, I thought the Pin Oak Farm project was more important than a $16 million mechanical engineering building UK had requested. I also omitted the $3.4 million UK wanted to finance the bonds it was using to build the William T. Young Library. UK had asked the General Assembly for the money during the 1994 legislative session and in the subsequent special session called by Governor Jones, with no success. UK president Charles Wethington then did an end run around the legislature by putting together a complex $41 million bond deal to build the library that involved the Lexington-Fayette Urban County Government, the UK Alumni Association, and the UK Athletics Association. Then he came, hat in hand, and asked the General Assembly and me to pay for it.

I saw no need to provide any funding whatsoever because UK had already found a way to fund the library project, and I knew it had cash reserves in the millions. Wethington had devised a plan to build the library, and he needed to adhere to that plan rather than trying to stick the state government with part of the bill. He had been too cute by half, in my opinion, in going ahead with the project in the first place. After the General Assembly turned him down, he said, "Well, I'm going to do it anyway because we're UK." I have to admit that Wethington was right about the need for a new library, which has been a great addition to the UK campus and the state. The legislative leaders and I were just offended by the method he used to try to force us to pay for it. We ended up funding construction projects at four universities, including $14 million for a new science building at the University of Louisville. The Jefferson County delegation was a powerful voting bloc in the legislature; they lobbied hard for the new science building, and I wasn't about to alienate them during the first year of my first term. I also included funding for construction at five community colleges, based on need. We didn't have the money to fund all the construction requests, so we had to choose strategically and politically.

My budget proposal included a 2.6 percent pay raise for teachers, calculated to keep pace with inflation, and a 5 percent increase for state workers, as mandated by law. During the house and senate conference committee on the budget bill, the legislature replaced the 2.6 percent raise for teachers with a flat, one-time $900 payment for each teacher, but state employees got their 5 percent increase. Eck Rose and Mike Moloney were against giving teachers a 2.6 percent across-the-board raise, which they claimed would hinder efforts to equalize funding between rich and poor schools. They believed any percentage raise should be funneled through SEEK, the funding system that gave more money to poor school districts to help them keep up with spending in wealthier districts. They also said the raise would violate the spirit of the Kentucky Education Reform Act, which allowed local school officials to make decisions based on what was best for their districts.

It seemed that the more I lobbied for the percentage increase for teachers, the more the opposition hardened against it. In late February I spoke at a meeting of the Kentucky School Boards Association and urged the members to contact their state legislators and encourage them to support the raise. As I left the meeting, I overheard some of the attendees saying that they would be happy to call their legislators to tell them to *oppose* the 2.6 percent raise. I guess I needed to work on my messaging! Admittedly, they knew much more about the Kentucky Education Reform Act than I did, and they were probably right. I had invested some of my early political capital trying to get the General Assembly to pass the raise for teachers, but I wasn't willing to make enemies over the issue.

I had also campaigned on the issue of collective bargaining for teachers, which was something the Kentucky Education Association (KEA) really wanted. However, during the legislative session, as opposition to the teachers' raise was coalescing, I decided not to lobby very hard for collective bargaining for teachers. House majority whip Kenny Rapier had told Leonard Gray, my legislative liaison, that he didn't think there were enough votes to pass a collective bargaining bill out of committee. Although I supported collective bargaining, I wasn't about to break any arms for it. I did what I could to satisfy the KEA, but I had bigger fish to fry during my first term.

The budget included small spending increases for most of state government. Both political parties looked upon my budget proposal favorably. The leadership in both the house and the senate publicly said they appreciated being included in the budget's formulation. I made it clear from the start that if they bought into the budget process, they would get a little bit of the gravy—what there was of it. I think that approach served me well, at least through my first term.

I did a lot of work later in my administration to eliminate many of the salary inequities in the merit system. We hired outside consulting firms to compare merit-system jobs with their private-sector equivalents. The salary structure of the merit system was out of balance. Theoretically, there was supposed to be a 5 percent salary increment between each grade level in the merit system. However, that structure had gotten out of kilter over time, and we were losing good employees to private-sector firms that could offer more money.

Some people had learned how to game the merit system by changing jobs within the state government and being allowed to keep their previous salary, even though they were starting at the bottom rung of a new department. As time went on and they continued to be promoted, some employees were making a lot more money than others with the same classification—sometimes as much as double—and some were making more money than their supervisors. As a result, state government was becoming a feeder system for the private sector as talented, underpaid employees and supervisors left for better pay. If that was allowed to go on long enough, state government and state services would suffer.

The Transportation Cabinet was particularly hard hit by this brain and talent drain. I remember UK professor Maurice K. Marshall telling us engineering students, "Now, I want you all to understand that you *are not* yet engineers. But we've given you the tools to where you *can become* an engineer." The Transportation Cabinet would hire young engineering graduates straight out of the universities, and they would spend five or ten years learning how to be actual engineers and then leave for more lucrative positions in the private sector. State government has to offer competitive salaries to attract and keep smart and talented people. I think we made progress doing that during my eight years as governor.

One of the issues that came up in early 1996 was the health insurance reform law passed during the Jones administration. Voters were complaining loudly about their inability to acquire health insurance and skyrocketing premium rates. By 1996, several insurance companies threatened to leave the state unless it repealed the health insurance law. An internal analysis initiated by Governor Jones and Don Stevens, commissioner of the Department of Insurance, in November 1995 indicated that insurance companies had charged too much on 80 percent of their plans. In short, insurance companies were gouging consumers. It was a real problem, and I certainly had no expertise on the subject, but I had to deal with it as governor.

Society exists through a codified social compact that the majority of people have agreed to abide by. As a society, we decided during the Great Depression that we would not let people starve to death in the streets. As a matter of public policy, through welfare, food stamps, Social Security, and the like, we protect people from starvation. Likewise, we decided to make affordable housing available to virtually all people. If someone doesn't have enough money to pay for housing, the government subsidizes housing for them or, under certain circumstances, might even purchase housing for those who can't afford it. These are the unalienable rights that the majority of Americans have determined are required to fulfill the "Life, Liberty and the pursuit of Happiness" phrase in the Declaration of Independence.

The amount of food people need and the cost of housing are relatively predictable. The cost of health care is *not* predictable. It can be zero, or it can be a million dollars, which is why health care is such a difficult issue. Social Security involves a similar problem: you may pay into Social Security all your life and then die the week before you retire and get none of your money back, or you may live longer than the national average and draw twice as much in Social Security benefits as you paid in. President Obama attempted to solve the health care problem by mandating, in the Affordable Care Act of 2010, that every American pay into the health care system, just like Social Security, so that everyone has access to affordable health care whether they are healthy, have a catastrophic illness, or are chronically ill. As a modern, civilized society, we decided that people shouldn't die simply because they can't afford modern medical care. The majority of Americans have decided that they *are* their brother's keeper; they will take care of one another and share the financial burden.

I believe Governor Jones tried to do the right thing by implementing health insurance reform. However, Kentucky is not an island; the plan would have worked only if the entire country had participated. People with preexisting conditions were moving to Kentucky to get health insurance, which the insurance industry used as an excuse to raise premiums. Insurance companies claimed that guaranteeing the issuance of policies, the renewability of coverage, mandatory coverage for people with preexisting conditions, and the right to keep coverage after leaving a job were the main factors driving up insurance premiums. Without the high premiums, the insurance companies wouldn't make any money, so it was strictly a financial decision for them. In my opinion, it is not a good idea to allow capitalism to control the health care system.

One of the problems for consumers was that the insurance industry divided Kentucky into individual markets. Only one company provided coverage for each region of the state, with the exception of Jefferson County, where two or three companies continued to operate. For example, only Blue Cross/Blue Shield offered health insurance coverage in eastern Kentucky. Consumers could either buy whatever plan the company offered, or they were just out of luck. The insurance companies were cherry-picking parts of the state where they offered their health insurance plans at very high rates, or they were leaving Kentucky entirely.

Governor Jones probably thought I didn't adequately defend his health insurance reform plan, which was one of his signature pieces of legislation, but I disagree. The truth is, there was no way to save it. In every progressive country in the world, with the exception of the United States, the national government guarantees or, in most places, provides basic health care to its citizens. Given the option, most private health insurance companies would insure only healthy people. They would like to be able to deny coverage to individuals with catastrophic or chronic illnesses and decline to renew the policies of those who get sick. That's why they offer only one-year plans. Health care for catastrophically or chronically ill people is very expensive, and that eats into the insurance companies' profits. They don't make money for their stockholders by insuring sick people. That stinks, but it is the essence of capitalism. If you have a managed 401(k) retirement plan, you may be one of those stockholders, and you expect the company to make money for you.

Health insurance is one of those issues governors have to deal with. The momentum to change the law was emanating from the legislature, not from my office. The legislative leaders were being besieged by their fellow lawmakers and their own constituents who either couldn't obtain health insurance or were paying exorbitant premiums. I tried to preserve the law, but it turned out to be impossible. The insurance companies had Kentucky over a barrel, and they knew it.

In mid-January I appointed eight legislators to an ad hoc committee to study the problems created by the health insurance law and come up with some possible solutions. The committee consisted of house speaker Jody Richards, house majority leader Greg Stumbo, house minority leader Danny Ford, representative Dr. Ernie Fletcher, senate president Eck Rose, senate majority leader David Karem, senate minority leader Dan Kelly, and state senator Dr. James Craise. It was my understanding that this was the first time in recent memory that a governor had formed an ad hoc commit-tee to study a legislative issue in the middle of a legislative session. I wanted the committee to be bipartisan because this was not a Democratic or Republican problem. This was a Kentucky problem, and the solution would need support from both parties.

I purposely didn't appoint any of the legislators involved in writing the health insurance reform law in 1994—namely, Ernesto Scorsone, Tom Burch, and Benny Ray Bailey. It was the leadership's responsibility to fix the law, and they could consult their experts in the house and senate if they wanted to—even though these experts had created the problem in the first place! The leadership didn't want to adjourn the session without finding a solution, so their goal was to come up with the least distasteful bill to ensure its passage.

The committee met at the governor's mansion several times, and I attended all those meetings. I didn't have an agenda for reforming the health insurance law. I didn't want the cheese; I just wanted out of the trap! In reality, the committee members would have preferred to repeal the entire law, but they were in a bind. The state couldn't live with the existing law, but it couldn't go back to the old way of doing things because that would leave too many Kentuckians without health insurance, which had been the rationale for passing the reform law in the first place. After much wrangling, the house and senate reached a compromise, and I supported the bill because it was obviously the best the legislature could do. The com-promise didn't solve all the problems, but I wanted the issue off my plate, so I signed the bill and moved on.

I was also committed to *fixing* the Kentucky Education Reform Act, not repealing it. In fact, if I didn't save KERA, there wasn't much hope of reforming higher education. In late February, during the legislative session, I formed an eighteen-member task force to study the problems associated with KERA. I wanted everyone on the task force to have skin in the game, so the senate appointed six members, the house appointed six members, and I appointed the other six. I formed the task force in response to a study—one of several sponsored by the federal government—documenting changes in twenty-one schools in four rural Kentucky school districts. According to the study, only a few of KERA's innovations had been fully integrated into school culture. Teachers were concentrating more on the practicalities of implementing those changes rather than their philosophical foundations. It was the task force's job to figure out how to fix KERA, and the members had eighteen months to do it. It was my job to figure out how to get the task done in the 1998 legislative session.

One of my most important accomplishments as governor was preserving the major elements of KERA. I didn't know very much about primary and secondary education, but I knew that KERA was a tsunami in terms of the changes it ushered in. KERA expected teachers to do the impossible from the get-go. In retrospect, it is not surprising that the reforms were slow to catch on. Most people are in favor of change, as long as it doesn't affect them. As a result, many experienced teachers and school administrators were leery of the changes.

I received a lot of good advice from my daughter Bambi, who was a schoolteacher. It took her a long time to make me understand what a rubric is. She was mentoring first-year teachers just out of college, and she reported that they had no concept of what KERA required. We discovered that most colleges in Kentucky were slow to teach their education majors how to teach according to KERA's guidelines. Additionally, some teachers and parents thought the changes implemented by KERA were detrimental. Almost all teachers complained that they were expected to do an impossible amount of additional work. They were right. By 1996, KERA was in jeopardy of collapsing.

The truth was, I had no idea how to fix KERA. However, I trusted the professional educators, the Prichard Committee for Academic Excellence, and the members of the legislature who told me that KERA was part of the solution to Kentucky's education problems and was worth saving. We had reached the six-year point, and the KERA-initiated changes were starting to become evident. At the same time, many educators, school administrators, parents, and altruistic types were beginning to question the viability of KERA.

Based on their own experiences in school, parents had preconceived ideas about what primary and secondary education and learning should look like. They were familiar with true-or-false and multiple-choice tests, but their children were being exposed to innovations designed to improve their critical thinking skills rather than just come up with the right answer. This was different from the parents' experience, and they were genuinely concerned.

Governors don't need to be experts in any given field. They need to understand the importance of an issue and provide the political leadership to make hard decisions. Therefore, my job was to be the political force behind the effort to fix KERA. I consulted legislators such as David Karem, Harry Moberly, Greg Stumbo, Jody Richards, Joe Wright, and David Williams—people who had been instrumental in writing and passing the original law. We held hearings all over the state to obtain local input and encourage people to accept the idea of fixing rather than repealing KERA. I was the repair shop supervisor, not the mechanic.

I believe that KERA is the single most important public policy decision made by the people of Kentucky in my lifetime. As governor, I was determined to derail the effort to repeal it. Formation of the task force bought us an additional two years to allow the changes brought about by KERA to take hold. The truth is, the task force was a delaying tactic. By the 1998 legislative session, people were beginning to understand KERA, so the pressure to repeal it had subsided to some extent. The task force devised some changes to the law that were mostly cosmetic, which bought *another* two years for the changes initiated by KERA to take effect. By the beginning of the 2000 legislative session, KERA reforms were finally showing positive results. Teachers, parents, and administrators had become accustomed to the changes, and strong opposition had dissipated. In 1996, during the peak of the opposition to KERA, the law's survival had been touch and go. By the end of the 2000 legislative session, KERA had become the national gold standard for education reform.

·Senate Bill 226 was the most contentious bill I supported during the 1996 legislative session. Its intent was to reform the prevailing wage law by lowering the monetary threshold required for the law to kick in on the construction of public buildings. At the time, public buildings had to cost at least $400,000 for the prevailing wage law to apply. Organized labor wanted the threshold lowered to $250,000, plus some other provisions.

Organized labor had attempted to pass similar bills in previous sessions. Those bills always passed easily in the house, even though some members weren't really on board, because they knew the senate would bury the legislation without even voting on it. During the campaign, I had promised organized labor that I would try to get a new prevailing wage law passed, as this was an important issue to the unions. Given the lack of success during previous legislative sessions, I decided to take a different route. Instead of starting in the house, I had senate majority leader David Karem introduce the bill in the senate.

Eck Rose and the senate Republicans opposed the bill. They argued that it would be a raid on local government budgets because it would increase the cost of building schools by 30 percent. They contended that local governments would be able to build schools only two-thirds the size they needed. However, my experience as a county judge told me that construction costs would rise only 3 to 5 percent, and the higher-quality work performed by skilled labor was worth it.

Rose thought he had the votes to beat the bill, but he didn't know that I had persuaded Tom Buford, a Republican from Jessamine County, and Paul Herron Jr., a Democrat from Crittenden County, to support it. After the bill passed in the senate, Rose came down to my office and chewed me out. He informed me that I had violated his earlier edict that I was not to go behind his back and talk to individual senators about specific pieces of legislation, and he wasn't going to stand for it! I sat quietly and took the verbal abuse. When he finished, I just smiled and said, "Have a nice evening, Eck." I didn't want to argue with him because I still had to get the bill passed in the house.

That task became a little more difficult when house speaker Jody Richards told me he had to oppose the bill for political reasons. However, Jody was a friend, and he had respect for me as governor and for the governor's office. He allowed the floor debate to drag on for two hours while we brought key legislators to my office to try to convince them it was a good bill. This was the closest I ever came to pressuring legislators to vote the way I wanted them to vote.

When school superintendents argued against the bill, house majority leader Greg Stumbo, who had agreed to push for the bill's passage on my behalf, threatened to retaliate by sponsoring a bill prohibiting school districts from paying superintendents more than teachers. Greg was good at that type of "negotiating." As a result, I persuaded about half a dozen representatives who were on the fence to support the bill, and it passed in the house by a bare majority of fifty-one votes.

During the 1996 legislative session, I made it clear to the legislative leadership and to the media that I would exercise my veto power only if I believed a law violated the Kentucky Constitution or if the leadership wanted it vetoed and promised not to override my veto. I wouldn't veto legislation simply because I didn't agree with it. In that case, I might not sign a bill and allow it to become law unsigned.

Overriding a veto required only a majority of the total membership of a chamber (a constitutional majority), not an overwhelming two-thirds majority. And in general, if a legislator had voted to pass a bill, he or she would vote to override my veto. Flip-flopping and voting both ways on an issue would be political suicide. I figured out pretty quickly that the only way to make a veto stick was if the legislative leadership wanted it to stick. If the leadership wanted to sustain my veto, they could simply not bring the issue up for a vote.

Several times during my eight years in office, the leadership came to me and said, "Governor, we made a mistake. Please veto that bill. We won't bring it up for an override vote." In general, when the legislature passed a bill, I believed it was my duty to either sign it or let it become law without my signature. I vetoed only one law passed in the 1996 legislative session, and the legislators didn't try to override my veto because they knew I was right.

Some legislators were disappointed that we didn't accomplish more during the 1996 legislative session, but the lack of money had a lot to do with that. I thought the session was a success, given the resources we had to work with. We put a Band-Aid on the health insurance reform law and laid the foundation for repairing the Kentucky Education Reform Act and reforming higher education. We also made headway in the areas of juvenile justice and domestic violence reform; my wife, Judi, lent her considerable influence to the latter.

Given the economic constraints we operated under during the 1996 legislative session, I thought it had gone fairly well, and I hadn't made any costly political missteps. I was eager to see what the rest of the year had in store for me.

I learned as county judge the importance of keeping in touch with the people. Here I'm speaking to the Kentucky Farm Bureau. (Courtesy of Kentucky Department for Libraries and Archives, Archives and Records Management Division)

I was in the office a lot, generally from 7:00 a.m. to 7:00 p.m. (Courtesy of Kentucky Department for Libraries and Archives, Archives and Records Management Division)

9

The First Year and Workers' Compensation Reform

When the General Assembly was in session, I had been obliged to remove my partisan hat because my job was to represent *all* Kentuckians, including those who had voted against me. Now that the session was over, I intended to be very political in supporting the principles of the Democratic Party and Democratic candidates. I made that clear in a mid-April 1996 speech to the Lexington Chamber of Commerce, where I also touted our accomplishments during the just-completed legislative session and reiterated that my administration was all about creating jobs.

There is no question that the policies and procedures I initiated and supported were influenced by the ideals and goals of the Democratic Party, but that didn't mean I was unwilling or unable to work with Republicans in the state senate and house. Similarly, I opposed Mitch McConnell every time he ran for the US Senate, and he opposed me in my first gubernatorial campaign. However, our political differences never interfered with our ability to work together in the interests of Kentucky. That said, I intended to promote the ideas and ideals of the Democratic Party in Kentucky and elsewhere.

I have always considered myself a generally easygoing person, but I can play hardball every once in a while. During my two terms as governor, I had a reputation for being tougher and meaner than I deserved, but I certainly didn't complain about it. I admit to being a hands-on administrator, and I worked at it 24/7/365. However, I wasn't a strong-arm governor in the mold of an Earle Clements, Louie Nunn, Wendell Ford, or Julian Carroll. I used persuasion rather than intimidation to get legislators to support my agenda. Overall, having a reputation for being tough wasn't a bad thing. Besides, I believed I was right most of the time!

The spring and summer of 1996 was a busy time. In mid-May I asked my secretary of natural resources and environmental protection, Jim Bickford, to review the state's environmental laws to determine whether some of them went beyond federal requirements and whether those laws might be driving existing businesses out of Kentucky or preventing new businesses from coming to the state. My guiding philosophy regarding environmental regulations was that responsible people intend to obey the law, and state government's job is to help them do that. However, if a company failed to comply with the state's environmental laws, it was penalized in the form of heavy fines, and I made it clear that the company was welcome to leave Kentucky.

During the last week of May and the first week of June, I traveled to China on a trade mission to explore economic development opportunities. Accompanying me was secretary of the Economic Development Cabinet Gene Strong, Jim Navolio and a couple of his staff members, my wife, Judi, my daughter Bambi, and events planner Donna Moloney. I was the first Kentucky governor to visit mainland China. I wanted to encourage the Chinese to invest in Kentucky, much like the Japanese had invested in Scott County with their Toyota manufacturing plant. Unfortunately, we discovered that the Chinese were not ready to start investing in the United States. We also found that selling Kentucky products in China was a little more difficult than getting the Japanese to eat Kentucky Fried Chicken.

The first thing we did in China was visit the US embassy, where the State Department briefed us on conditions there. Our trip to China coincided with the battle over intellectual property and proprietary patents, which didn't make things easy for us. Our Chinese hosts must have thought we were a lot more important than we were. We were treated to a state dinner in the Great Hall of the People, and the entrée was authentic Peking duck. My daughter didn't eat much, so we bought her a hamburger at McDonald's on the way back to the hotel.

The next day we had a formal meeting with a high-profile official in China's Commerce Department. During my discussion with the Chinese official, she did a full-court press, presenting China's side of the intellectual rights issue, which I couldn't do anything about, as it was a national, not a state, issue. We concluded afterward that there wasn't much potential for either Chinese investment in Kentucky or a Chinese market for Kentucky products, so we never returned to China while I was governor.

I went back to China in 2009, and it had changed significantly in thirteen years. In 1996 rush-hour traffic in Beijing consisted of mostly bicycles. By 2009, it was mostly cars. In 1996 the airport bathrooms reeked of urine, but in 2009 they were more modern than restrooms in the United States. The hotels in China had been modernized too. We took a two-hundred-mile bus trip to the Chinese interior. Interestingly, Chinese civil engineers don't follow the natural topography when building highways; they bore straight through any obstacles they encounter. The modern four-lane highway we traveled on went through a mountain range with ten or more tunnels, one of which was thirteen miles long. We would go through one tunnel and then onto a bridge across the valley into another tunnel. There was practically no traffic in China's interior. The Chinese were building for the future.

This experience was quite different from my trips to Japan. I went to Japan once as a private citizen, twice while I was lieutenant governor, and eight times while I was governor. I've eaten all the sushi I ever need to eat. Japan is a modern, impressive country—very clean and safe, and the people are very polite. During my trips to Japan, we would meet with the representatives of eight or ten Japanese companies already doing business in Kentucky, as well as the representatives of eight to ten prospective Japanese companies we had targeted. If a company's top representative was unable to attend, the governor would have to sit out the meeting because, according to Japanese custom, the participants had to be equal in rank.

I also went to Korea twice when Kentucky was in the running for a Hyundai manufacturing plant. Korea was more crowded than Japan, and I didn't care for the garlic they seemed to put in everything. However, the Koreans treated us very courteously and were receptive to our incentives. Hyundai eventually chose to build a plant in Alabama instead of on the eighteen hundred acres in Hardin County we had suggested. We recognized how good the Hardin County property was and purchased it, and that is where the Ford Motor Company built its new battery plant more than twenty years later.

After the 1996 legislative session ended, I was kept busy. In addition to traveling overseas and out of state, I was in my office dealing with whatever issues emerged. I also spent a great deal of time traveling throughout the state. I wanted the people of Kentucky to know that I hadn't forgotten them, that I was concerned about their welfare, and that I wanted to help them as much as I could. It's not difficult for a governor to get exposure on Lexington and Louisville television stations, but I wanted the people in Garrard, Pulaski, Fulton, Crittenden, Laurel, Boyd, Mason, Christian, Knott, Logan, Pike, and all the other counties to know that I was thinking about them, too.

I also maintained a good relationship with state legislators. I didn't want to ignore them after the legislative session ended and they left Frankfort. I wanted them to know that I recognized their importance and intended to keep them involved in my decision-making process.

Small gestures from a governor can have immense value. For instance, after I got involved in Wendell Ford's 1971 gubernatorial campaign, I received a Christmas card from him. I had that Christmas card framed, and it's still in my home today as one of my most treasured possessions. Similarly, as a reward for my involvement in Julian Carroll's 1975 gubernatorial campaign, he sent me an invitation to the Kentucky Derby in 1976. My parents had never been to the Derby, so I took them as my guests. At the pre-Derby breakfast in Frankfort, I introduced them to Governor Carroll, and the staff photographer took a photograph of the governor shaking hands with my mother. She considered that one of her most prized possessions until the day she died. She told everyone she knew that she had shaken hands with the governor. I never forgot that, and I was very proactive in maintaining visibility throughout the state. I believe it was a good use of my time and helped maintain my influence among the people.

Over the course of my political life, I have discovered that personal contact can overcome many sins. If the people had confidence in me as their governor, they would be more likely to acquiesce when I made a tough decision that required sacrifice on their part. The only way I knew how to build that kind of confidence was to visit all 120 Kentucky counties and listen to what the voters had to say. Every year of my governorship except the last, I visited every county in Kentucky at least once. Take my word for it: political leadership is much more complex and challenging than business leadership.

For most of my life, I have been too much of a hands-on administrator when I should have spent more time looking at the big picture. However, as governor, I think I maintained a good balance. I was certainly a hands-on administrator, but I also focused on the economy, jobs, education, and running an efficient and honest administration. Fortunately, I had many good people working with me, and I delegated a lot of the hands-on stuff to them, such as secretary of the cabinet Crit Luallen, who decided which cabinet administrators needed to meet with me personally. As a result, as governor, I didn't neglect the big picture nearly as badly as I did in my personal life and business affairs.

After being in office a few months, I had a talk with Lieutenant Governor Steve Henry about his political future. I tried to help Steve's political career as much as I could. During the first year of my first term, after Anne Northup defeated Mike Ward in Kentucky's Third Congressional District, I urged Steve to run against her in 1998 because he already had a strong political base in Jefferson County. I pointed out that if he won and held that congressional seat through the 2000 and 2002 election cycles, he would be able to circle back and run for governor at the end of my second term. Unfortunately, Steve didn't take my advice, and he spent eight years as lieutenant governor. Had he run against Northup and won, he would have helped both his own political fortunes and the Democratic Party in Kentucky.

In mid-August we created the Renaissance Kentucky program to revitalize the downtown areas of small communities across the state and demonstrate my commitment to improving the lives of rural Kentuckians. Only small communities were eligible to apply for Renaissance Kentucky funding. I created a twenty-six-member board to guide the program and appointed Lynn Luallen, head of the Kentucky Housing Corporation and husband of Crit, to chair it. The board's task was to approve the plans of applicants. Each participating community had to develop a long-range plan to improve its core downtown area. The goal was for the community to coordinate governmental and private resources to revitalize its downtown area and to prioritize projects efficiently. As county judge, I had seen towns repave a major downtown street, only to tear it up the next year to replace a sewer line. Seventy-five towns, mainly county seats, took advantage of this program, and I was very proud of it.

I had the honor of speaking for three minutes at the Democratic National Convention in Chicago near the end of August 1996, when President Clinton was nominated for reelection. Terry McBrayer lobbied hard for me to be one of the speakers. I was still the "golden boy" among the national Democrats for beating a Republican, so I was given a three-minute slot in the middle of the afternoon, when the convention center was nearly empty. My speech wasn't broadcast live on television, but it was still a thrill for a country boy from Kentucky!

In early September Fred Mudge, the secretary of transportation, was the first member of my administration to resign. He had accepted a senior executive position with RJ Corman Railroad Group. Fortunately, deputy secretary Jim Codell was interested in moving up, and he turned out to be one of the best cabinet members I appointed. He was sensitive and responsive, but he could tell people no, including me.

The first real crisis I faced as governor involved workers' compensation insurance. Soon after my election, friends in the coal industry began to complain about dramatic increases in the premiums for workers' compensation insurance when their policies came up for renewal. Some coal operators were paying premiums equal to 100 percent of their payroll. No company can afford that.

Herbie Deskins, Greg Stumbo, Kelsey Friend, and other legislators from the coal regions developed what essentially became a coal miners' retirement program called the Subsequent Injury Fund. If a person who had worked for multiple employers over the course of a career contracted a disease such as black lung or developed a progressive physical disability due to a back injury, the question arose: which company was responsible for the former employee's disability? The answer: the Subsequent Injury Fund, which was subsidized by a percentage fee on all workers' compensation insurance premiums. Eventually, the majority of people awarded claims from that fund were former coal miners. Many older coal miners, who lost their jobs as the coal industry declined, viewed these lifetime awards as pensions. Almost all coal miners viewed a black lung award as their right if they had worked underground in the mines for twenty years or more. Over time, the award process became ridiculous as office workers, truck drivers, and coal operators filed for and received disability awards. It was a gravy train that the coal industry couldn't afford, and it was becoming an unacceptable cost to *all* employers in Kentucky.

Black lung is not difficult to diagnose. The law at the time stated that if a doctor said you had coal dust nodules on your lungs, even if your breathing wasn't impaired, you had black lung and were eligible for workers' compensation benefits. Based on that, I could have filed a claim for black lung. I have nodules on my lungs, and I still have coal dust embedded in my hands, even though I haven't worked in a mine in decades! However, I am certainly not disabled. Most claimants were not even physically impaired, much less disabled, yet they received lifelong awards. It was unfair because *all businesses* in Kentucky funded the program, not just the coal industry. Therefore, most businesses had to pay into a fund that their workers rarely needed. It was an enormous cost of doing business, and they were tired of paying it.

In 1994 Kentucky legislators passed a law that created a new Subsequent Injury Fund for coal industry employees subsidized only by the coal industry. That law also increased workers' compensation benefits for all recipients, but it made those benefits harder to get so that businesses would save money. However, every time the legislature tightened eligibility requirements, the courts loosened them again. As a result, the number of claims awarded doubled from five thousand in 1994 to ten thousand in 1996.

The problem was just coming to a head as I took office. The 1994 legislation became effective in the middle of July 1994. Many coal companies' workers' compensation policies had already been renewed by July 1, so the effects of the new law were not reflected in those premiums. By July 1995, most of the existing policies had expired, and premiums skyrocketed.

Early in the 1996 session, I called house majority leader Greg Stumbo into my office and told him that we had to make the fund solvent. He convinced the house to pass a temporary funding bill that utilized money from the coal severance tax, which was part of the General Fund, but it didn't pass in the senate.

The coal industry was not the only one begging for relief from workers' compensation costs, which were still very high across the board. In early February 1996 the Economic Progress Initiative Council held a news conference and declared that the Kentucky workers' compensation insurance program was in crisis. The council claimed that the high cost of insurance, legal fees, and settlements for injured workers made Kentucky economically uncompetitive with other states. After the legislative session ended, I wanted to determine whether the council's charges were valid, so in mid-April, at a hearing of the sixteen-member Workers' Compensation Advisory Council, I challenged them to prove that costs were too high for Kentucky businesses. The council made a very impressive case. I put together a task force to research the problem and develop recommendations to be considered by a special session of the General Assembly. I wanted to wait until after the November election and after the Thanksgiving holiday to call the special session to deal with this issue.

Initially, house and senate Democrats could not agree. They even disagreed about whether I should call a special session. Legislators from the coal counties, legislators from non-coal but strong union counties like Jefferson, and legislators from rural agricultural counties all had different opinions on the subject. Some legislators from coal counties, such as Herbie Deskins, wanted to wait a while longer and let the previous changes to the workers' compensation law take full effect.

This was a politically dangerous issue to tackle so early in my first term, as reforming workers' compensation would upset the apple carts of some of the legislature's most powerful members. However, I didn't believe in kicking the can down the road when it came to taking on tough issues. This was a problem that had to be fixed, whatever the political cost.

Pro-business legislators such as senate president Eck Rose and almost all the Republicans thought I should take the lead on this issue. They thought I should make proposals to fix the problem before calling a special session. Once again, I didn't have any specific recommendations. As a coal operator, I had paid millions of dollars in workers' compensation insurance premiums, but I didn't know why the cost had gone up so much until I did some research. I had been out of the coal industry for eighteen years, so I didn't have firsthand knowledge of the current situation. The administrator of the state workers' compensation insurance program, Walter Turner, educated me and helped develop the program passed by the General Assembly during the 1996 special session.

Some people were abusing the law by treating workers' compensation as a form of social welfare. Many claimants were capable of working but had lost a job and couldn't find another, so they were using the system, with the aid of their attorneys and doctors, as a lifetime pension plan. Anyone who had been an underground coal miner for twenty years was almost assured of qualifying for black lung benefits. It was seen as an entitlement. People felt they were owed the benefits. That's just the way it was.

I knew the growing number of claimants was unsustainable, but I didn't want to jeopardize compensation for truly ill or injured workers. The law had to be fixed for the system to remain solvent and for Kentucky to compete with surrounding states in attracting and retaining businesses. The workers' compensation law was pointless if people couldn't find a job in the first place.

Having been the secretary of the Cabinet for Economic Development, I already knew that workers' compensation insurance costs were too high. Kentucky was one of the top five states in the country in both the number of claims and the amount of monetary awards. When Gene Strong, my secretary for economic development, told the Workers' Compensation Advisory Council that Kentucky's costs were among the highest in the nation, the members were genuinely surprised. I wanted the advisory council to identify specific problems so we could educate the public before searching for solutions.

At the annual meeting of the Kentucky Coal Association in late October 1996, I told the coal operators they would have to continue to shoulder most of the financial burden of their employees' claims for injuries and chronic illnesses. However, I also told them that my goal was to reduce the number of black lung and coal-related injuries by half by rewriting the law.

A couple of days before I called a special legislative session and released the reform plan, I met with a group representing organized labor and a group representing the business community. I went back and forth between two rooms in the capitol for almost twelve hours as they discussed the plan and tried to come up with a compromise. In the end, organized labor decided to oppose the plan.

Ron Cyrus was president of the AFL-CIO, and he had played a key role in getting me elected governor. I thought Ron was a reasonable person, and he understood that the workers' compensation insurance law needed to be fixed. We had been working together on the reform plan, but when it got down to crunch time that day, Ron said the unions wouldn't support it, so we parted ways. Labor leaders vowed not only to oppose my reform plan but also to make sure I wasn't reelected.

After organized labor dropped out of the negotiations, we took a wrecking ball to the existing law and moved the needle much closer to what industry wanted. This made the reform law more severe than it should have been, all because organized labor got huffy and dropped out of the process. I don't like to be blackmailed, so I took the attitude that if the unions weren't going to support the compromises we had proposed, we'd just go ahead and do whatever the business community wanted.

Eck Rose, minority floor leader Dan Kelly, Walt Turner, and I extensively rewrote the workers' compensation law. The two major issues we tackled were lifetime benefits and black lung and back injuries. Our program for job-related back injuries and black lung claims relied on objective medical evidence and therefore reduced the need for attorneys. We added a qualifier to the black lung provision that required claimants to demonstrate impaired breathing as tested by a spirometer (a device that measures breathing capacity), not just X-ray evidence of coal deposits on the lungs. Individuals with slightly impaired breathing who could still work would be enrolled in a paid retraining program to qualify them for some other job. Only those with stage 3 black lung, which was rare, qualified for total disability. We estimated that this would reduce claims by as much as 75 percent. We also cut off workers' compensation benefits at age sixty-five, based on the theory that workers' compensation insurance was meant to replace earnings lost due to a work-related physical impairment. Once recipients reached retirement age, they would be eligible for Social Security and Medicare.

Our plan set up a system whereby benefits reviewers, who were state employees, would evaluate each claim before the worker hired a lawyer. The reviewer would also help the worker file a claim with the employer's insurance carrier. If the worker deemed the amount of an award unfair, he could file an appeal with an administrative law judge, much like Social Security. The worker could also hire a lawyer to contest the amount awarded, and the lawyer's fee would be based on only the *increase* in benefits secured. Lawyers didn't like that provision. Our reform plan was a radical change, but I thought it was fair.

At the start of the special session on December 2, 1996, I had house majority whip Kenny Rapier file the bill. Three other members of the house leadership signed on as cosponsors; Greg Stumbo was the only one who didn't. The bill went to the Labor and Industry Committee, chaired by Ron Cyrus and dominated by other supporters of organized labor. I expected that committee to rewrite substantial portions of the bill to favor the unions, so I had a duplicate bill sent to the Appropriations and Revenue (A&R) Committee, which was much friendlier.

Harry Moberly from Richmond was chair of the A&R Committee. Richmond had a substantial business community, and those business leaders were tired of paying so much for workers' compensation. Even though Moberly and Stumbo were friends, Harry led the charge for me and did an excellent job. I sat next to Walt Turner while the A&R Committee debated the bill, and we answered questions during the proceedings. Then the committee approved the bill and sent it to the house floor for debate and a vote.

The fight in the house was a knock-down, drag-out battle that resulted in some bruised feelings. The biggest sticking points were the diminished involvement of lawyers in the process, the definition of particular injuries based on accepted medical practice, and the one-size-fits-all award amounts. In the end, the bill passed overwhelmingly in the house by a vote of eighty to seventeen. After Stumbo lost, he stood up and said, "Mr. Speaker, I'm not used to getting beat that bad." The bill then sailed through the senate without many amendments and passed by a vote of thirty-two to six.

I had always been confident that I would get something passed, but I couldn't predict the precise outcome. I don't remember cajoling anybody during the debate on the bill; the legislators knew something had to be done, and the majority of them were willing to listen. We logically explained our objectives, and at the end of the day, they knew it was the right thing to do. Workers' compensation was completely out of control, and the legislature understood that reality, as the final votes demonstrated.

Reforming workers' compensation insurance was not part of my plan when I was elected governor, and it wasn't something I wanted to do. It was something I had to do, and it complicated my life politically. On the one hand, that fight got me on the wrong side of Greg Stumbo and organized labor, which was not a politically smart thing to do. On the other hand, I convinced the Republicans and the business community that I was fair and would do what needed to be done, not what was politically expedient. It dramatically improved my image among Republicans, which may explain why they mounted only token opposition to my reelection campaign in 1999.

The reform plan effectively "cured" black lung because most miners didn't want to be retrained for another job. Many people with back injuries were physically able to do other work if they underwent retraining, making them ineligible for full workers' compensation benefits. As a result, we drastically cut the number of claims in Kentucky, and that was good for the state's business climate.

Let me make one thing clear: there *is* a disabling condition called pneumoconiosis, commonly referred to as black lung, that was prevalent in the coal industry in the past. If the work environment is dusty, very fine coal dust particles become embedded in the lungs of coal miners who have worked in the mines for a long time. My grandfather Roscoe Borders died from black lung, and it is a terrible disease. The federal government passed the Coal Mine Health and Safety Act of 1969, which dramatically reduced the amount of dust allowed in coal mines. That didn't cure black lung for those who already had it, but the new standard likely prevented new miners from contracting it *if the mine actually complied with the law.* Most did. By the 1990s, few miners were developing the disabling disease. However, I have heard that the recent practice of mining lower-quality coal in low seams has increased the amount of dust created, resulting in more cases of black lung.

The workers' compensation insurance law was one of the most personally troubling issues I faced during my eight years as governor. My political mentor Kelsey Friend was one of the most prominent black lung lawyers in Kentucky. I was acquainted with many coal miners, and I sympathized with all of them. Unions had helped elect me governor, and I believed in the overall goals of organized labor. I had many friends in unions, such as Phinis Hunley, Larry Sanderson, Charlie Cantrell, and dozens of others all over the state. It was a particularly difficult issue for some of the people on my staff, including my secretary of labor, Joe Norsworthy, his number-one assistant, Eddie Jacobs, and my labor liaison, Danny Ross. I had one-on-one conversations with them and apologized for the difficult position I had put them in. I guess Eddie summed it up best when he said, "Governor, our hearts are in one place and our asses are in another."

Less than a week after the bill's passage, two of Gene Strong's economic development initiatives came to fruition. The first one pertained to a Japanese auto parts manufacturer, AISIN World Corporation of America, which announced that it would invest $41.5 million to build a factory in London. The second announcement pertained to the Pittsburgh Tube Company's decision to build a $35 million plant in Hopkinsville. Vice president for corporate development Donald Nelson specifically mentioned passage of the workers' compensation reform legislation as a major factor in his company's decision to build in Kentucky. It was nice to receive that kind of affirmation.

After the bill passed, I held a celebration on a hastily constructed stage in the rotunda of the capitol. In retrospect, that event was probably a little over the top. At the time, I didn't realize the full ramifications of the new law, but it didn't take long for me to find out. I had inadvertently made it so difficult to obtain workers' compensation benefits that many people are still angry with me. My bill went too far. I later acknowledged that mistake and tried to make it less draconian in subsequent sessions.

During this time, I made one of the biggest mistakes of my governorship. My disagreement with Greg Stumbo had become so bitter that I wrote a very intemperate letter to him and released it to the press without consulting Skipper or Crit. They never cussed me out over it, but I'm sure they wanted to! I think my reputation as a hard-nosed fighter intimidated them a little. They later learned that my tough-guy persona wasn't all it was cracked up to be. Nevertheless, it took a long time for Stumbo, one of the most capable, powerful, and influential members of the General Assembly, to get over the animosity caused by our disagreement. His dislike of me carried into the 1997 special session on higher education reform. Though my actions were shortsighted and stupid, no one could have foreseen how my fight with Greg would undermine my ability to get some of my other initiatives passed. But the storm clouds were gathering.

At the time, my staff and I thought the workers' compensation issue had damaged me politically. I had no idea that it actually *enhanced* my standing throughout the state. Getting that bill passed was a big victory for me. It demonstrated that I had a lot of political capital and knew how to use it. Many in the legislature and in the media gave me high marks for the political acumen I exhibited during my first year in the governor's office. That, too, was gratifying.

As 1996 ended, I considered my first year in office a success, and I couldn't wait to tackle higher education reform in 1997. In August 1996, in front of 250 people I had invited to Frankfort, I outlined a strong position and said I was staking my entire governorship on the issue of higher education reform. I let them know that I was serious about this subject, and I wouldn't tolerate selfishness, shortsightedness, or turf wars. If I thought workers' compensation reform had been a sticky wicket, I was in for a surprise. I had no idea what kind of hornets' nest I was about to disturb.

My first difficult issue was workers' compensation reform. Here I'm signing a bill to improve the law as coal miners look on approvingly. (Courtesy of Kentucky Department for Libraries and Archives, Archives and Records Management Division)

Jody Richards was the speaker of the Kentucky House of Representatives for all eight years of my governorship and a loyal supporter throughout. (Courtesy of Kentucky Department for Libraries and Archives, Archives and Records Management Division)

In her role as First Lady, Judi served as hostess for many different events at the governor's mansion, including tours for school groups. (Courtesy of Kentucky Department for Libraries and Archives, Archives and Records Management Division)

10

Postsecondary Education Reform and Other Issues

My primary legislative goal heading into 1997 was postsecondary education reform. In my opinion, Kentucky had a fundamental decision to make: would the commonwealth retain a postsecondary education system based solely on the raw political power of the state's public universities, or was it ready to adopt a coordinated system in which the public universities worked together to achieve long-range goals and move the state into the twenty-first century?

Shortly after my inauguration, Skipper and I had sat down to talk about the direction we wanted to take this administration. He asked me directly and I replied: "I want to reform higher education in the commonwealth of Kentucky. I want to be a leader of change in the way we look at our colleges and universities to be sure they are educating with an eye toward our future." Skipper meekly asked, "Paul, couldn't we do that in the second term?" I responded, "Skipper, if I can't do something bold and decisive in the first term, there won't be a second term." Skipper replied, "Amen."

I had no delusions that reforming postsecondary education in Kentucky would be easy. I understood that this would be the biggest challenge of my political career. Unlike workers' compensation reform, where there had been an impetus for change in the business community and the legislature, there wasn't any widespread dissatisfaction with the existing public university, community college, and technical school system. I knew that broaching this issue would make some people uneasy. However, after looking at what other states had done and consulting education experts, I knew that for Kentucky to move forward educationally and economically, the postsecondary education system had to undergo a fundamental change.

It wasn't like I hadn't been warned of the difficulties by people I knew and respected in and out of the state legislature. David Karem, who had been a legislator for about twenty-five years and had dealt with just about every issue, told the media that passing workers' compensation reform would seem like a cakewalk compared with higher education reform: "Whenever you're talking about getting into higher education, legislators immediately see the chamber of horrors that it can be politically. It's difficult to even get a logical discussion going. As soon as you start talking about something, somebody's back gets up, the political wheels start turning, and you almost crush the dialogue. You get pummeled politically over it."

Former governor Edward "Ned" Breathitt, who chaired the University of Kentucky's Board of Trustees, told the media, "If we get into the governance issue, I think we will have a confrontation in the legislature of epic proportions. We will dissipate our energies fighting over an issue that was settled years ago."

House speaker Jody Richards said, "I think everybody agrees there needs to be some substantive changes. I think everybody also agrees, it's one of the most difficult areas to make changes in."

Mark Chellgren, a veteran reporter for the Associated Press, called postsecondary education reform "the swamp where seasoned legislators fear to tread!"

Complicating the already contentious and complex postsecondary education reform issue was another development I had to deal with. In the state senate, the Democratic Party had been losing seats to Republicans since the early 1990s. We Democrats took the loss of those seats as isolated occurrences, not recognizing that Kentucky's conservative political swing had become a broad-based movement. We were so brainwashed by the mythology that Kentucky was a Democratic state and that state government was the fiefdom of the Democratic Party that we didn't consider the possibility of an alternative. We ignored Republican gains in the state senate until we could no longer bury our heads in the sand, and by then, it was too late.

In the November 1996 election the Republicans picked up another state senate seat when Joe Meyer lost in the Twenty-Third District in northern Kentucky to Jack Westwood. I considered Joe's loss a great disappointment because it left the Democrats with only a slim majority in the senate—twenty seats to eighteen. Senate Republicans were just one seat away from being able to block Democratic legislation and my legislative agenda. However, never in my wildest dreams did I think the Republicans would actually win enough seats to become the majority party in the senate or, worse, that any senate Democrats would defect to the Republican Party, until it happened in late 1999.

The immediate result of Meyer's loss was that it split the senate's Democratic caucus. Before the 1996 election, there had been rumors that some

Democrats were unhappy with Eck Rose's leadership style as president of the senate, and it was possible they might break ranks when it came time to elect the senate leadership in early January 1997. Back in November, Eck had dismissed those rumors and told the media that he was confident the Democratic caucus would stick together and reelect the leadership team that had been in charge during the 1996 legislative session. In late December Larry Saunders indicated that he intended to challenge Rose for senate president. Walter Blevins told the media that he and three other Democratic senators from eastern Kentucky—Benny Ray Bailey, Glenn Freeman, and Gary Johnson (who had defeated Kelsey Friend in the Democratic primary in May before winning in November)—wanted a change in leadership. He claimed they were angry because they hadn't been appointed to chair the most important committees, which seemed strange to me because Freeman and Johnson had just been elected. I suspect they had been promised committee chairs and additional funding for their districts if they supported a change in leadership. Whatever their reasons, those five Democrats made a deal with seventeen of the eighteen Republicans to combine forces, vote Rose out as president, and install Saunders in that position. David Williams was the only Republican who didn't join the cabal because he and Rose were friends.

It is my understanding that Benny Ray Bailey, a Democrat from Knott County, and Dan Kelly, the Republican minority leader from Washington County, led the effort to depose Rose. Larry Saunders was just the front man. Saunders wanted the prestige of being senate president, but Bailey's goal was to chair the Appropriations and Revenue (A&R) Committee, which controlled the money. Long-serving A&R chair Mike Moloney had decided to retire after the 1996 legislative session, and as the ranking Democrat on the committee, Bailey should have been the heir apparent. However, Rose considered Bailey a loose cannon, so shortly after the November election, he told Bailey in no uncertain terms that he wasn't going to appoint him chair of the committee. As a result, Bailey decided to join forces with Kelly and the Republican caucus to take control of the senate. Rose didn't know about that plan; he thought he had enough votes in the Democratic caucus to be reelected president of the senate. The members of each political party generally vote together in what is called a "binding caucus" to make sure the majority party gets to elect the leadership, even if some of the caucus members don't want a particular person elected. Rose was in for a rude awakening when the senate met to elect its leadership on January 7, 1997.

As minority leader, Kelly was merely looking to increase the Republicans' influence in proportion to their growing numbers in the senate, and he saw the split in the Democratic caucus as the perfect opportunity to do this. Kelly and his caucus just wanted to have meaningful input into legislation. In exchange for the Republican caucus's support in deposing Rose, Bailey promised Kelly that the Republicans would receive fair representation on committees and would be able to choose their own committee members. That was the deal struck by Kelly and Bailey. It had nothing to do with public policy or political philosophy. It was all about power and who chaired the senate's committees.

I took a hands-off approach to electing the leadership in the senate and house. Having established coequality with the executive branch of government, the legislature would have been offended if I had tried to insert myself into the legislative leadership battle, so I stayed out of it.

Gary Johnson from Pikeville, my own Pike County senator, had been county attorney when I was county judge. As a courtesy to me, he came to my office on the morning of the leadership election and told me that he and four other Democrats were going to vote for Larry Saunders as senate president. I said I thought they were making a mistake, but I thanked him for telling me. I decided not to warn Rose because I had nothing to gain by getting involved in the legislative leadership drama. In fact, it would have damaged my relationship with the leadership, even if my preferred candidates had prevailed, because then they would have gone out of their way to prove they were not beholden to the governor.

In retrospect, Rose should have done the right thing and appointed Bailey chair of the A&R Committee. By all rights and custom, Bailey was next in line for the chairmanship, but Rose ruled the senate with an iron fist, and he wasn't going to let someone he didn't trust control the flow of money. Bailey had a reputation for fudging the truth; whenever he sponsored a bill or attached an amendment, his colleagues wanted to take a good look at it and make sure there was nothing fishy going on. As governor, I didn't want Bailey to be the A&R Committee chair either, and he proved me right. He refused to do what I requested and did whatever *he* wanted to do. He was too independent.

On the afternoon of the leadership elections, Karem made a motion to recess so the Democrats and Republicans could retire to their respective caucus rooms to select their candidates. Rose immediately declared that the motion had passed without actually taking a vote, and Kelly and Saunders objected. As the other fifteen Democrats left the chamber, Saunders and his four Democratic coconspirators and the eighteen Republicans remained glued to their seats. Those twenty-three members in the senate chamber constituted a quorum. Seventeen Republicans and five Democrats voted for

Saunders as senate president, and they immediately passed new operating rules that gave Republicans everything Kelly had requested as part of his bargain with Bailey. Rose and the other fourteen Democrats could do nothing about the coup that had occurred in their absence. I have to admit that it was brilliant political and parliamentary strategy on the part of Bailey and Kelly. However, their pact was merely a marriage of convenience. The five Democrats and the Republican caucus still had major ideological and policy differences, and to my knowledge, they never voted as a bloc and never felt any loyalty to one another.

After Rose was deposed, everyone knew that Bailey was behind it, and that, of course, caused hard feelings between the two men. In addition to Bailey's chairmanship of the A&R Committee, as a reward for their part in the cabal, Glenn Freeman was appointed chair of the Economic Development and Labor Committee, and Gary Johnson was appointed chair of the State and Local Government Committee. Walter Blevins was elected president pro tem.

Bailey and the other four dissident Democrats found themselves barred from caucusing with the fifteen Democrats who had supported Rose. Those five were persona non grata within the Democratic caucus, and the Republicans didn't want them in their caucus room either.

I made it clear that although I supported the fifteen "loyal" Democrats, I was determined to work with whoever was in charge. We would have to work together if we hoped to get anything done legislatively. I also believed the fifteen loyal Democrats would reclaim leadership of the senate after the 1998 elections.

I didn't get into politics because I loved the political game. I got into politics to run for governor, and once I was elected, my goal was to move Kentucky forward. I wanted to avoid becoming entangled in the internal politics of the General Assembly, as previous governors had.

That didn't mean I forgave the five Democrats who revolted. As the titular head of the Kentucky Democratic Party, I believed they were wrong; they had abandoned the party and had to pay a price for that, even though I didn't consider myself a "revenge" politician. However, I wanted the legislators to know that I rewarded my friends. Although I had to work with those five Democrats and the Republican caucus, I let them know that they weren't going to get any special favors from me, and it complicated my relationship with the senate.

Out of necessity, I maintained a civil relationship with Benny Ray and Larry. I gave Saunders the respect he deserved as president of the senate, but Bailey was the person I negotiated with because I knew he was the brains behind the senate leadership team. In fact, I always thought he was an intelligent and effective legislator. The fifteen loyal Democrats asked me to communicate directly with majority leader Karem rather than either Saunders or Blevins. I agreed to recognize Karem as the titular leader of the senate Democrats, and I even supported their refusal to accept the new leadership's committee assignments. However, I was determined to play the hand I had been dealt. I had to figure out a way to work with the five dissident Democrats and navigate around the hard feelings within the Democratic caucus. I had to ensure that policy issues were decided on their merit rather than on personal relationships. The fifteen Democrats later relented and reluctantly accepted their new committee assignments. The Republicans were never successful in convincing Bailey to be more conservative on policy issues. He was a proud liberal, and nothing would change that.

My relationship with Dan Kelly and the Republican caucus remained the same. I understood that his role in the cabal had been based on political opportunism. He was only trying to obtain more influence for his party. Both of us understood that we would work together when we could and work against each other when we had to. I had no problem with a healthy give-and-take between political adversaries. I always had a good working relationship with Kelly. I respected him and understood where he was coming from. By the time I called the special session in May to deal with postsecondary education reform, the political situation in the senate had settled down, and I thought we could move forward on that issue.

I have always advocated for postsecondary education, whether public or private. I joined the Pikeville College Board of Trustees in 1970 because I strongly believed that a college-educated workforce would elevate Kentuckians' standard of living and quality of life. I think even one year of college has tremendous value for young people. Exposing young people to a college curriculum and environment for even a short time improves their critical thinking skills and gives them a better perspective on the world, how they fit into it, and what they need to do to be successful.

I knew reforming Kentucky's public system of higher education was going to be difficult, but I was somewhat confident that logic would ultimately prevail. It turned out to be more challenging than I had anticipated.

Truthfully, I didn't know what reforms needed to be implemented. The only thing I knew was that our public universities were the key to Kentucky's future, and the system needed to be improved.

After the 1996 General Assembly adjourned, I hired consultants to evaluate the Kentucky system of higher education and offer suggestions to make it more efficient and readily accessible to all Kentuckians. To prepare for the special session and help me get a postsecondary education reform bill passed, I hired Paris Hopkins to be my liaison with the senate and former state senator Ed Ford as an adviser. Hopkins had previously worked for former senate majority floor leader Joe Wright and former senate president Eck Rose. At the time I hired him, Hopkins was working for Larry Saunders in the senate president's office. I expected Hopkins, Ford, and house liaison Leonard Gray to stay in touch with the legislators, attend our staff meetings, and tell us where the vote count stood and what we needed to do to pass a bill.

Ford was knowledgeable about the actual concept of postsecondary education reform, whereas Hopkins was more of a good old boy who could schmooze with the senators and take a reading on whether they were leaning for or against our proposal. He wasn't as deeply immersed in the details of the reform bill, and he didn't need to be. Both Ford and Hopkins provided a valuable service during and after the debate on postsecondary education reform.

I established a committee to study the issues and hold hearings throughout the state to educate people about the problems and opportunities relevant to Kentucky's public universities. I discovered an elitism among four-year degree-granting institutions. For example, I attended a dinner at the University of Louisville, and a professor told me that every person should have a bachelor's degree. I asked him why, and he said to make money. I told him that I knew a diesel mechanic who made more money than he did. His attitude stuck in my craw. After all, medical school, law school, engineering school, and business school constitute vocational education. My reaction to that bias among the faculty at Kentucky's public universities was to call my initiative *postsecondary* (rather than *higher*) education reform. I wanted to emphasize that my proposal would address *all* forms of state-supported education after high school, including vocational education and adult education.

The advisory committee could not agree on a proposal, so the bill we developed was based on what my staff, many of whom were educators, and my consultants thought would work for Kentucky. I let the experts decide what to do and then figured out how far to go. It was up to me to make the political argument and get the bill passed. I knew I wouldn't get everything I wanted, and if I asked for too much, the whole proposal might go down in flames.

In early March 1997 my administration issued a report that identified the inadequacies of the current postsecondary education system in Kentucky. In our opinion, there was too much duplication among the state's universities, community colleges, and vocational schools. The Council on Higher Education, the state's coordinating body, was not effective in setting postsecondary policy or coordinating subject majors, let alone course offerings among the state's public universities. The universities could no longer afford to be all things for all people. Most of the universities were offering the same subjects and the same courses. Kentucky is a relatively small and poor state, and we simply couldn't afford the duplication, which was wasting Kentucky's finite financial resources and holding the state back educationally and economically. I told the members of the Council on Higher Education they had fallen short in controlling the public universities' excesses, largely because of political interference. The council had little real authority because the individual universities wanted direct access to members of the General Assembly in order to use their political influence to get what they wanted, rather than having their wants and desires filtered through the Council on Higher Education. Leonard Hardin, who was chair of the council, agreed with me.

One of the early debates was whether Kentucky should have one unified statewide system like that in North Carolina, California, Texas, and Alabama or stick with the current system of a coordinating body to ensure adequate services and reduce duplication. We concluded that one statewide system wasn't the best way to go, and politically, it would have been far more difficult to get that type of system adopted and implemented. Therefore, we decided to give the coordinating board real authority, and this required a change in name and leadership. We named the new coordinating body the Council on Postsecondary Education (CPE).

I didn't want the individual public university presidents to be subordinate to the head of the CPE because that would hinder the universities' ability to hire top-flight administrators. On the one hand, we didn't want the president of the University of Kentucky to have to answer to some person in Frankfort that nobody knew. On the other hand, we didn't want the head of the CPE to have to deal with eight strong-willed university presidents with more powerful political constituencies than the council president had. One proposal intended to increase the CPE's influence was to pay the council president a salary equal to that of the highest-paid university president. In later years, as the presidents' salaries escalated, this provision went out the window.

My vision was for the budget proposals of the eight public universities to come directly from the CPE to the governor. I wanted the CPE president to present the overall higher education landscape to the governor and the General Assembly. I wanted the governor and the legislature to become dependent on the CPE for advice on issues pertaining to postsecondary education, rather than allowing the individual universities to lobby the governor and the legislature. University presidents have a lot of political influence in their communities and in the legislature, and we were trying to thread the needle on that issue. It wasn't an easy task, which is why previous governors and legislatures wouldn't touch it with a ten-foot pole.

As I examined postsecondary education in the commonwealth, I saw that each public university acted like its own little fiefdom, and the university presidents jealously guarded their domains. They generated a lot of revenue through tuition, out-of-state students, graduate courses, and other programs, but they all wanted state money too. During every budget cycle, all the university presidents went to Frankfort to lobby the individual legislators from their regions and the chairs of the Education and A&R Committees. They all wanted a bigger slice of the budget pie, and it was a free-for-all. As the state's flagship university, the University of Kentucky always received the biggest slice, and the other university presidents resented that. UK administered the Agricultural Extension Service, with agents in all 120 counties, and the statewide popularity (Big Blue Nation) of UK's basketball program gave the university enormous political influence in Frankfort. The regional university presidents also resented UK's control of the community colleges, which offered some of the same courses as the regional universities but much more cheaply, cutting into their enrollment and budgets. The regional presidents therefore had no interest in coordinating their instruction efforts with UK or any other public university because they were busy building their own empires. They didn't want to cede any of their course offerings to another university because that might hurt their enrollment and affect their political influence in the General Assembly. When I broached the idea of reforming postsecondary education in the state, the regional university presidents were among the first to support the idea in the hope that it would reduce UK's influence in Frankfort while increasing their own.

As I looked forward to the twenty-first century, I envisioned UK becoming one of the country's top-twenty public *research* universities. I understood that it still had an obligation to teach undergraduate students the basics, but I wanted UK to focus on and specialize in basic and advanced research. This meant attracting the best and the brightest scientists, medical professionals, and engineers in the country, and I was willing to provide the funding to make that happen. But first I had to convince UK president Dr. Charles Wethington, the presidents of the other universities, and the members of the state legislature to follow my lead. Dr. Wethington proved to be particularly tough to convince.

Based on my consultants' conclusions, I thought the community colleges were a drag on UK and would prevent it from becoming a top-twenty research university. Conversely, I thought UK hampered the community colleges' ability to react to the particular economic conditions in their respective communities. As the consultants explained it to me, the community colleges had to meet the workforce needs of their communities. They also had to offer general education courses that could be transferred to a four-year institution and count toward a bachelor's degree, but that wasn't their main mission. The community colleges had to be flexible and adapt to changing circumstances. For instance, the workforce needs of Ashland, with a manufacturing economy in flux, were different from those of Bowling Green, which was expanding rapidly with many high-tech companies.

I didn't think it was necessary for UK to oversee the largest community college system in the nation. UK had done a great job building the community college system, but that system had matured to the point where it could become a separate entity. The people of Kentucky needed UK to become a leading research university to help drive and modernize the state's economy, and I didn't think UK could do that if it continued to be distracted by the community colleges. The community colleges were like colonies, and UK treated them as such. UK was happy to take advantage of the political influence the community colleges had with legislators, but it wasn't interested in nurturing the community colleges and helping them reach their full potential.

As I envisioned it, the mission of the seven regional comprehensive universities was to provide bachelor's degrees to all Kentuckians who wanted a basic college education and offer master's degree programs to those specializing in subject areas such as business administration or social work. The regional universities would accomplish this by offering students several options. One option was the traditional on-campus experience. I believe the residential college experience helps young people transition from dependence on the family to independence. Both classroom and out-of-classroom experiences on a college campus have great value in promoting critical thinking and socialization skills, and the importance of exposure to a multicultural college campus cannot be overemphasized. In my estimation, participating in academic discussions in the classroom led by an expert in the relevant field and learning to articulate one's opinion are greatly undervalued. Although I advocate a fully immersive on-campus experience for students whenever possible, for some students, living at home is the best option, so we funded several satellite campuses for the regional universities to make in-person learning available within driving distance of every Kentuckian. We funded extension campuses for regional universities in Prestonsburg, Ashland, Corbin, Hopkinsville, Elizabethtown, Glasgow, Owensboro, and Paducah.

For other Kentuckians, an on-campus experience is simply impractical due to geographic location, family obligations, or time constraints. I envisioned the regional universities providing educational opportunities for these nontraditional students too. In particular, I thought providing a "virtual" college experience for these students and getting seriously involved in distance learning would be an innovative direction for the regional universities to take. I envisioned utilizing Kentucky Educational Television (KET), one of the best public television networks in the nation, in this distance learning effort, along with the internet. I thought the regional university presidents would share my vision, and I was very disappointed when they didn't. As it turned out, the community colleges have taken advantage of the online education option, but not to the extent I had imagined.

I also wanted to provide funding for each regional university to establish a "center of excellence" in a subject or discipline in which it could excel or already excelled. For example, Eastern Kentucky University had a nationally recognized law and criminal justice program, and Western Kentucky University had a nationally recognized journalism school. I wanted the regional universities to continue to excel in those areas that set them apart from one another, and I wanted to prevent other universities from duplicating those existing programs.

The consultants emphasized that research universities tend to be cautious about change, and faculties often undertake lengthy reviews when determining the substance of any new academic offering. In contrast, community colleges need to be nimble to fulfill their workforce development mission. The consultants advised us that the worst way to run a community college or technical school system was through the bureaucracy of state government, and the second worst way was through the bureaucracy of a large university. At the time, Kentucky did both. UK administered the community college system, and the state administered the technical school system. The consultants recommended that a new statewide entity, the Kentucky Community and Technical College System (KCTCS), administer both community colleges and technical schools. We knew that merging the two systems would cause problems, so we proposed that they be governed by a common authority while maintaining their separate identities. The KCTCS president would be responsible for administration of the entire entity. However, each community college and technical school would have a chancellor to administer the school.

I wanted this new postsecondary education system to specialize in workforce development, in addition to the community colleges' traditional mission of providing the first two years of a bachelor's degree program. New businesses and new technologies can't wait a couple of years while a degree curriculum is designed, reviewed, and implemented by a university faculty committee. If a business needs a hundred welders, they have to be trained *now*, and the community colleges and technical colleges require the flexibility to do that.

I received a stark reminder of how difficult my task was going to be in late March when I appeared on a KET program with UK president Dr. Wethington, University of Louisville president Dr. John Shumaker, and Murray State University president Dr. Kern Alexander. Before the program began, I was a little nervous because I'm not a lawyer, a professor, or a trained debater, and I knew all these gentlemen were sharp individuals. However, I was the governor and this was my plan, so I felt obligated to defend it.

The discussion largely devolved into a debate between Dr. Wethington and me. I hadn't anticipated this turn of events, as Wethington and I had always gotten along quite well in the past. I was a little surprised when he adamantly opposed my plan to remove the community colleges from UK's control and accused me of trying to damage UK. I questioned why he thought I would want to damage UK when my children and I were graduates of that institution. I said if he could present evidence that my ideas were wrong, I would be happy to listen and modify them. He surprised me again when he dismissively described my plan as "fundamentally flawed" and told me I had been "ill advised."

The intransigence demonstrated by Dr. Wethington was incomprehensible to me, particularly since my original plan designated UK as the state's *only* research university. Had he supported my plan at the outset, UK would have been given all the financial resources it needed to turn itself into a true research university. But when Dr. Wethington decided to dig in his heels and oppose my plan, I had to find other allies, such as the Louisville and Jefferson County business community and their representatives in the General Assembly. Unfortunately for Dr. Wethington and UK, in return for their support, those constituencies wanted the University of Louisville to be designated the state's second research university. So instead of UK being the *sole* research university in the state, it would now have to compete for funds with the University of Louisville.

After the KET program, Dr. Wethington began a sustained public relations campaign to oppose my plan to separate the community colleges from UK. He turned almost all the UK basketball radio commercials into attacks against postsecondary education reform and me. UK also ran a full-page advertisement in the *Lexington Herald-Leader* that consisted of photographs of a vocational school T-shirt and a UK community college T-shirt with the caption, "Don't let the governor make us vocational schools." He was trying to make vocational education look inferior.

The year before, UK had won the NCAA basketball championship, and I had appeared at the victory celebration in Rupp Arena to congratulate the team when it arrived back home. In 1997 UK lost to Arizona in the championship game right in the middle of the fight over the community college issue. Although I wanted UK to win, I wasn't looking forward to making another appearance at the victory celebration. I might not have made it out of Rupp Arena alive because Dr. Wethington had labeled me Public Enemy No. 1!

Dr. Wethington appealed to in-state and out-of-state UK alumni to contact members of the General Assembly and pressure them to oppose my postsecondary education reform plan. UK used every bit of political influence it had to try to stop the plan dead in its tracks. I understand that people were betting on who had more political power, the president of UK or the governor of the state. I could only hope that I would win that battle.

For me, separating the community colleges from UK was the one non-negotiable issue. Everything else was on the table. I spoke to many groups and influential individuals, seeking their advice and help, including the Prichard Committee for Academic Excellence. I had served on that committee in the 1980s and resigned when I ran for lieutenant governor in 1987. (I am a member now.) The Prichard Committee had spearheaded the effort to reform elementary and secondary education in Kentucky a decade earlier. We found three different studies (one commissioned by the Prichard Committee) that recommended separating the community colleges from UK because their missions were so different. After I appeared before the Prichard Committee, explained my position, and pointed out that its own study supported that position, the committee voted to endorse my reform plan. In fact, I had the support of the Kentucky Chamber of Commerce, the Louisville business community, the regional universities, and many other people and organizations throughout Kentucky. UK was the only influential entity against the plan, and it *almost* succeeded in defeating it.

I knew I could not impose my will on the legislature. I had to be reasonable and not let the "perfect" get in the way of the "good." For example, my plan called for a new body with a powerful executive at its head to replace the Council on Higher Education. One of its powers would be to appoint members of the universities' board of trustees or board of regents. House speaker Jody Richards and A&R Committee chair Harry Moberly objected to that provision. They were afraid it gave the new council and its president too much power and might make the head of the council a czar, so I relented and removed that provision.

I had to have some legislative buy-in and support, and I knew that house majority floor leader Greg Stumbo would certainly oppose my plan. He had previously been on record as favoring the removal of the community colleges from UK's control. He realized UK was using the community colleges as a political weapon and was not giving them the resources they desperately needed. However, Stumbo was still smarting from the workers' compensation debate in 1996, and after he lost that fight, he abruptly changed his mind about the community colleges. I understood why: he was going to oppose anything I supported until he got over his last defeat. Therefore, I needed the backing of house speaker pro tem Larry Clark, Richards, and Moberly for the plan to have any chance of passing in the house.

In early April I decided to go into the lion's den and present my post-secondary education reform plan directly to the UK Board of Trustees. I didn't receive a hero's welcome. In fact, I learned that immediately before I arrived, the board had passed a resolution in support of Dr. Wethington and his position regarding the community college issue. I told the board members that Wethington was more interested in playing politics than in moving the state forward. I told them I had lost confidence in Wethington's ability to be objective and in his ability to lead Kentucky's flagship institution. And I told the board members that they were complicit, since Wethington reported to them, not to me. I felt the chill in the boardroom drop below zero.

In response, Dr. Wethington told the board that, for UK to become a top-twenty public research university, it would need $691 million in capital investments over a fifteen-year period and an additional $104 million every year thereafter for recurring costs, including the hiring of 640 additional faculty members. At the time, UK's national ranking was sixty-sixth among all universities and forty-fourth among all public universities, so it had a long way to go to reach top-twenty status. Dr. Wethington said the university was willing to begin a private fund-raising initiative to help defray the cost to the state, but the legislature would have to substantially increase its monetary support for the university in the state budget.

I called his estimates "academic fraud" intended to discredit and embarrass me. I had already stated that I was willing to give the university an extra $20 million to $30 million a year to fuel its new research mission. I called on the UK board to investigate the accuracy of the budget figures cited by Wethington, but it ignored my request, which I found very disrespectful. I think Dr. Wethington was trying to make reaching top-twenty status seem impossible, and maybe it was, but I thought we should try. In my opinion, there is nothing wrong with having lofty goals. I would rather reach for the stars and fail than reach for the mediocre and succeed.

To say I was hot under the collar after I left the UK board meeting would be an understatement, particularly when the board gave Wethington a standing ovation. He and the board had openly defied me, and I was not going to back down. I went back to Frankfort and promptly appointed my own committee to evaluate the budget estimates Wethington had submitted. I appointed Louisville attorney Sheryl Snyder, who happened to be a UK Law School graduate, as the committee's chair. When the committee made its report, it stated that Wethington had vastly overestimated the costs, which came as no surprise to me.

Prior to calling the special session, I visited each of the community colleges and held open forums to take questions and comments from faculty, administrators, and students. I wasn't exactly greeted with open arms at these institutions. When I visited the campus of Ashland Community College, interim president Roger Noe, a former state legislator and former chair of the House Education Committee, had arranged a pep rally *against* my plan. I felt like General George Armstrong Custer arriving at the Little Big Horn at every campus forum.

The administrators, professors, and students at the community colleges liked their affiliation with UK because having the UK imprimatur gave them a certain panache and prestige. Even though the community colleges went through a separate accreditation process and the faculty and students had no official standing with UK, they were determined to keep that affiliation. When a couple of Owensboro Community College students held up a sign supporting my plan, it was such a singular event that I actually commented on it to the media that accompanied us on those trips.

After visiting the individual community colleges, I realized that their administrators were largely inbred. There were few "outsiders" who came from other states. Most of them were loyal to Charles Wethington, who had risen through the community college system himself and had been chancellor of Maysville Community College. Governor Wallace Wilkinson had orchestrated Wethington's appointment as president of UK after Dr. David

Roselle left for the University of Delaware. Wilkinson and Wethington were both from Casey County and were friends. Wethington's appointment did not sit well with the university's faculty because he was not considered a real scholar like his predecessors Otis Singletary and Roselle, and he never had a warm and fuzzy relationship with his faculty. He ruled UK like an autocrat.

The one message I delivered at each community college was that the University of Kentucky was not an entity in and of itself. I directed that message at Dr. Wethington, who liked to say that UK was not a "state university" but a "*state-supported* university" that controlled its own destiny. I reminded the attendees at those open forums that UK existed to serve the people of Kentucky, not its own agenda. I considered separating the community colleges from UK an integral part of reshaping postsecondary education for the good of the state. I tried to convince them that UK and the community colleges would be among the beneficiaries.

My disagreement with Dr. Wethington over the community college issue was never personal. He and the members of the UK Board of Trustees believed that the university was an autonomous entity that charted its own course and did not answer to the governor or the state legislature, and they believed the state should continue to fork over ever-increasing amounts of money. Wethington accused me of interfering in the university's operation and trying to intimidate him and the board. In my opinion, Wethington just wanted to preserve his kingdom. He wanted to be in total control of UK; he wanted to preserve the statewide political power the community colleges provided, and he was willing to fight anybody who tried to chisel away at that control and power.

I thought Wethington's view was very parochial and that he failed to see the big picture. In my opinion, he and the UK Board of Trustees were being extremely selfish. We had fundamentally different visions of what kind of institution Kentucky's premier university should be and what his job as its leader should be. The difference was that I had the bully pulpit to convince the public that I was right. I had hired experts who said this was what Kentucky needed to do to improve postsecondary education. My only objective was to move Kentucky forward into the twenty-first century. I had no interest in getting into a drag-out, down-in-the-dirt, personal spat with Dr. Wethington. After the reform bill passed, I certainly did not embark on a crusade to remove him as UK president because of his opposition. My involvement in his removal came later, after he went around the established process to oppose one of my selections to the UK board.

Every regional university and most Chambers of Commerce across the state supported my postsecondary education plan. It was endorsed by the

Council of Independent Kentucky Colleges and Universities, which consisted of the presidents of Kentucky's nineteen private colleges, including Centre College and Transylvania University, as well as by the National Education Commission of the States, an influential policy group. Even the *Lexington Herald-Leader*, UK's hometown newspaper, and the *Louisville Courier-Journal* supported my plan. The only holdouts were Charles Wethington and the UK Board of Trustees.

I'm sure Dr. Wethington felt beleaguered. The only organization that supported UK's position was the Farm Bureau, probably because UK controlled the Agricultural Extension Service. However, the Farm Bureau was only an insurance agency, so I'm not sure how active it was in the community college debate. Wethington probably believed it was UK against the world. However, he had many UK resources that he called on to fight me. In mid-April the UK Alumni Association began a massive letter-writing campaign to all UK graduates, urging them to oppose my plan. They numbered in the tens of thousands inside and outside the commonwealth.

I had not anticipated this. In addition to being UK alums, many of these people were Kentucky voters, so I knew the community college issue might cost me politically across the state. Shortly after the UK letter-writing campaign began, I literally stayed awake one night thinking about it. I knew that if I took the community college issue out of the reform plan, UK would fall into line, the bill would pass easily in the legislature, and I could declare victory. However, postsecondary education wouldn't change enough. Future Kentuckians would not thank us for passing up this golden opportunity to fix higher education in the commonwealth. That night, I decided to stay the course and do what I thought was right. I would fight for my reform plan, and if I lost, I lost. The next morning I told my staff that we were going to fight for the community college issue, and that's when everyone said, "Hell yes!" They all pitched in and cranked up our publicity campaign. They understood what was at stake.

If I had lost the community college battle, I would not have run for reelection in 1999 because the only thing the voters would have remembered was that I tried to destroy the University of Kentucky. I would have to go back to Pikeville and mine coal or something. Additionally, if I lost the battle, the legislature would have treated me like a lame-duck governor for the remainder of my term. I decided to continue to champion my plan, despite the potential political fallout. As a result, the community college issue became a publicity battle. It became a fight for the hearts and minds of Kentuckians, including community leaders and state legislators.

I did everything I could to promote my plan. In early April the Kentucky Chamber of Commerce decided to mount an advertising and lobbying campaign in support of it. This was very beneficial because the organization had more than three thousand members, and it had leaders in every community. Some state legislators across the commonwealth understood the big picture and supported my reform plan on its merits, despite UK's political influence. There weren't many of them, but there were some, so I shifted into high gear and started lobbying legislators to support my proposal.

On a Saturday morning in mid-April I asked Dr. Wethington to come to Frankfort for a private meeting at the governor's mansion to try to resolve the community college issue. I also invited Skipper and former senator Mike Moloney, whose senate district had included UK. I thought the four of us could surely work out some sort of compromise to meaningfully reform postsecondary education without anyone losing face. The meeting, which lasted about an hour, took place in the sunroom of the governor's mansion, and everyone was cordial. However, it became clear that Dr. Wethington was unwilling to budge one iota from his position and fully expected me to cave in. He indicated a willingness to join the technical schools with the community colleges, but only if UK continued to control the whole system. I think he believed he had the upper hand and assumed I had called the meeting in desperation. He might have been right about the former, but he was wrong about the latter. The meeting ended without a resolution.

I met in early May with senate minority leader Dan Kelly and senate president Larry Saunders to discuss my postsecondary education reform plan. I knew I would need some Republican support in the senate, and now that Eck Rose was no longer in charge, I had to deal with a new set of political circumstances. Even though Saunders had the title, I understood that the powers behind the throne were Kelly and Benny Ray Bailey. Saunders and Bailey supported the plan, but Kelly opposed it, not because of the community college issue but because he didn't know how I planned to pay for the $100 million increase in the postsecondary education budget I had promised ($38 million in 1998 and an additional $62 million in 2000). He was also concerned that the new governing authority I championed would undermine the universities' local autonomy. I was afraid that his opposition to the reform bill would influence other members of his caucus to oppose it, and I needed every vote I could get. I addressed Kelly's concerns by telling him I intended to pay for the budget increase through cost savings achieved by streamlining government, but he still voted against the

plan, probably for political reasons. He didn't want me to have a big political victory that might help me get reelected in 1999. I worked well with
Kelly for the rest of my tenure as governor, but this time, I felt he let me
down for purely partisan political reasons.

After the meeting with Wethington at the governor's mansion, I
expected to face a stiff headwind. UK had a lot of resources, a lot of political
influence, and tens of thousands of alumni in the state. Before I called the
special session, polls indicated that UK was winning the publicity war.
Forty-eight percent of people polled in early April indicated that they
knew about the community college dispute, and of that number, 62 percent
supported UK's position. I had my work cut out for me.

On the Sunday before the session started, I called the state senator from
my district, Gary Johnson, and invited him to my house in Pikeville to discuss
my proposal. He said there was no reason for us to meet: if I just told him
what I wanted him to do, he would do it. Truth be told, I don't think he was all
that interested in serving in the state senate. He had just wanted to beat
Kelsey Friend, a member of the other Democratic faction in Pike County.

I knew I didn't have the votes to pass my plan. I lobbied every undecided legislator, identified through information supplied by Leonard Gray,
Ed Ford, and Paris Hopkins. Jim Callahan (now deceased), the representative from Wilder in northern Kentucky and a member of the house leadership team, had agreed to sponsor House Bill (HB) 1, the postsecondary
education reform bill. That was huge! I had positive commitments from all
the house leaders except Stumbo.

In the top right-hand drawer of my desk in the governor's office, I kept
a list of every legislator who had promised to support the reform bill. As the
special session progressed, I called in every legislator who I thought might
vote for it, looked them in the eye, and told them what was at stake. Before
they left my office, I asked, "Can I count on your vote?" If they said yes, I
wrote their name down on a legal pad. One by one, that list grew longer.
The day of reckoning was fast approaching, and you could have cut the
tension in the capitol with a knife.

I even invited members of the UK Board of Trustees to meet with me
individually and in small groups in the governor's office in an effort to convince them that HB 1 was in the best interests of UK and the commonwealth. I didn't invite Dr. Wethington to any of these meetings. I knew his
position and assumed he wouldn't have anything constructive to add. I
sought support from every corner and tried to convince everybody that this
was the right thing to do. I don't think I convinced many of the UK board
members, but I did my best.

We finally decided it was time to introduce the bill and let the chips fall where they may. It was clear that I needed some Republican votes to pass my bill in the senate. I had enough votes to pass a bill of some kind, but I didn't have the votes to defeat Senator Ernesto Scorsone's amendment designed to keep the community colleges under UK control. I was one vote short. I had worked the Democrats as hard as I could. I had three Republicans on my side, and I needed one more. I had a good relationship with Charlie Borders, who represented Boyd County, which had a community college. I talked to Charlie in my office, and he was receptive to my position but wanted to study it. He said, "I need to talk to some people this weekend and pray about it." Much to my relief, on Monday he agreed to support my plan.

I still had some work to do in the house. I eventually got John Will Stacy from Morgan County to agree to support my plan. I had fifty-three yes votes in the house, which was two more than I needed. I had twenty yes votes in the senate, which was the bare minimum I needed. I called Stumbo, who was leading the opposition, to my office at around five or six o'clock on May 16 and told him I had the votes to pass my postsecondary education reform bill. I showed him the list of legislators who had agreed to vote for it. I told him I hoped to avoid a bloodbath that would split the Democratic Party. Stumbo looked at my list, left my office, and went upstairs to talk to house member Joe Barrows and Dr. Wethington, who were waiting in his office. Stumbo certainly didn't want to lose another major legislative battle with me, having already lost the fight over workers' compensation.

Dr. Wethington probably believed that if he lost this battle, I would engineer his removal as president of UK. In fact, that didn't enter my mind. I respected Wethington as an administrator. I thought he was wrong on the community college issue, but I didn't have any animosity toward him, and his resistance didn't diminish my support for UK. I believed my plan would strengthen the university's research mission, and that turned out to be true. Two or three hours later, Stumbo returned to my office and said, "Okay, Charles is willing to talk."

As a good-faith gesture, I accompanied Stumbo to his office to meet with Wethington and Barrows, where we discussed a compromise for about an hour and a half. After a short break, we moved the meeting to my office and continued the discussion. We reached what I thought was an agreement on all the major issues at two o'clock in the morning. I agreed to allow community college degrees to retain UK's imprimatur, and I had no problem with the community colleges keeping UK's name on their campus buildings. I was even willing to let UK continue to act as the "pass-through" for the community colleges' budgets, with the caveat that UK would not have the authority to alter those budgets. In the middle of the night, I called the rest of the house and senate leadership to my office to fill them in on the details.

Even though I already had enough votes to pass HB 1 in both legislative chambers, I made several concessions to assuage UK supporters in and out of the state legislature. I didn't consider any of the compromises I offered to be substantive. We agreed that an independent board of the community colleges would manage the system and make decisions on important issues such as approving academic programs, hiring faculty, and devising budgets. The community colleges would no longer be under UK's control. I thought these compromises would ease HB 1's passage in the legislature without creating any hard feelings. Before the late-night meeting broke up, we agreed to hold a press conference in the morning, which was a Friday, to announce what I thought was an agreement but Wethington apparently thought was only a truce.

After members of the news media and the General Assembly arrived in Room 110 of the Capitol Building, I stood next to Dr. Wethington and announced that he and I had reached an agreement on all the major outstanding issues pertaining to HB 1. The sigh of relief among the legislators was almost audible. I was all smiles, but Dr. Wethington looked like he had just swallowed a spoonful of castor oil. I later discovered that after the press conference, he immediately began to lobby legislators against HB 1's passage. After defeating an amendment (by a vote of 62–37) to allow UK to retain control of the community colleges, the house passed HB 1 by an overwhelming bipartisan majority (76–24) on May 30.

The battle now switched to the senate, and I felt good about the bill's prospects there. Scorsone, whose district in Lexington included parts of UK, intended to introduce an amendment to keep the community colleges under UK control. His first attempt to add the amendment had failed in the Senate Education Committee by just one vote, so now he introduced it as a floor amendment. Just before the senate was about to take up the bill, Gary Johnson came to my office and said, "Governor, I'm going to vote for your bill, but I promised Glenn Freeman that I would give him one vote during this session, and he asked me to vote for the amendment to keep the community colleges with UK." I shouted, "But Gary, that *is* the issue! You said you would vote for whatever I wanted!" He replied, "But I promised Glenn!" And I pointed out, "You promised me!" I couldn't convince him to change his vote on the community college issue, and to this day, I don't understand why.

Johnson volunteered to try to convince Walter Blevins to support me on the community college issue. Johnson didn't have a community college in his district, but Ashland Community College was located in Blevins's district. The senate was already in session, and debate on the bill was under way. I called Johnson, Blevins, Bailey, and Saunders to my office. Karem agreed to keep the debate going while we worked on Blevins. After we figuratively beat him over the head with a rubber hose, he finally agreed to vote with us. I don't like using strong-arm tactics, but I couldn't afford to lose on this issue. There was too much at stake for both the state's future and my own political ambitions.

After they left my office, I called Karem on the senate floor and told him to take a vote. The roll is called alphabetically, so Blevins's name came up early, but when his name was called, he wasn't in the chamber. After everyone had voted except for Blevins and Johnson (who wasn't present when his name was called either), the vote was eighteen to eighteen. Blevins then returned to the chamber and asked for the opportunity to explain his vote. As he began to speak, I said to the group assembled in my office, "He's going to vote for the amendment," and that's what he did. Scorsone's amendment passed by a vote of nineteen to eighteen because Blevins reneged on his promise to vote against it. Johnson's vote in favor of the amendment would have made it twenty to eighteen, but he ducked out of the senate chamber and didn't cast a vote, saying he couldn't make up his mind. After the amendment vote, the entire postsecondary education reform package passed in the senate, twenty-three to fifteen.

This was a dangerous time for HB 1 in the legislative process. When one chamber changes the other chamber's bill, the usual procedure is for the first chamber to agree to the second chamber's changes and pass that version of the bill. If the first chamber doesn't accept the second chamber's changes, it asks the second chamber to rescind its revisions of the measure. If it refuses, both chambers will probably vote to send the bill to a conference committee, where they discuss only the issues on which they disagree. Most of the time, the conference committee can't reach an agreement, so they go to a "free" conference committee, where anything in the bill can be discussed and changed. All Stumbo had to do was make a motion to accept the senate's version, which he actually preferred, and he might have had enough votes in the house to pass it. However, much to my relief and gratitude, he did not do that.

I never discussed this sequence of events with Stumbo, but I think, deep down, he knew I was right. He sent HB 1 to the free conference committee, where I knew I would be in good shape. Saunders and Bailey had promised to appoint senators to the committee who would support my plan, and Richards had promised the same thing in the house. On the last day of May, the committee eliminated Scorsone's amendment, and both chambers passed the bill (73–25 in the house and 25–13 in the senate).

As it turned out, the community college issue had so dominated the discussion that the rest of the bill sailed through the legislature without much contention. In fact, Dr. Wethington supported the bill, except for the community college provision, because it gave UK many goodies. If Wethington had gotten on board earlier, UK would have benefited even more. His resistance proved detrimental to the interests of his university, and he must shoulder the blame for that. It was a monumental error in judgment on his part.

Although postsecondary education reform was landmark legislation, I never thought that passage of HB 1, combined with workers' compensation reform, assured my reelection. I had demonstrated that I was a strong governor, but I had angered many UK supporters and coal miners in eastern and western Kentucky. And I had enough political experience to know that a lot can happen between the last day of May 1997 and Election Day 1999 that might derail my plan to serve a second term.

I knew when I signed HB 1 into law that it was just a framework; many details would have to be worked out as reforms were implemented over the next few years. Many of those details could make or break the entire effort. Even though the community college issue had received the most attention by far, the law was much more comprehensive. The foundation of the reform legislation consisted of six specific goals that the new Council on Postsecondary Education was supposed to attain by the year 2020:

1. Achieve a seamless, integrated system of postsecondary education strategically planned and adequately funded to enhance economic development and quality of life.
2. Make the University of Kentucky a nationally ranked, top-twenty public research institution.
3. Make the University of Louisville a nationally recognized metropolitan research institution.
4. Establish at least one program of distinction at each of the six regional universities.
5. Establish a comprehensive community and technical college system that ensures access to two-year courses of study leading to a bachelor's degree and meets employers' workforce training needs.
6. Ensure efficient and autonomous institutions that deliver educational services comparable to the national average in terms of quantity and quality.

One of my first important tasks was selecting the members of the new CPE. Of the thirty-nine names submitted by the nominating committee, I selected fifteen, six of whom had been members of the old Council on Higher Education: Leonard Hardin, chair of the old council; Marlene Helm, head of the elementary school system in Fayette County and secretary of the Education, Arts, and Humanities Cabinet during the Jones administration; Charles Whitehead, a member of my gubernatorial transition team in 1995; Dr. Lee Todd, founder of Databeam in Lexington; Walter Baker, a Republican state senator from Barren County who had served on the Kentucky Supreme Court; and Shirley Menendez, an administrator in the Livingston County school system. I thought it was important for the new council to have some member continuity and institutional memory of previous attempts to fix the system.

Dr. Gary Cox, outgoing director of the Council on Higher Education, played a key role in establishing the new council and was a great help to me. The passage of HB 1 meant that he was going to lose his job, but he understood that postsecondary education reform needed a fresh start, and he unselfishly supported it 100 percent. He advised me through the entire implementation process and then departed quietly and honorably, and I admired him for that. I was happy when he landed on his feet and found employment as president of the Association of Independent Kentucky Colleges and Universities. Cox was a real statesman, which I define as a person who does what's right for the whole, even if it doesn't serve his personal best interests. There are few real statesmen in government, and he was one.

I let the new council fill in most of the details of postsecondary education reform and intervened only when I felt it was necessary. For example, I was instrumental in hiring Jeff Hockaday as the interim president of the new community and technical college system because we needed somebody fast and he was qualified and available. Later, I played a role in hiring Mike McCall as the permanent president.

One of the key details was hiring someone to head the new CPE. That person would play a crucial role in the success or failure of HB 1's reforms. I was not involved in the search to fill that position. I left that decision to the council members. When they hired Gordon Davies, the former head of a similar entity in Virginia, I believed they made a good choice at the time, but I was wrong. He was the reason the new council didn't become as strong as I had hoped. He was personally too strong and failed to use good judgment or diplomacy, particularly when dealing with influential members of the legislature such as Moberly and Richards, who were interested in specific universities. Growing the power and independence of the council had to be a slow process.

My vision was that the CPE would become an entity that both the governor and the General Assembly could rely on for advice and guidance. However, I knew the new council would have to prove its worth and earn our respect over time.

The first challenge after passage of HB 1 was the postsecondary education budgets for the 1998–1999 and 1999–2000 fiscal years. It was up to the CPE to make a recommendation to me regarding the details of the budget, after I had given the council the bottom line. I didn't review the specifics of the CPE's first budget proposal in 1998, as I was committed to supporting the council's recommendation. But Harry Moberly, chair of the House A&R Committee, sure did. He believed that Eastern Kentucky University (EKU) had not received its fair share. Davies's failure to understand Moberly's legislative role and establish a dialogue with him raised many eyebrows, including mine. I had to violate my own rule of accepting the CPE's budget recommendation on its face. I told budget director Jim Ramsey to step in and settle the dispute. I thought Davies would have learned his lesson, but in fact, he never did. He thought he was a czar who could force his will on the legislature. He was wrong.

The CPE's next budget proposal in 2000 was even worse. It was obvious that Davies, perhaps as revenge, had been even more unfair to EKU, and once again I had to step in to resolve the dispute. Davies, however, was still not contrite, and as far as I was concerned, he had to go. Unfortunately, my vision of the CPE becoming the governor's and the General Assembly's primary adviser on postsecondary education policy went with him.

As the framework for implementing HB 1 evolved, I had other issues to deal with after the special session adjourned at the end of May 1997. In June I had to make the difficult decision whether to commute the death sentence of an inmate at the state prison at Eddyville to life without parole. Forty-four-year-old Harold McQueen's execution by electric chair was scheduled for July 1. He would be the first inmate executed in Kentucky in thirty-five years. McQueen's crime was particularly heinous. After robbing a Minit Mart convenience store in early April 1981, he had brutally murdered twenty-two-year-old Rebecca O'Hearn, the unarmed store clerk. As governor, I had the power to pardon, commute, or reduce the sentences of state prisoners, a responsibility I did not take lightly. In my opinion, a few governors in other states *do* take a rather cavalier attitude about it, using executions to score political points with certain segments of the electorate.

Ben Chandler, the Kentucky attorney general, had made the death penalty an issue during his 1995 campaign. In 1976 the US Supreme Court had ruled that capital punishment was not cruel and unusual, but over the next nineteen years, Kentucky's attorneys general did not forward any death warrants to the governor for signature; they were content to pass the buck to the next attorney general and governor. During the 1995 campaign Chandler promised to forward the death warrants of all death-row inmates who had exhausted the appeals process. In Kentucky, death sentences are automatically appealed to the Kentucky Supreme Court, and Chandler's position was that after an inmate had exhausted the appeals process, it was the attorney general's sworn *duty* to send the death warrant to the governor. He had a valid point, but I have always thought that Chandler was also politically motivated in case he decided to run against me in the 1999 Democratic primary. If I commuted McQueen's sentence to life without parole, I would be handing Chandler an issue he could run on.

Harold McQueen had started down the wrong path long before he murdered Rebecca O'Hearn. He was hooked on drugs and had an arrest record for burglary and pandering. I eventually decided to sign McQueen's death warrant, but I agonized over it. He had committed a terrible crime, but he was still a human being. The evening of June 30 was a long one as we waited quietly in the basement of the governor's mansion for word of McQueen's execution. When confirmation arrived shortly after midnight, I felt sick. I consoled myself by reasoning that the people of Kentucky supported the death penalty, and a jury of his peers had found McQueen guilty. He had run out of appeals, and I had sworn to uphold the law, regardless of my personal opinion. It was the toughest decision I made in my eight years as governor.

During the 1995 campaign I had talked about the need to reform the state's juvenile justice system. One of my ideas was to establish boot camps for nonviolent juvenile offenders, similar to those in Louisiana, Ohio, Alabama, and Colorado. I believed that locking up nonviolent juvenile offenders without introducing them to a structured alternative environment and positive instruction was counterproductive. I strongly believed that with early intervention by the state, these young people could turn their lives around and avoid ending up like Harold McQueen. Therefore, I was eager to tackle the issue of the entire justice system, including juvenile justice.

In mid-July I decided to form a twenty-nine-member task force consisting of prosecutors, law enforcement officers, and other justice department officials to study how to improve the state's courts and corrections department. I wanted to reap the benefits of their expertise and make sure the plan I introduced to the legislature reflected the input and buy-in of those involved in all aspects of the criminal justice system. The overall objective was to be tougher on serious crime and more lenient on less serious, nonviolent crime.

When the task force presented its report in early December, just ahead of the 1998 session of the General Assembly, it contained 108 recommendations. I was somewhat taken aback by the report's scope. It included subjects I was not prepared to tackle at a cost beyond the state's means. One of the recommendations I fully supported was creation of the Kentucky All Schedule Prescription Electronic Reporting System (better known as KASPER) to monitor prescription drugs. I take great pride in that system because it was the first of its kind in the country, and it has proved very effective.

Another task force recommendation I supported was based on my experience as a county judge. At the time, a person arrested for violating a state law and tried by a state court was incarcerated in a county jail, and the county had to pay the cost of that person's incarceration. I didn't think this was a legitimate county expense. The counties were stuck with the bill for housing state prisoners. That provision of the criminal justice reform law did not pass, due to a lack of funding, but it is something I still support.

The juvenile criminal justice system was in even worse shape. County jails were not healthy environments for juvenile offenders, and the recidivism rate among juveniles was high. I wanted to build state-run juvenile-only facilities all over Kentucky to remove the counties from the juvenile justice system. I didn't know how many of the task force's recommendations we might be able to get passed during the 1998 legislative session, but juvenile justice reform was my top priority. It was one of my most important accomplishments as governor.

Before tackling criminal justice reform, I called another special session of the legislature at the end of September to try, once again, to fix Brereton Jones's health insurance reform law. Since that law passed in 1994, some forty-five insurance companies had left the state because they couldn't make a profit. This left an insurance vacuum that limited consumers' options and drove up insurance premiums and deductibles because there was less competition. The pressure to fix the law was even more intense in the fall of 1997 because price freezes that had allowed people to hold on to insurance policies purchased before July 1, 1995, were due to expire on October 15, 1997. Thousands of Kentuckians were on the brink of losing their health insurance, and I had to try to fix the problem.

I was the first to admit that I was not an authority on health insurance. Whatever expertise there was in Frankfort was in the legislature. I had inherited this health insurance mess, and in my mind, it was the legislature's problem to fix. At the beginning of the special session I made it clear that I was not going to take the lead on this issue. I had demonstrated with workers' compensation and postsecondary education that I was willing to get involved in controversial issues, but I simply had no solution to the health insurance problem. I told legislators that I was content to be an observer and would sign any bill they sent me.

Before calling the special session, I thought the legislative leadership had reached a consensus on how to fix the law. The primary problem was how to provide affordable health insurance to chronically ill people. Senate Bill (SB) 1, sponsored by Democrat Tim Shaughnessy, allowed insurance companies to charge chronically ill people up to 150 percent of standard health insurance rates and also created a high-risk pool. Funding for the high-risk pool would come from an insurance premium tax collected from out-of-state indemnity insurers and existing assessments on insurance companies. If those sources proved inadequate, the legislative leadership had tentatively agreed to add $5 million from the General Fund to the high-risk pool.

If SB 1 passed, the Kentucky Department of Insurance estimated that five thousand people would buy insurance through the high-risk pool, but about half a million others would be unable to afford it or just wouldn't buy it. From the outside looking in, I thought the legislature had few options. There was no easy solution that would make everybody happy. Kentucky is one of the poorer states in the nation and has one of the unhealthiest populations, so I knew we lacked the capacity to solve the health insurance problem. Absent national health insurance reform, I thought a free, competitive market was probably the consumer's best chance to get a quality product at a fair price in the long term.

Before I called the special session, leaders in both chambers had led me to believe that SB 1 would pass. Unfortunately, it didn't turn out that way. Several amendments were added to and then withdrawn from the original bill. Several substitute bills were introduced and then discarded. The special session ended in failure, and feelings got hurt in the process. Greg Stumbo and I had another little dustup when he called me an ineffectual governor and a liar, and I made the mistake of retaliating in kind. That marked the low point of our relationship. Stumbo and I managed to patch things up before the start of the 1998 legislative session, but health insurance remained a problem.

On December 1, 1997, I received the worst news a governor can hear. A student at Heath High School in West Paducah had shot and killed three of his classmates and wounded five more in a premeditated attack. As Pike County judge, I had dealt with several destructive floods and mine disasters, so I was used to dealing with crises caused by nature or accident. This was my first experience with such a senseless, tragic, and wholly avoidable catastrophe like the Heath High School shootings. The event traumatized the entire state and the country. I grieved for the victims and their families and for the young man who had committed this atrocity. This event was very difficult from both a personal and a political standpoint, as my staff and I debated when I should go to Paducah. There was no question that I needed to meet with the families and express my condolences. But I wanted to avoid the appearance of grandstanding or seeming to take political advantage of the tragic event.

What do you say to grieving parents after such a tragedy? The only thing I could think of was, "I'm sorry. I don't know why this happened, but know that I, Judi, my staff, and all Kentuckians grieve with you. If you ever need anything, let me know." It felt inadequate. Nothing I said would make those parents feel any better or fill the holes in their hearts. When the funerals were over and the country moved on, those parents would still have empty beds in their homes. I also grieved for the family of the shooter, Michael Carneal. Their lives had also been shattered. It was determined that Carneal was mentally ill, and he was sentenced to life with the possibility of parole in twenty-five years on the condition that he receive treatment. None of those families' lives will ever be the same, and they may never know why it happened.

My second year as governor of Kentucky ended on a tragic note, so I was looking forward to the challenges ahead and was optimistic that 1998 would be better. I was riding high politically, with victories on both workers' compensation and postsecondary education reform. With the national and state economies on the upswing, I was eager to start the 1998 legislative session and augment our progress on education reform. I was also beginning to think that my prospects for reelection in 1999 were looking very good!

Education was the focal point of my eight years as governor, and the state slogan was "Education Pays." (Courtesy of Kentucky Department for Libraries and Archives, Archives and Records Management Division)

The highlight of my administration was passage of the Postsecondary Reform Act of 1997, better known as House Bill 1. I signed it into law on the steps of the capitol with a group of children in attendance. Standing behind me is Terry McBrayer, who was instrumental in getting me elected governor, and Bill Stone, who was the legal adviser for my opponent Larry Forgy during the 1995 gubernatorial campaign. Bill later became a good friend of mine. (Courtesy of Kentucky Department for Libraries and Archives, Archives and Records Management Division)

11

Let the Good Times Roll, 1998

In 1996, during my first legislative session as governor, I presented to the legislature what was essentially a bare-bones budget. I, along with the independent, nonpartisan Consensus Forecasting Group (CFG), honestly believed that the state would be strapped for cash over the next two-year budget cycle. We were wrong. In mid-November 1997 I received some very good news when the CFG reported that the state treasury would have a surplus of approximately $156 million for fiscal year 1998–1999! The federal budget also had a sizable surplus, as the national economy was really humming along in the mid to late 1990s. As it turned out, the CFG's initial November forecast was low, and by early December it had increased the estimate to $222 million. Jim Ramsey, the state budget director, told the legislature's A&R Committees that, based on conservative estimates, the budget surplus would amount to another $250 million to $300 million in the second year of the biennium, for a two-year surplus of $400 million to $500 million! With that kind of political capital, I knew my second legislative session as governor would be a lot different and a lot more fun than my first had been. I was going to be the first governor since Julian Carroll who had *real* money to spend. To quote Charles Dickens in *A Tale of Two Cities,* if 1996 was the "worst of times," 1998 was the "best of times." The mood in the legislature was "let the good times roll," and boy, did they ever!

In my opinion, we introduced real pork to Frankfort in 1998. On January 20 I presented a $12.6 billion two-year state budget to the legislature. In it, I proposed borrowing $970 million to finance several major new initiatives—a record amount of borrowing at the time. The 1998–2000 budget was one of the most generous the Kentucky General Assembly has ever passed, and it didn't include a tax increase. The national and state economies were in good shape, and thanks to the bare-bones budget passed in 1996, we now had a substantial surplus and uncommitted revenue to spend, and we had increased the state's bonding capacity. As a result, we had a *ton* of money available!

Our general rule was to limit debt service to about 6 percent of the General Fund, so the dramatic increase in revenue meant a corresponding increase in borrowing power. I believe in long-term borrowing for capital projects that will last twenty years or more because citizens who will benefit from the projects should help pay for them. It's not wise to borrow to pay for ongoing programs that need new funding each year. I also believe that when a government has an extraordinary income year that is unlikely to be repeated in the near future, it's not wise to invest all that extra money in recurring programs. Therefore, we decided to spend some cash on capital expenditures in the budget adopted during the 1998 legislative session.

As governor, I wanted to decide how to spend most of the state budget, but I wanted to give the leadership some of the largess and the credit too. For instance, I called Greg Stumbo and offered to put another $5 million in the budget for Floyd County, his home county. After our previous disagreements over workers' compensation and community colleges, I thought spreading a little honey in his district couldn't hurt and might help repair our relationship. "What do you think we ought to use it for?" I asked. "You have any ideas?" A little surprised, Stumbo replied, "Well, John Rosenburg has some kind of astronomy program or something he's been talking about. Let me have him call you, and he can tell you what it's all about." Rosenburg, a liberal lawyer from Floyd County, explained the idea to me, and I liked it. Prestonsburg now has a nice astronomy science center run by the community college, courtesy of the 1998 state budget surplus. There is nothing else like it in the commonwealth.

Of course, it wasn't totally up to me to decide how the state's money would be spent. In fact, the legislature had the final word. I sent my budget proposal to the house, where it could be changed, and then to the senate, where it could also be modified. The two chambers must agree on a final budget before sending it back to the governor. The governor can use his line-item veto to reject any part of the budget, but the General Assembly can override a governor's veto with a constitutional majority vote in each chamber.

I had exceptionally good relationships with most members of the house, both Democrats and Republicans. That wasn't the case in the senate. After the coup against Eck Rose, the senate remained severely divided. Benny Ray Bailey was chair of the senate's A&R Committee, which has the first shot at changing the budget bill sent from the house. In general, the senate passes whatever budget bill the A&R Committee sends to the floor for a vote, with little or no change. But with Bailey in charge, all bets were off. The budget I sent to the legislature appropriated money in a way that I thought would benefit the entire state. Bailey, however, was much more parochial in his approach to the state budget.

Majority floor leader David Karem, minority floor leader Dan Kelly, and I tried to constrain Bailey's worst impulses and control the votes of the A&R Committee. One day late in the legislative session, Kelly came into my office and told Karem and me, "I've lost Charlie Borders. He's going to support Benny Ray's version of the budget." Dan explained that Bailey had put so much money in the budget for Charlie's district that he couldn't turn it down. I looked at Bailey's budget and saw that he had added $500,000 for a fire department in Greenup County, part of Borders's district. Of course, Bailey had added $5 million to the budget for fire departments in Knott County, in his own district. It turned out he had bought Borders cheap!

With the help of the house, we managed to get a pretty fair and progressive budget adopted by the General Assembly. Bailey maintained a good relationship with me because he knew I still had some control over the state budget "cookie jar" (money the governor could spend at his discretion), but he occasionally tried to do an end run around me. Even though Bailey's version of the budget failed, Borders got his fire department. And over the next year, we kept finding additional goodies in the budget for Bailey's Knott County, to the tune of about $34 million.

Generally, when there is a state budget surplus, the governor and the legislature should put some of that money in the rainy-day account because it's pretty obvious that this situation happens only once in a blue moon. However, in 1998 we had two pots of money to dip into—the surplus forecast for the new biennium, plus a lot left over from the 1996–1998 biennium—in addition to a substantially increased debt capacity. When economic times are good, the leadership has to be cautious about committing the state to too many ongoing obligations. A one-time outlay for a brick-and-mortar project is not a bad way to spend surplus money because once construction is complete, that's the end of the state's obligation, other than maintenance costs if ownership stays with the state. However, commitment to a long-term, ongoing program entails the likelihood of having to cut that program's funding in lean economic years, which can be painful and can have a negative impact on legislators' (or a governor's) reelection prospects.

As a county judge, I went through two budget cuts in ten years. With that in mind, I made it very clear that I didn't want to commit the state to ongoing programs that might hamstring future legislatures and governors, including myself. If I was reelected to another four-year term, I wanted to have some money stashed away in case the economy went south again. I didn't want to spend my second term as governor being unable to accomplish anything because I had no money.

Soon after the CFG made its initial estimate of the budget surplus, I knew the legislature would devolve into a spending free-for-all unless I controlled it. Therefore, I announced that I would be accepting applications for one-time expenditures in anticipation of the budget surplus. I specifically mentioned that it was a good time to invest in infrastructure projects because of the booming economy, low interest rates, and Kentucky's strong credit rating. Besides, I wanted to fund projects that I could get credit for, rather than just saying, "Here's $300 million: have at it!" I wanted the budget surplus to be already committed so the legislature couldn't monkey around with it after I submitted the budget for its consideration. Once I included something in my budget proposal, the legislators would have to take money away from some project if they wanted to spend it elsewhere. My experience as a county judge taught me that having the first shot at the budget was better than having the last.

By the time the 1998 session began, I had a notebook filled with 139 applications and project proposals submitted by state legislators and local officials from all over the state. The cost of those projects totaled more than $638 million, which exceeded the projected budget surplus, so we prioritized them and stopped when the money ran out. I listed veterans' nursing homes in Madisonville and Hazard as my top two funding priorities. I also made sure the house and senate leadership got funding for their pet projects to keep them happy. For projects that couldn't be funded immediately, I promised those legislators and local officials that they would get preferential treatment in the next budget cycle, assuming those projected budget surpluses materialized.

Forty projects proposed by legislators were included in the original budget I sent to the General Assembly on January 28. I wanted them to feel like they already had ownership of the budget. If the two A&R chairs, Benny Ray Bailey in the senate and Harry Moberly in the house, wanted to spend the money on other priorities, they would have to eliminate their colleagues' pet projects from the budget and face the heat for doing so. My original list of projects survived mostly intact. Bailey and Moberly might have moved small amounts of money around, but almost everybody was happy. In that way, I was able to control the spending spree that occurred during the 1998 legislative session.

When I put that project list together, I listened to everybody—Democrat or Republican, it didn't matter. I tried to be fair and distribute money equitably across the state, without regard to party politics, although some Republicans might disagree with that statement for partisan reasons. For example, I allocated $5 million of the budget surplus to each of three south-central Kentucky counties—Green, Adair, and Russell—even though they were heavily Republican, to augment their local economies after Fruit of the Loom and OshKosh B'gosh closed their textile plants and laid off hundreds of people. At the same time, I wasn't going to penalize a legislative district just because one of my political friends or donors lived there. We funded projects that benefited many people, no matter who submitted them for consideration. We had a lot of money, and I thought everybody—Democrats and Republicans—should reap the benefits of this once-in-a-generation opportunity. I believe it was a fair process.

Golf courses were also high on my agenda during my two terms as governor. On the face of it, this might seem frivolous, but I had a specific plan. Using Alabama's Robert Trent Jones Golf Trail as a model, I hoped to make Kentucky a destination for avid golfers. During my governorship, we built or expanded a number of courses around the state, including in Middlesboro, Falmouth, Bardstown, Dale Hollow, Mineral Mound, Louisa, and Grayson. My plan to make Kentucky a golf destination withered on the vine after I left office, and I think my successors missed an important economic development opportunity.

During the 1998 legislative session, I also proposed a change in how coal severance tax revenue was spent. Under a law passed during the Jones administration, this money was largely limited to projects approved by the Cabinet for Economic Development that led directly to the creation of jobs. The counties could use the money to buy land, construct factory buildings, build access roads, lay water and sewer lines to an industrial park, and the like. Two-thirds of the money was allocated to the county that had mined the coal, and the rest was allocated for projects proposed by more than one coal-producing county. We called this the Multi-County Fund.

By 1998, a lot of the coal severance tax revenue was still sitting in the coal counties' accounts because there wasn't enough flat land or enough money to build an industrial park in every county. I concluded that using the money in the Multi-County Fund to build twelve regional industrial parks— nine in eastern Kentucky and three in western Kentucky—made more sense. However, I still had to figure out some way for these counties to spend the money in their single-county accounts. I started personally approving line-item projects in the budget that the counties had requested and that would contribute to their economic development, even if the projects weren't directly related to new job opportunities. They used the money mostly for infrastructure projects such as water and sewer systems. All this was part of my plan to bring jobs to the coal-producing counties of Kentucky.

One of the items on my 1998 agenda was ensuring that more children were enrolled in the federal Children's Health Insurance Program (CHIP).

Congress had passed the law establishing the program the previous year, and it required investment by the individual states to be eligible for federal matching funds. The program provided health insurance to children whose family income was below 200 percent of the federal poverty level. At the time, the federal poverty level was about $16,000 for a family of four. I estimated that CHIP would provide coverage for more than ninety-one thousand Kentucky children. You can't move a state forward if the children who live there aren't healthy.

Throughout my two terms as governor, I made children's issues, including education, health care, domestic abuse, drug addiction, and the juvenile criminal justice system, one of my primary focuses. "Education Pays" was the slogan of my two administrations. In fact, after my political career was over, I continued to invest my time and energy into improving and enhancing the lives of young people through my work as president and chancellor of the University of Pikeville and as chair of the Council on Postsecondary Education. If you get right down to it, though, the main objective of my two administrations was jobs. And the most important thing a state can do to create jobs is to have a healthy, educated workforce. I love children, and the way you show your love for them is to make sure they are healthy, educated, and safe. Creating a plethora of good-paying jobs was my objective, and I saw improving education at all levels as the strategy to achieve that goal.

Another issue that was high on my 1998 legislative agenda was the criminal justice reform Ben Chandler and I had talked about in 1997. After the task force I had appointed in July 1997 made its report, Chandler and I agreed to join forces to overhaul important aspects of the criminal justice system in Kentucky. At the beginning of the 1998 legislative session, we stood together and announced that we were collaborating on a bill that incorporated initiatives from our earlier independent plans.

Despite Chandler's investigation of my 1995 campaign, I was able to work with him on other issues to benefit the commonwealth. By combining forces, we persuaded the legislature to substantially increase the state's expenditures on juvenile justice. In 1998 I persuaded the legislature to approve the construction of juvenile-only detention facilities in Barren, Adair, Campbell, Hardin, Breathitt, McCracken, Madison, Bourbon, Rowan, Boyd, Casey, Carroll, and Warren Counties. Just before she left office in 2001, US attorney general Janet Reno came to Kentucky and commended us for having the best juvenile justice system in the country. I am extremely proud of the improvements we implemented.

Although I supported the prevailing wage law passed in 1996, which was a high-priority item for organized labor, I had decided to put off collective bargaining until the 1998 legislative session. Now I felt compelled to fulfill my campaign promise to get a collective bargaining bill passed, but I wasn't encouraged when I had difficulty finding a sponsor for it. I had to twist the arm of J. R. Gray, chair of the Labor and Industry Committee and one of the strongest supporters of labor in the legislature, to sponsor House Bill 760. Skipper and Leonard Gray advised me to stay as far away from the bill as possible; they knew it had no chance of passing, and they saw no profit in my involvement in a lost cause. I would have taken that advice if Greg Stumbo hadn't become critical of me after HB 760 stalled in committee.

Stumbo, still smarting from workers' compensation reform, laid the blame for HB 760's lack of progress at my feet, saying that I should have used the budget surplus to bargain for votes to move the bill through the committee. He questioned whether I actually supported collective bargaining for public employees and warned organized labor not to trust me. Even though I knew HB 760 had no chance of passing, I couldn't let his challenge go unanswered. I held a press conference and threw my support behind the bill while wearing a "Trust" sticker on the lapel of my suit jacket. During a three-day hearing in the Labor and Industry Committee, I argued the merits of the bill for more than an hour. Afterward, J. R. Gray admitted he didn't have the votes to get HB 760 out of committee, let alone pass it on the house floor. At that point, I decided not to expend any more capital on a lost cause, so when union activists held a last-gasp rally on the steps of the capitol in the middle of March, I chose not to saw off the limb I was already out on and didn't attend. The collective bargaining issue would have to live to fight another day.

During the run-up to the debate on collective bargaining, I experienced a personal loss I had to process. My mother died on March 12 in the governor's mansion, six months shy of her eighty-second birthday. My sisters and I had planned to take her to New York on her eightieth birthday in 1996, but just a few weeks before we were scheduled to leave, she was diagnosed with kidney cancer, so we postponed the trip. She continued to live at her own home in Louisa, but after six or seven months, we realized she was unable to take care of herself and moved her into the governor's mansion. My mother couldn't tolerate the chemotherapy she was receiving at the Markey Cancer Center at UK, so she halted treatment, and her condition slowly deteriorated over the next year and a half. My sister Jo came to Frankfort and looked after her until she required around-the-clock care. My mother's passing certainly got me thinking about my own mortality and the legacy I wanted to leave behind. I think that is something everyone should consider, no matter their station in life. I knew my legacy depended on what I accomplished as the governor of Kentucky, and I was nowhere near finished with my agenda.

One of the pressing issues we had to tackle during the 1998 legislative session was how to implement HB 1, the contentious postsecondary education law passed the previous May. The primary challenge was allocating the state's higher education budget. The Council on Postsecondary Education's first task was to examine the existing budgets of all the state's public universities, as well as each university's budget request for the new budget cycle. The council's second task was to take the money in the state budget committed to higher education and distribute it as fairly and equitably as possible.

I wanted us to make these budget decisions based on the state's *needs* and not necessarily on the public universities' *wants*. I wanted to give the higher education community the first shot at the state budget, but the universities' funding had to become more pragmatic and less political. With two years to go in my first term, and assuming I was reelected to a second, I would have six years to establish this funding pattern. I believed that would be sufficient time for higher education reform to take root.

I wasn't naïve enough to think that the old rivalries would magically disappear and the University of Kentucky, the University of Louisville, and the regional comprehensive universities would suddenly agree to abide by the CPE's budget recommendations. I understood that if UK was the eight-hundred-pound gorilla, the other seven state universities were a school of barracuda.

Shortly after I took office in 1995, I had dinner with David Hawpe (now deceased), editor of the *Courier-Journal.* That newspaper had been instrumental in my underdog election victory, and Hawpe had been largely responsible for its endorsement of me. I wanted to hear his ideas about improving Kentucky. He knew that higher education was a priority for me, so he suggested that the state's two research universities, the University of Kentucky and the University of Louisville, needed to have endowed chairs so they could attract some of the best and brightest researchers and scholars in the country. When David brought up the subject, I honestly had no idea what an endowed chair was! After he explained the concept to me, I thought it was a very good idea. That conversation convinced me to allocate $10 million a year in my 1998 budget proposal as an ongoing appropriation for endowed chairs at the two research universities.

During the 1998 legislative session, Jim Ramsey and I had a meeting with Ron Greenberg (father of current Louisville mayor Greg Greenberg) and Hank Wagner at Jewish Hospital in Louisville. At the meeting Ron said, "Instead of allocating $10 million for endowed chairs at UK and U of L, why don't you float a twenty-year, $100 million bond issue? You can't count on future legislatures funding, on an ongoing basis, that kind of program out of the state's General Fund, but you *can* commit them to paying off a twenty-year bond issue. And you'll demonstrate that you're serious about jump-starting the research missions you envision for these two universities and really give this initiative momentum." Jim and I talked about it on the way back to Frankfort, and we decided to try it. We also decided to make it a matching fund program: to receive money from the fund, a university had to find a donor to match that amount.

I frankly don't remember who came up with the phrase "Bucks for Brains," and I certainly don't take credit for it, but we decided to sell it to the legislature as a one-time initiative. Out of the $100 million, UK would receive two-thirds and the University of Louisville would receive one-third. We proposed that the entire amount come out of the budget surplus if the money was available, and we would use the authorization to sell bonds as a backup plan. I think we anticipated a lot more opposition from the legislature than we actually encountered.

I believed then, and I still believe, that luring top researchers and scholars to Kentucky's two research universities would lead to new discoveries, inventions, and innovations, which in turn would fuel Kentucky's economic growth by creating new businesses and good-paying jobs. It worked in North Carolina's Golden Triangle, and I believed it would work in Kentucky. Unfortunately, Kentucky has underfunded higher education since I left office. The 2008 national financial crisis and subsequent economic recession contributed to that, but even after the economic recovery, the legislature has not restored funding for higher education to its inflation-adjusted pre-recession levels, and that is a huge, shortsighted mistake, in my opinion.

As I traveled around Kentucky, I found that people believed Governor Wilkinson had proposed the state lottery as a means to increase funding for education. That belief was wrong. Wilkinson had proposed that lottery proceeds be allocated for a one-time veterans' bonus, senior citizens' programs, and early childhood programs, but the legislature refused to approve that type of earmarking and added lottery revenue to the General Fund instead. I decided the time was right for the legislature to reconsider that allocation. I proposed to earmark lottery proceeds for college scholarships. At the time, the budget contained modest funding for the College Access Program (CAP), which provided a small scholarship to any Kentucky undergraduate attending an accredited college in Kentucky who qualified for a federal Pell Grant. This was a limited pool of about $10 million. Awards were made on a first come, first served basis, and there was not nearly enough money to cover all eligible students. The budget also included about $5 million a year for the Kentucky Tuition Grant (KTG) program, which awarded grants to Kentucky undergraduates eligible for Pell Grants and enrolled at any private, independent, not-for-profit accredited college in Kentucky. Those scholarships, worth about $3,000 a year per student, were also distributed on a first come, first served basis.

I proposed the gradual conversion of all lottery proceeds to support the CAP and KTG programs, along with a new scholarship program based on academic merit. There was some opposition to giving money to children from wealthy families. Obviously, some of these high-performing students would be from wealthy families. But a significant part of the approximately $1 billion a year Kentucky allocated to state colleges and universities went to the children of well-off families anyway. I didn't see any difference, and my proposal eventually prevailed.

I proposed that 50 percent of lottery proceeds be allocated to the state's two need-based programs (CAP and KTG) and 50 percent to the new merit-based program, which we called the Kentucky Education Excellence Scholarship (KEES). At some point in the legislative process, the proportions changed to 55 percent based on financial need and 45 percent based on academic merit. KEES allows high school students to earn scholarship money based on their grade point average (GPA) beginning when they are freshmen. We modeled KEES on Georgia's HOPE (Helping Others Pursue Education) scholarship program, established in 1993 when Zell Miller was governor. The Georgia program was an all-or-nothing proposition. If students achieved the required high school GPA, they got the full amount of the scholarship. If their GPA was one-tenth of a point below that, they got nothing. I felt that was too steep a cliff.

Under KEES, freshmen who maintained a 2.5 GPA earned a $125 college scholarship for up to four years of college. The better the GPA, the more scholarship money they earned. Those who ended their first year with a 4.0 GPA earned a $500 four-year college scholarship, for a total value of $2,000. Based on their yearly GPAs, students could earn the same amounts in their sophomore, junior, and senior years. Recognizing that GPAs can vary based on the academic rigor of individual high schools, we also created a four-year scholarship based on students' ACT scores. The annual scholarship amounts ranged from $125 for an ACT score of 18 to $500 for a score of 28 or higher. By the time students graduated from high school, they could have earned up to $2,500 in scholarship money for each year in college, for a total of $10,000. Thanks to the KEES, CAP, and KTG programs, a college education was within reach for nearly 75 percent of the state's high school students. These scholarships were also first come, first served, but the money was almost sufficient to meet the demand. The KEES program was so popular that the General Assembly has used General Fund money to make up any shortfall. Most of this scholarship distribution system has remained intact over the various gubernatorial administrations that followed mine. Without the KEES, CAP, and KTG scholarship money, many small private colleges and universities in Kentucky would not exist today.

Again, my underlying objective was to create more good-paying jobs in Kentucky, and I knew an educated workforce was essential to achieving that goal. I wanted to ensure that more Kentucky children could afford to go to college and get that education. The lottery revenue stream for college scholarships in Kentucky has grown to about $250 million a year. That program is one of my proudest achievements as governor. Relative to population, Kentucky provides more state scholarship money to students than almost any other state.

In the senate, A&R chair Bailey moved funding for all 145 budget surplus projects ahead of funding for the Bucks for Brains initiative, thinking he would get the support of senators representing the districts where those 145 projects resided. However, the majority of senators were on my side because many of those projects were already included in my budget, and few senators, Democrat or Republican, respected or trusted Bailey because of his role in deposing Eck Rose as senate president. I also had the support of the house leadership. Therefore, when the budget bill went to a conference committee near the end of the legislative session, my version prevailed with only minor tweaks. Several legislators added $18 million in pork for their districts, which I expected, so I wasn't surprised or angry. In a $12.6 billion two-year budget, $18 million was not a lot of money, so I wasn't going to pitch a fit over that.

As it turned out, I believe the budget surplus was adequate to fund the entire $100 million Bucks for Brains program in its first iteration. In fact, the initiative was so popular that I included it in my next budget proposal too, and the legislature approved it a second time in 2000. In 2002 the legislature agreed to fund Bucks for Brains by selling bonds. Philanthropists liked the idea of their donations doubling in size when the state matched them dollar for dollar. In those three budget cycles (1998, 2000, and 2002), the legislature provided $300 million for the Bucks for Brains initiative, which turned into a total of $600 million: $400 million for UK and $200 million for the University of Louisville. I think that money made a substantial difference at both universities and certainly boosted their national reputations and rankings as research institutions. We even included a separate $10 million matching fund for the regional universities, which gave them a new fund-raising tool. Prior to the Bucks for Brains initiative, they relied mostly on state support for basic operations, along with a few generous alumni who contributed relatively small sums of money.

The 1998 legislative session was the best one I presided over as governor and one of the best sessions the General Assembly has ever had. Money can't solve every issue, but it can certainly solve a lot of them! At the conclusion of the 1998 session, I was very pleased with the way my administration was going, and I was excited about our progress in the areas of economic development and education. A mid-March Bluegrass State poll showed that I had a 71 percent approval rating among adults—the highest of any modern governor of Kentucky—and only a 17 percent disapproval rating.

Several members of my administration departed in 1998. First, Margaret Handmaker resigned as secretary of the Revenue Cabinet, and I appointed Sarah Jane Shaaf, a Louisville financial planner, to replace her. I didn't know Shaaf personally, but she came highly recommended by friends in the Louisville accounting community.

The second change came when I had to fire Alice McDonald, head of the Governmental Services Center. Alice got into some legal trouble when she was accused of tampering with evidence during an investigation by the attorney general's office, which was looking into her alleged misuse of state funds and resources while she was the elected superintendent of public education in a previous administration. Robert Peters, secretary of the Personnel Cabinet, replaced McDonald as head of the Governmental Services Center, and deputy secretary of personnel Carol Palmore, a veteran of state government, moved up to replace Peters. Later in the year, state budget director Jim Ramsey left to become the vice-chancellor for administration at the University of North Carolina at Chapel Hill. I replaced him with Crit Luallen, who was also my secretary of the cabinet. Fortunately, I later convinced Ramsey to come back as state budget director, and he stayed until 2002, when he became the president of the University of Louisville. I had nothing to do with that hiring, and I wasn't too happy about it. I had hoped Ramsey would stay and finish out my second term.

In early July I was selected to chair the Education Commission of the States (ECS) due to my efforts to reform higher education in Kentucky.

That position was another feather in my cap and validated the intent of HB 1. Such positions are more ceremonial than substantive. Organizations like the ECS have professional staff who do most of the actual work advocating policy endorsed by the nation's governors. Other than attending ECS meetings, my primary point of contact with the organization was through Ed Ford, who had helped guide HB 1 through the legislature and had a good understanding of education-related policy issues. Ed was my go-between with the ECS, and he told me whatever I needed to know.

In the summer of 1998 Ashland Incorporated announced that it was considering moving its corporate headquarters out of Kentucky. That would have been a huge economic loss for the state because Ashland was one of the five biggest corporations in Kentucky, along with Ford, Humana, Toyota, and UPS. Those five entities were good corporate citizens; they supported education initiatives at all levels and were responsible for a multitude of spin-off companies in the state. Ashland also sponsored three cultural performing arts programs each year called "In Performance at the Governor's Mansion," featuring artists with Kentucky roots. Judi and I hosted those events all eight years I was governor.

In an effort to convince Ashland to stay in Kentucky, I met with corporate officials and escorted them around northern Kentucky, the Greater Cincinnati Airport, and several nice residential communities in the area. I suggested that Ashland relocate its corporate headquarters to the Towers of RiverCenter in downtown Covington, and the company agreed to do that. Unfortunately, Ashland eventually moved its headquarters to Wilmington, Delaware, in 2020.

Another potential setback to Kentucky's economy came to light when UPS revealed that it was thinking about moving its national hub from Standiford Field in Louisville. It was planning a major expansion and thought it would be unable to hire enough workers to fill its odd schedule of three- to four-hour shifts in the middle of the night. The pay and benefits were good, but these were only part-time jobs. Company representatives told us that college students made the best employees, but because they had to work at night, few students were willing to take the jobs. I tasked Jim Ramsey and Crit Luallen to work with University of Louisville president John Schumaker and leaders of the Jefferson County Community and Technical College to try to meet UPS's workforce needs. The university and community college developed unique schedules for students working at UPS and designated special dorms for them to live in. UPS provided scholarships, benefits, and a special bus service for its student employees. It is hard to overestimate the importance of UPS to the Kentucky economy.

Although we failed to lure Hyundai, the South Korean automobile manufacturer, to Hardin County, a good result came from that effort. Hyundai eventually decided to build its plant in Alabama, but we went ahead and purchased approximately eighteen hundred acres of land about fifty miles south of Louisville that bordered both Interstate 65 and the CSX main rail line, believing the property would attract a similar project someday. We were right. In 2020 Governor Andy Beshear announced that Ford would join with SK Innovation, a South Korean company, to invest almost $6 billion to build two factories on the property we had purchased more than twenty years ago, providing jobs for about five thousand people. These manufacturing facilities are likely to create many spin-off support businesses in the area.

In mid-September 1998 members of the Cabinet for Economic Development accompanied Judi and me on a nine-day working trip to Spain, Germany, France, and England. In Spain we met with officials of Acerinox, one of the world's largest stainless steel producers. When Brereton Jones appointed me secretary of the Cabinet for Economic Development in 1991, Acerinox had already started building a plant in Carroll County along the Ohio River. By 1998, that plant was thriving, so I wanted to see whether we could get the company to expand the plant and create more jobs, which it eventually did. Prince Philip, who is now King Philip VI of Spain, later visited us in Frankfort, and I gave him a tour of the plant.

Next, we visited the headquarters of Montaplast in Germany. That company had built a plant in Frankfort in 1992, when I was secretary of economic development, and we talked about expanding its operation in Kentucky. In France, we convinced Lafarge to build a large gypsum wallboard plant in Silver Grove in northern Kentucky. That trip definitely paid dividends by bringing good-paying jobs to Kentucky.

In mid-November of 1998 the four major tobacco companies—RJ Reynolds, Lorillard, Brown and Williamson, and Philip Morris—reached the Master Tobacco Settlement Agreement with several tobacco-growing states. Ever since 1964, when the US surgeon general warned that smoking cigarettes could be dangerous to one's health, the tobacco industry had been under attack, and consumption declined over the next several decades. The selling of tobacco products was still legal, but the use of tobacco was getting less popular every day. The states were able to sue the tobacco companies because they had intentionally withheld information about the health hazards associated with tobacco use, including the extent to which nicotine is addictive. Phase I of the Master Tobacco Settlement Agreement was worth $206 billion to the states.

Although Kentucky had not joined the initial lawsuit against the tobacco companies, it could choose to do so now. Ben Chandler and I had to decide whether to join the twelve other states that had sued the tobacco companies and had already accepted the Master Tobacco Settlement Agreement or file our own lawsuit. On a Monday in November, the tobacco companies presented Kentucky with an offer to accept phase I of the agreement and gave us until noon on Friday to decide. It was an easy decision. Kentucky was in no position to take on the tobacco companies alone. Under phase I, Kentucky would receive some $3.4 billion over twenty-five years, with more than 70 percent going to repay the federal government for Medicaid costs. That left Kentucky with $40 million a year to spend on other things.

At the time, Kentucky still had about sixty thousand tobacco farmers. The original settlement did not include specific compensation for those farmers hurt by the agreement, but the tobacco companies were willing to meet with the officials of tobacco-producing states to discuss growers' concerns and the establishment of a $5 billion Growers' Trust Compensation Fund called phase II. Chandler, Kentucky agriculture commissioner Billy Ray Smith, and I boarded the state's plane and flew to Durham, North Carolina, to meet with representatives of the tobacco companies, North Carolina governor Jim Hunt, and North Carolina attorney general Mike Easley. The tobacco companies were under no obligation to meet with us, but to their credit, they did.

Our little group argued that phase I harmed farmers in Kentucky, North Carolina, and other tobacco-producing states by reducing the demand for tobacco. As a result, representatives of Philip Morris, Brown and Williamson, and Lorillard orally agreed to contribute to the Growers' Trust Compensation Fund to help tobacco farmers transition to other crops. RJ Reynolds initially resisted contributing to the trust fund, offering to buy additional domestic tobacco instead. If RJ Reynolds didn't participate in the trust fund, the other tobacco companies would have been financially disadvantaged and wouldn't have participated either. Our Kentucky delegation took the RJ Reynolds representatives into another room, and I held my own "come to Jesus" conversation with them. I phoned the president of RJ Reynolds and asked him to come to Durham to join the discussion, but he refused. That made me mad, so I told him I would be in his office at eight o'clock the next morning, and he should be ready to receive me. Later that evening, his representative meekly told us that RJ Reynolds would participate in the Growers' Trust Compensation Fund. I guess my undeserved reputation as an eastern Kentucky tough guy reached all the way to the RJ Reynolds corporate office!

Under phase II, Kentucky would receive an additional $1.6 billion to $2 billion to help tobacco farmers transition to alternative crops. These amounts were estimates for the next twenty-five years, but the payments are supposed to continue as long as the companies sell tobacco. We allocated the phase II money during the 2000 legislative session. Half was appropriated for the development of new or improved agricultural products to allow farm families to stay on their farms and prosper economically, 25 percent was allocated to early childhood development programs, and 25 percent was allocated to health care programs. I believed then, and I believe now, that Kentucky benefited from both tobacco settlement agreements.

As part of the settlement, the tobacco companies agreed to dramatically revise how they sold and marketed cigarettes in the United States. They agreed to take down all billboards advertising tobacco products and to stop using cartoon characters such as Joe Camel for marketing and promotion. They agreed to limit brand-name sponsorships of entertainment and sporting events and end the sale of promotional merchandise with tobacco logos. The companies also agreed to pay $25 million a year for ten years for a national study of smoking among youth and $1.5 billion over a five-year period for a national antismoking campaign.

One of the biggest sociological changes in my lifetime has been the public's attitude toward smoking. Smoking is no longer socially acceptable in most places in this country. I quit smoking not long after I became governor when I realized that I was setting a bad example for young people in the state. During much of the twentieth century, smoking was so ubiquitous in homes, businesses, and public buildings that you barely noticed the odor. Nowadays, I can smell someone smoking a cigarette five cars ahead of me at a red light! This is a huge societal change that will be of immense benefit to the nation's health and economy as we move forward.

Shortly after Kentucky agreed to join the tobacco settlement agreement, Philip Morris closed its plant in Louisville, a decision that caught me off guard. The plant's closing cost fourteen hundred people their jobs. I flew to New York and met with the chair and CEO of Philip Morris, Michael Szymanczyk, hoping to convince him to change his mind, but to no avail. It was a done deal. The plant's closing also drove home the point that tobacco's days as a major industry in Kentucky were over.

Later in 2000 I created a twelve-member board to decide how to allocate the 50 percent of the phase II money designated to diversify the agricultural industry in Kentucky. I appointed myself chair, Billy Ray Smith vice-chair, and Ben Chandler secretary-treasurer. Paul Hornback, president of the Council for Burley Tobacco, told the media that being a member of that board was a no-win situation. "Everybody says this is the last board they'll ever sit on because they're going to make so many people mad, they'll never get elected to anything again!" According to Hampton "Hoppy" Henton, executive director of the Farm Service Agency, which administered the US Department of Agriculture's tobacco quota program, "People on this board will have to be wise beyond their years. You can be expedient, and you can be fair and equitable, but it's awfully hard to do both at the same time."

I was a hands-on chair because I wanted the board to direct the money wisely and appropriately. As a general rule, the board would fund half of each project, and the farmer would fund the other half. One program consisted of an effort to improve the genetics of the state's beef herds. Its objective was to help farmers buy bulls with superior genetic characteristics. There has been measurable improvement in the quality of the Kentucky beef herd since then. Another program emphasized grapes as an alternative crop, and Kentucky now has some thriving wineries. We also subsidized goat ranches, with limited success. I had high expectations for shrimp and catfish farms, and we put a lot of time, effort, and money into them, but they just didn't work out. Kentucky couldn't compete with Louisiana in those areas. We supported a bass farm in western Kentucky that catered almost exclusively to Chinese businesses in the Northeast. Despite a few failures, for the most part, I think we delivered the goods for Kentucky's farmers.

By the middle of the summer of 1998, I turned more attention to my reelection campaign. In the Democratic primary to fill the US Senate seat of Wendell Ford, who had announced his retirement, Scotty Baesler, the former mayor of Lexington and congressman from the Sixth District, defeated Louisville business executive Charlie Owen and Lieutenant Governor Steve Henry. I didn't support anyone in the Democratic primary, but privately I thought Henry's candidacy was a mistake because he wouldn't be able to raise enough money to be competitive, and I was right. Baesler's Republican opponent in November was Jim Bunning, and Bunning won the election in one of the closest races in Kentucky history. Both of Kentucky's US senators were now Republicans.

Shortly after the 1998 Democratic primary, Brereton Jones began to hint that he was thinking about running against me in the 1999 gubernatorial primary. When Jones appeared at an event in Prestonsburg earlier that year, Greg Stumbo had introduced him as "the next governor of Kentucky." I guess Brereton thought he might be able to use workers' compensation reform against me in eastern Kentucky and the community college issue against me all over the state. Maybe he thought Chandler's ever-widening investigation of my 1995 gubernatorial campaign made me vulnerable. In addition, he probably thought I hadn't done enough to protect health insurance reform, one of his signature pieces of legislation.

In mid-August, on the same night I held a $25-a-ticket fund-raiser for the Kentucky Democratic Party at party headquarters in Frankfort, Jones hosted a free picnic at Airdrie Stud, his Thoroughbred horse farm off Old Frankfort Pike in Woodford County. My fund-raising event drew about six hundred people, while Jones's drew more than a thousand. Apparently, someone was handing out "Flatten Patton" bumper stickers at Brereton's event. Being an engineer, I had always been good at math, so even I could add two plus two. It sure seemed like Jones was testing the water for a campaign against me.

Had Jones run, I believe it would have been a competitive race, and I'm not sure who would have won. The campaign finance law was still in force, so financially, we would have been on a level playing field. He had his circle of friends and supporters, and I had mine. We also had many mutual friends who would have found themselves in a difficult situation. However, I believed Jones didn't really like being governor that much, and I may be wrong, but I had the impression that his wife, Libby, didn't enjoy the lime-light that came with being First Lady of Kentucky. She always seemed happiest when she was working on their horse farm, and everyone in Frankfort knew that. Ron McCloud, whom I had recommended as Ken-tucky Democratic Party chair, told the media that he was surprised Libby hadn't volunteered to be on my reelection exploratory committee to keep her husband from running!

I think Brereton liked the *title* of governor, but he preferred to go home at five o'clock and didn't want to schmooze with legislators. He was a "big picture" kind of administrator, not a policy wonk like I was. I didn't have a close personal relationship with him, but it wasn't adversarial either. I have always been grateful to him for appointing me secretary of the Cabinet for Economic Development for sixteen months, which helped get me elected governor.

Jones said he wouldn't decide whether to run against me in the pri-mary until sometime in December 1998 or early January 1999, and frankly, I wasn't overly concerned. He had his record to run on, and I had mine. And there wasn't anything I could do about it anyway. When Brereton announced his decision not to challenge me in the primary on December 1, I suspect Greg Stumbo was disappointed. In reality, I knew by early Novem-ber that he wouldn't run. When I contacted people associated with his 1991

Judi and I enjoy the view from the front porch of the governor's mansion. (Courtesy of Kentucky Department for Libraries and Archives, Archives and Records Management Division)

gubernatorial campaign or people who had served in his administration and asked if they were interested in helping me, they all said yes. I named Mark Guilfoyle, Jones's cabinet secretary, as my campaign committee chair. Pat Mulloy, Jones's finance secretary; Kevin Hable, state budget director in the Jones administration and later cabinet secretary; and Joe Prather, chair of Jones's 1991 campaign, all agreed to serve on my campaign committee by mid-November. Kevin and Pat were my friends as well, and they may have stuck with me had Jones decided to run, but Mark and Joe definitely would have gone with Brereton.

Then, in mid-December, Ben Chandler announced that he would be running for reelection as attorney general rather than challenging me in the primary. With both Jones and Chandler out of contention by the end of

Walking with Lee Todd, who became the president of the University of Kentucky in 2001. Todd and state budget director Jim Ramsey implemented postsecondary education reform (HB 1) and made it work. (Courtesy of Kentucky Department for Libraries and Archives, Archives and Records Management Division)

1998, I was ready to kick my own campaign into high gear. Based on what I had accomplished in my first three years as governor, I felt confident the people of Kentucky would agree that I had earned another four-year term. By the filing deadline for the primary, there was no one running against me. I ran for elective office thirteen times, and the 1999 Democratic primary for governor was the only time I was unopposed.

12

Making Modern History

The constitutional amendment passed by Kentucky voters in 1992 allowed the governor to succeed himself. Up to that point, only James Garrard had served two consecutive terms as governor, and that happened in 1796 and 1800. When the Kentucky Constitution was amended during Garrard's first term, the new limit didn't take into account that he had already served one term. The 1992 constitutional amendment allowing succession went into effect in 1995, meaning that I was the first governor it applied to, and I fully intended to run for reelection in 1999 and make modern Kentucky history.

I felt good about my reelection prospects, but I didn't make the mistake of thinking I was bulletproof. I faced some substantial negatives heading into the 1999 campaign. I had made plenty of enemies in eastern Kentucky over my reform of the workers' compensation law, which enraged many working and retired coal miners and other people performing dangerous jobs. Ben Chandler's investigation of my 1995 campaign was ongoing, and my chief of staff, Skipper Martin, was under indictment because of it. I had alienated some state and union workers over my refusal to go to the mat over collective bargaining. I had upset legions of UK alums over the community college issue. Any one of those factors, let alone a combination of them, might have been the death knell for a politician running for governor of Kentucky. I was fully aware that I could encounter a substantial headwind in my attempt to get reelected.

I was unopposed in the Democratic primary, and I liked it that way, but I thought the Republicans would present a political heavyweight to challenge me. I half expected Larry Forgy to force a rematch of our 1995 race, which I had barely won. I was unaware that the Republican Party was in such disarray. The only candidates running in the Republican primary were Peppy Martin, an unknown former publicist from Louisville who was living in Bonnieville, and David L. Williams, not the state senator but an unknown utility contractor. I was frankly shocked, but I certainly wasn't going to complain!

Rumors were circulating among the news media that US senator Mitch McConnell and I had reached a gentleman's agreement about the

1999 gubernatorial race. Supposedly, Mitch had pledged not to recruit a strong Republican candidate to run against me if I agreed not to run against him when he came up for reelection in 2002. Let me state unequivocally that there was absolutely no truth to that rumor. We never had a discussion like that, and as far as I know, nobody associated with either my office or his ever talked about such an arrangement on our behalf. I had no interest in running for Mitch's Senate seat. If Kentucky voters deemed me worthy, I fully intended to serve all four years of my second term as governor because I still had things I wanted to accomplish. I admit I had my eye on Jim Bunning's US Senate seat; he was up for reelection in 2004, which fit my personal political timetable perfectly. My own shortcomings and mistakes permanently derailed that idea, but in 1999, that was my plan.

Peppy Martin won the Republican primary. She was an unknown quantity. Gatewood Galbraith, a Lexington lawyer, had also entered the race as an independent. His major platform was the legalization of marijuana, so I never considered him a major threat. However, politics can be full of surprises, and I didn't want to be surprised. Therefore, I launched my campaign in early February and ran as if I were behind in a race against a strong candidate.

One thing I had to guard against was complacency among my campaign staff and my supporters. So I issued a warning by invoking the name of Jesse "The Body" Ventura, the former US Navy underwater demolition team member, Vietnam War veteran, and professional wrestler who had shocked the nation by winning the Minnesota governor's race in 1998 as the Reform Party candidate. I had met Ventura at various governors' meetings, and he came across as a bombastic person who had no political philosophy or knowledge of government, but I guess Minnesota voters got what they wanted: an outsider to shake up the system. I don't know anything about Ventura's accomplishments as governor, but he sure enjoyed the limelight.

I enjoy campaigning. I believe there is therapeutic value in getting out in public, shaking hands, and engaging in old-style politicking. I had improved my speechmaking to the point where I felt comfortable getting onstage in front of a crowd of strangers and firing them up.

It soon became apparent how weak Peppy Martin was as a candidate. By the end of February, I had raised almost $250,000 for my campaign, while Peppy's campaign was more than $3,000 in debt. Shortly thereafter, my campaign stopped actively soliciting money, but donations were still welcomed. By early May, I had almost $500,000 to spend on the campaign, compared to Peppy's less than $10,000. Dale Emmons, a Kentucky political consultant, compared Peppy to a mule running in the Kentucky Derby: her only chance of winning was if the other horse (me) dropped dead! I was in good health, so I felt confident heading into the fall election. I wasn't concerned about losing, that's for sure.

I believe the Republican Party did the people of Kentucky a disservice by not running a credible candidate against me in 1999, even though I was the beneficiary of that decision. Senator McConnell and the state Republicans regarded me as a strong administrator and politician in the mold of Wendell Ford, Louie Nunn, and Julian Carroll, and they didn't think I could be beaten. Many Republicans seemed to appreciate my policies as well as my candor. However, in the absence of competent competition, politicians can get lazy and take their eye off the ball. I didn't intend to let that happen to me. Since the outcome of the November election looked like a sure thing, I continued to govern as if I were already into my second term. I had established an eight-year agenda from the outset in 1995, so we didn't have to shift gears when we put together our agenda for the 2000 legislative session. I had a good staff in the governor's office and good cabinet secretaries, so we just kept going.

Early childhood development and adult education became two of my legislative priorities in 2000. I had earlier appointed my daughter Nicki to head a twenty-five-member task force charged with developing a twenty-year plan to improve learning among Kentucky children in their first five years of life. I was able to put 25 percent of the tobacco settlement money toward funding the early childhood program.

At the end of April 1999, officials from Toyota came to Frankfort and invited me to test-drive the first Prius to roll off the assembly line in Scott County. The Prius was Toyota's brand-new hybrid car, and I drove it up Dead Man's Hill on Old Louisville Road in Frankfort to test the vehicle's handling and acceleration. Toyota had notified the news media, so when I came back down the hill and parked the car on the east side of the capitol, there were at least two reporters waiting. I took the opportunity not only to congratulate Toyota on its hybrid technology but also to float an idea I had been contemplating as I looked ahead to the 2000 legislative session.

My idea was to establish fourteen gambling casinos in Kentucky: three casinos in Louisville, two in Lexington, and one each in northern Kentucky, Pikeville, Owensboro, Paducah, Ashland, London, Henderson, Hopkinsville, and Bowling Green. I believed casino gambling, which I euphemistically called "congregate gaming," could provide a dedicated source of revenue to bolster the state treasury, help the horse racing industry compete with gambling in surrounding states, and preserve Kentucky's wetlands, farmlands, mountains, and other natural treasures. In addition, casinos could stimulate the growth and renewal of the blighted urban areas where they should be located. Estimates were that casinos could generate $100 million to $300 million a year for Kentucky.

In October two Kentucky economists, Lawrence Lynch at Transylvania University and Paul Combs at the University of Louisville, conducted a study at the behest of the Kentucky Economic Development Corporation, whose board included forty of Kentucky's most prominent business executives. Their report asserted that Kentucky was losing more than $159 million a year to Ohio River casinos outside of the commonwealth, based on zip code and license plate surveys conducted at those casinos. However, other studies emphasized the downside of casino gambling. For example, a South Carolina study found that casinos led to an increase in compulsive gambling, bankruptcy, and personal debt that cost the people of South Carolina $171 million a year—far more than the $60 million the state took in each year by taxing the gaming industry. In addition, most of the money made by the casinos flowed out of the state to the casino owners. The National Gambling Impact Study Commission concluded that, although casinos led to jobs and economic opportunities, they took a heavy social toll in the form of bankruptcy, gambling addiction, broken families, and moral turpitude. Religious conservatives such as the Reverend Nancy Jo Kemper, executive director of the Kentucky Council of Churches; the Reverend Claude Witt, director of the Kentucky Temperance League; Republican state senator Tom Buford; and my 1995 gubernatorial opponent Larry Forgy used these negative aspects of casinos to oppose my idea.

I was surprised by the uproar generated by my casino proposal. I suddenly found myself portrayed as Satan incarnate! I tried to keep my response to opponents simple: Kentucky already had legal gambling that provided a relatively small revenue stream. If people had a proclivity to jeopardize their economic well-being by gambling, they could do it by buying lottery tickets, betting on horse races, patronizing the bingo parlors run by charities, or playing poker in private card games. If there are four liquor stores in town and you open one more liquor store, does that lead to more alcoholics? Establishing casinos in Kentucky wouldn't have created a worse problem than already existed, and there was an obvious demand for casino gambling. Why shouldn't Kentucky receive some of that gaming money instead of watching it flow out of state to private investors or the coffers of surrounding states?

I think the worst form of gambling is bingo, and these games are usually run by charities. For many elderly people and retirees, bingo is their only means of social interaction, and they really can't afford to play when they're on a fixed income. I had an aunt in Morehead who was hooked on playing bingo. A friend of hers would take her to the bingo parlor, and we later discovered that she had been writing bad checks to pay for her bingo habit, which we eventually covered.

The second worst form of gambling is the lottery, which is operated by the state. Rich people generally don't play the lottery because the odds of winning are astronomical, and they aren't taken in by the pitch that "someone is going to win, so it might as well be you!" The people who typically play the lottery go into the convenience store to buy a loaf of bread or a gallon of milk and decide to put down a couple of hard-earned dollars on a lottery ticket in the hope of hitting it big and leaving their financial troubles behind. I am not against gambling, but I have never bought a lottery ticket.

I don't worry about people who gamble on horse racing or in casinos because they can generally afford to lose. They see gambling as entertainment, not as a way out of their immediate or long-term financial predicaments. Betting on horses and playing the slots are the least pernicious forms of gambling, in my opinion.

In early July I flew to Washington, DC, for the sole purpose of flying back to Kentucky with President Bill Clinton on Air Force One. He was beginning a six-state tour through America's poorest communities, and he planned to stop in Jackson and Perry Counties in eastern Kentucky and had asked me to accompany him. I couldn't have devised a better image for my campaign than being seen in eastern Kentucky escorting President Clinton. We traveled to McKee and Hazard, and it was as hot as it could be. During that trip, Clinton announced his New Markets Tax Credit Program, which became part of the Community Renewal Tax Relief Act passed by Congress in 2000. The tax credit program financed commercial development, not residential development. The idea was for the federal government to make direct allocations to communities for redevelopment projects that needed more support, rather than funneling the money through the state government.

In early August I directed the Finance Cabinet to employ the accounting firm PricewaterhouseCoopers to study the social and economic impact of expanding gambling in Kentucky and to produce a report by December 1 so that the lawmakers and I had the information before the 2000 legislative session began. PricewaterhouseCoopers had already conducted similar studies for other states and had generally found that the expansion of gambling, including casino gambling, would benefit their economies.

That's why I wanted this particular firm to conduct the study. Its final report estimated that more than half of adult Kentuckians gambled in some fashion and that the state had lost more than $200 million in gambling revenue to riverboat casinos in Illinois, Indiana, and Missouri in 1998 alone. The report estimated that casino gambling would add nearly $1.1 billion to the state budget by the year 2003. That did nothing to mollify the evangelical Christians who viewed casino gambling as a moral issue. I seemed to have a knack for alienating voters. By the middle of the summer, Peppy Martin was using the casino issue against me, but I didn't care.

At a campaign stop at Stark in Elliott County, I floated another controversial idea by suggesting that the legislature raise the gasoline tax by 10 cents a gallon. I may have been a little cocky at that point in the campaign, but my basic philosophy was to tax people who can't vote against you, and I knew that people traveling through Kentucky on their way to another destination purchased at least a third of the gasoline sold in the state. Therefore, I thought Kentucky should have a high gas tax. Although it made good economic sense, proposing to raise the gas tax probably didn't enamor me with trucking companies in the state or with any Kentuckians who owned a car or a truck. Fortunately, I don't recall encountering any hostile crowds during my campaign stops or rallies around the state.

As expected, Peppy Martin and the Republicans attacked me for suggesting a hike in the gas tax. They called me "Ten-Penny Paul," but that derisive nickname didn't have any legs. As far as I was concerned, as a political opponent, Peppy was just a speed bump on my way to reelection. I was never mean to her; I just ignored her. Gatewood Galbraith was a more credible candidate, but he had no chance either. KET held only one gubernatorial debate, citing a lack of public interest in the election. I directed most of my questions and responses to Gatewood during that debate. He was entertaining, and he was right about the marijuana issue—a man ahead of his time.

Peppy ran an odd campaign. For example, she said she could eliminate 50 to 75 percent of Kentucky taxes if the voters gave her eight years in office. Her economic "plan" was to shift state functions to private investment in the form of tax-exempt bonds sold by churches. No prominent Republican endorsed her, not even Mitch McConnell or David Williams, who later became president of the state senate. In fact, Williams stated publicly that he would vote for me because Peppy was unqualified. Even though I ran a vigorous campaign, I never sweated the outcome. In November I received 60.6 percent of the vote, and Peppy barely got more votes than Gatewood, a one-issue candidate.

My challenge after the election was to get state legislators to support casino gambling and the gas tax increase. That task became more difficult when two Democratic state senators switched political parties in 1999 and became Republicans, giving that party a majority in the senate. In mid-July Democrat Dan Seum from Louisville announced that he was changing his party affiliation. Seum said he had always considered himself more of a conservative than a liberal and felt uncomfortable in the Democratic caucus. Casino gambling was the final straw that pushed him over to the Republican side of the aisle. There may have been some truth to his explanation, but I also knew that Seum and Larry Saunders were political enemies, even though they were both Democrats from Louisville. As senate president, Saunders had treated Seum badly, and in return, some of Seum's speeches on the senate floor were critical of Saunders, so there was bad blood between them. I had no warning about Seum's defection. If I had known, I might have been able to call Seum and Saunders into my office and get their dispute straightened out, but I wasn't aware of how badly their relationship had deteriorated. Seum's switch meant that the senate would be deadlocked—nineteen Democrats to nineteen Republicans. Terry McBrayer, former chair of the Kentucky Democratic Party, summed up the Republicans' new status best when he said, "They will be hard dogs to keep under the porch." We didn't know the situation was about to get a whole lot worse.

In mid-August state senator Robert J. "Bob" Leeper announced that he too was joining the Republicans, even though 80 percent of the registered voters in his southwestern Kentucky district were Democrats, albeit conservative ones. I had known for weeks that Leeper was thinking about switching political parties, and his dislike of Saunders was no secret. During the legislature's organizational meeting in January 1999, Leeper had not joined the Republicans in supporting Saunders's election as senate president, as he was a friend of Eck Rose. To punish Leeper, Saunders removed him as chair of the Agriculture and Natural Resources Committee, which Leeper had chaired for six years, and took him off three other committees as well. The media reported that Mitch McConnell had played a key role in convincing Leeper to join the Republicans and that McConnell and David Williams had promised Leeper a seat on the A&R Committee if he switched parties.

Before Leeper made his announcement, I knew that if the Republicans gained control of the state senate, it would affect my legislative agenda. Even at that late date, I still thought the Democrats would win back the seats they were about to lose and that the Republican surge was only a

My staff and I discuss an issue with the house leadership team. My second term was devoted to implementing the programs adopted during my first term, as well as addressing early childhood education, adult education, and the tobacco settlement program. (Courtesy of Kentucky Department for Libraries and Archives, Archives and Records Management Division)

short-term aberration. I didn't recognize that the political landscape of Kentucky had shifted so dramatically toward the Republican Party. If the Republicans controlled the senate during the 2000 legislative session, collective bargaining for public employees would be dead in its tracks. And I could probably forget about casino gambling and my plan to place video lottery terminals (VLTs) at the racetracks. I also figured the opportunity to pass any real tax reform would evaporate. Therefore, I flew to Paducah to talk to Leeper. I pleaded with him to remain in the Democratic caucus. I warned him that I didn't think he could get reelected running as a Republican in his district and that I would certainly recruit and support a Democrat to run against him. I didn't threaten to use the line-item veto to eliminate projects from his district in the next budget cycle, but in retrospect, maybe I should have. Shortly thereafter, he announced that he was switching political parties. So much for my powers of persuasion!

The casino gambling issue became more problematic in mid-November when attorney general Ben Chandler issued an opinion that the Kentucky Lottery Corporation could not operate casino-style gambling or

I invited nine former governors to spend an evening with me at the governor's mansion for dinner and conversation. Wallace Wilkinson was unable to attend. (Courtesy of Kentucky Department for Libraries and Archives, Archives and Records Management Division)

VLTs without a public referendum to amend the state constitution. The 1891 revised Kentucky Constitution expressly prohibited casino-style gambling. Although Chandler's opinion did not carry the force of law, I reluctantly had to agree with him. By mid-December, on the eve of the 2000 legislative session, I concluded that there was little to no support in the General Assembly for amending the constitution. It was not an auspicious start to my second term as governor, and as I looked ahead to the 2000 legislative session, I could only play the hand dealt me. David Williams and the senate Republicans had arrived. They now had a power base from which to operate, and for the most part, they used it superbly. I knew I was going to have to alter a few of my legislative priorities, but my biggest mistake was thinking that I knew what to expect from the Republican leadership. I was used to working both sides of the political aisle and had been successful doing that. However, I didn't realize just how much the Republican takeover of the state senate had changed the political landscape. I was about to find out.

13

A Second Term, or Be Careful What You Wish For

The 2000 Legislative Session

I was pleased with what my staff and I had accomplished in our first four years, but there was still work to do. Early on the morning after Election Day 1999, I was back at my desk, as if it were just another day at the office. One of my top priorities was to meet with the leadership of both legislative chambers in an attempt to foster bipartisanship, now that the Republicans controlled the state senate. I let the leadership know that I intended to introduce an aggressive legislative agenda and would work diligently with members of both political parties.

The Democratic leadership of the house, particularly A&R Committee chair Harry Moberly, and the Republican leadership of the senate—David Williams, Dan Kelly, and Richie Sanders (who succeeded Benny Ray Bailey as A&R Committee chair)—were included in our budget discussions and decisions. Both chambers' leadership had a hand in writing the 2000 budget proposal that emerged as House Bill (HB) 502. It was ready to submit to the legislature by mid-December.

My second inaugural ceremony in 1999 was much more subdued than the first one in 1995. In fact, my second inaugural speech lasted only sixteen minutes, which might still be a record for brevity. I enjoy history, and although I was fully cognizant of the historical significance of my reelection, the pageantry of the occasion was just a distraction from planning for the opening of the 2000 legislative session. I wanted the General Assembly to know that I didn't intend to be a "caretaker" governor during my second term. I was fully committed to the job for the next four years, and I wouldn't be distracted by my personal life or by political ambition.

Heading into my second term, I was in a strong position politically. One of the keys to my successful first term was that I insisted on keeping the legislature involved and informed. I didn't keep secrets, and I didn't make any important announcements that surprised either the legislative leadership or the media. I respected the media, and that played a large role in my success. That kind of leadership style builds trust, and trust is the coin of the realm in Frankfort—or at least it used to be.

In December 1999 Skipper and I met with David Williams, who would be the leader of the Republicans in the upcoming session of the General Assembly. We met in the basement of the governor's mansion to discuss the political reality of his party being in control of the senate and which issues we might be able to work on together. The major topic was substantive tax reform. Aware of the bleak revenue picture, Williams was very agreeable to comprehensive tax reform, especially an increase in the gas tax to add to the Road Fund.

It would be fair to say that during the previous twenty-eight years, when the Democrats controlled the governor's office and the two legislative chambers, districts represented by Democrats had received far more funding for local road projects than those represented by Republicans. Understandably, Williams wanted to play catch-up. He said, "I want to build roads in Kentucky that can be seen from the moon, and I want one of them to go through Burkesville." Burkesville was David's hometown. I stuck out my hand and said, "You have a deal!" I lived up to my end of the bargain, but unfortunately, he didn't.

Heading into the 2000 legislative session, Williams and I were on good terms, and I never anticipated an adversarial relationship merely because of our different party affiliations. However, there had been several warning signs that Williams was thin-skinned and that his imminent election as president of the senate had gone to his head. On the day of my second inauguration, I held a reception for state legislators at the governor's mansion. At one point, I saw Crit and Williams arguing face-to-face and asked them what was going on. Crit said, "David is upset that he wasn't given the seat on the inaugural platform that's reserved for the president of the senate." I replied, "Well, Larry Saunders is officially still the president of the senate, and we gave him that seat. I'm sorry if that offended you, David, but that was simply proper protocol." Williams backed off, but I could tell he was still upset. Later, I learned that he had tried to convince the Republican caucuses in both the senate and the house to boycott the inaugural ceremonies because of the perceived slight against him. They defied him and attended anyway. In retrospect, I should have seen this as a warning shot across my bow, but at the time, I viewed the incident as merely a hiccup. It was my understanding that we had an agreement to take on comprehensive tax reform as well as the gas tax increase.

In fact, just prior to the start of the 2000 legislative session, Williams said nice things about me to the media. He even sponsored Senate Bill (SB) 1 at my request, which would expand and increase funding for adult education. I had been working with Ed Ford, my special assistant on educational issues, on the bill, and I knew Williams was interested in that issue too. Although SB 1 was my bill, I didn't really care who got credit for it. I just wanted it passed quickly, and Williams seemed eager to sponsor it.

During the 2000 legislative session, I didn't take the attitude that it had to be my way or the highway in my dealings with the legislative leadership. The house Democrats and I were generally on the same page, and they supported my legislative agenda. My attitude toward the Republican leadership in the senate was one of compromise. I wasn't going to get everything I wanted, and they weren't going to get everything they wanted. That is how governance ought to work, particularly when there is a politically split legislature.

I intended to focus on early childhood development. In February 1998, while attending the National Governors Association meeting in Washington, I heard leading neuroscientists explain that the brain is the only organ not fully developed at birth. I had always thought a child's brain was like a computer, all wired up and ready for data (knowledge) entry. However, I learned that a newborn's brain is actually more like an Erector set. Infants are born with all the neurons they need, but those neurons aren't wired yet. I was like Saul on the road to Damascus regarding early childhood development. I saw the light!

I realized that to get a full return on our previous investments in education through the Kentucky Education Reform Act (KERA) and higher education reform, we had to support early childhood development. I created the Governor's Office of Early Childhood Development and appointed Dr. Kim Townley as its executive director, reporting directly to me. In March 1999 I established the Early Childhood Development Task Force and appointed my daughter Nicki as chair. Dr. Townley and Nicki were the only two early childhood experts on the task force. The other twenty-three members were influential individuals representing a wide variety of businesses (e.g., UPS, Toyota), professions, and organizations across Kentucky, as well as Republican and Democratic state and local officials. This was a conscious decision. The task force needed to convince noneducators that early childhood development was vital to Kentucky's future.

I charged the task force with developing a long-term strategy—specifically, a twenty-year plan to enhance Kentucky children's prospects for success. I recognized that supporting high-quality early childhood experiences would require a significant financial investment over an extended period of time. The task force approached this assignment by establishing working groups to examine children's needs and then present recommendations. They devoted thousands of hours to reviewing current circumstances and existing service gaps affecting the state's children and their families. In addition, hundreds of citizens voiced their concerns and suggested improvements during ten community forums held across the state. I believe the decision to involve many people at the grassroots level contributed significantly to the long-term success of our new program, called the KIDS Now initiative.

While the task force was working on its twenty-year plan, I set out to educate legislators about the importance of early childhood development. We sent all legislators articles and DVDs about early brain development. For a year and a half I wore "Save the Children" neckties as a conversation starter. By the beginning of the 2000 legislative session, Kentucky lawmakers probably knew more about early brain development than any other legislators in the country. Nicki and I also spoke to local business leaders and elected officials about early brain development and the connection between early childhood education and workforce development.

In November 1999 the task force presented a twenty-year plan that included more than sixty recommendations, the major ones being:

- Establish a state-funded scholarship program to attract and retain child-care workers.
- Establish a state-funded health insurance plan for child-care workers.
- Develop a four-star rating system for all child-care programs, including those for school-age children.
- Provide prenatal vitamins and other health care services and screenings for all new Kentucky mothers and their babies.
- Expand Medicaid.
- Provide eye exams for children before they start their first year of school.
- Increase tax exemptions for dependent children.

We funded six of these seven priorities identified in the twenty-year plan. I worried that state-funded health insurance for child-care workers would be politically unacceptable and might torpedo the entire bill.

Improving early childhood development was not going to be easy. Like most problems, if an easy fix existed, somebody would have implemented it already. The real issue came down to money. We needed more money and a restructuring of state government, particularly the Cabinet for Health Services and the Cabinet for Families and Children. Bob Sexton, executive director of the Prichard Committee, believed that improving early childhood development could be as important to Kentucky's future as the passage of KERA had been in 1990.

My early childhood development initiative ran into some trouble in the Republican-controlled senate. Led by majority floor leader Dan Kelly, the Republicans wanted to spend $56 million to expand existing education programs and let the counties decide how to fund their early childhood development efforts through public health education, home visits, better child-care facilities, nutrition programs, or other initiatives. Although the senate Republicans agreed with some of my proposals, such as funding universal vaccinations and vision and hearing screening, their plan had key differences.

For years, early childhood experts in northern Kentucky and Cincinnati had worked to educate business and community leaders about the importance of early childhood education and its relationship to workforce development. Northern Kentucky and Cincinnati have strong economic and social ties, and business leaders on both sides of the Ohio River were interested in improving the quality of life in their communities. During the 2000 legislative session, executives from Procter & Gamble and northern Kentucky businesses convinced their senators, including president pro tem Dick Roeding, to support the bill, which eased its passage in that chamber.

The Republicans' plan included setting up local early childhood partnerships, county by county. It did not provide funding for improving day care, which was a major part of my plan, probably because they believed mothers should stay at home. However, it expanded existing early reading and literacy initiatives and an existing substance abuse program for pregnant women. Kelly seemed more interested in utilizing current programs rather than establishing an entirely new agency, but he was open to compromise. I thought the Republican plan had little substance, and I warned the senate's A&R Committee not to play politics with Kentucky's children. I had really studied this issue and knew the subject.

As a county judge, I had recognized the importance of county health departments, and I knew elected officials would support legislation that brought money to their counties. Therefore, we placed all the health-related components of the KIDS Now program in local health departments. Task force member Darrel Beshear, the Republican county judge in Pulaski County, suggested sending annual reports to all elected county officials and legislators that specified how much KIDS Now money their counties received each year. We did this to maintain the political support of these local officials.

Near the end of the legislative session, Kelly and the senate Republicans backed down and passed my version of the bill by a unanimous vote. Passage of this early childhood initiative had been my number-one priority. Along with KERA and the Higher Education Reform Act, this new program would be the third rung on the ladder that gave Kentuckians a leg up.

Before the end of my second term, I transferred the Office of Early Childhood Development to the Kentucky Department of Education. Although Dr. Townley and Nicki argued strenuously against this move, I knew that new governors don't always support their predecessor's major initiatives, and I hoped this transfer would protect the program. During my successor's first budget cycle, I called my daughter every day to ask whether the KIDS Now program was still being funded. The fact that the program exists more than twenty years later is a testament to the popularity and importance of the original legislation.

During my pre–legislative session meetings with the house and senate leadership, I asked them to think about reforming Kentucky's tax system. Unlike 1998, when the state treasury was flush with cash, the nonpartisan Consensus Forecasting Group (CFG) had predicted a significant budget shortfall for the coming biennium, as the national dot-com bubble was about to burst. It did, and with it came the 2000 stock market crash. Kentucky's tax structure had long been in need of a complete overhaul, but a lack of political will had killed any real reform effort. With a new century approaching and the forecast of a significant budget shortfall, I thought the timing might be right for tax reform.

Tax reform is just about the most difficult and touchiest political issue to tackle because you are bound to make somebody—or a bunch of somebodies—mad. Whenever you pass tax reform legislation, someone always pays *more* in taxes while others pay *less*. Of course, you never hear from the latter. I had just been reelected to a second term by a landslide, so I thought I was in a strong political position to advance a tax reform initiative.

I also thought I could use some of my political capital to increase the gasoline tax by 7 cents a gallon. Gas tax money is used to build and repair roads, and I knew that the road projects contained in the existing six-year road plan would cost $600 million more than the state's anticipated revenue. The Road Fund's primary revenue streams are the gasoline tax, the sales tax on motor vehicles, driver's license fees, and the car licensing fee. The legislature had to either remove projects from the existing road plan (or let us do it) or increase the gas tax to make up the shortfall. Increasing the gas tax by 7 cents a gallon would raise an additional $196 million a year.

Frankly, most people have no idea how much the gas tax is. They just pump their gas and pay whatever the amount is, although they may gripe about the cost per gallon. As cars have become more fuel efficient, gas consumption has decreased over the last thirty years, but the cost of building and maintaining highways has increased, so there is less money to go around for roads. As a former county judge, I know firsthand that drivers let you know when there are potholes in the road! The Road Fund will be in big trouble when electric cars and trucks become ubiquitous and people stop buying gasoline. My guess is that people will have to pay a tax when they recharge their electric car batteries at charging stations along the highways and interstates.

At the time, Kentucky had one of the lowest gas taxes in the nation; it ranked forty-sixth out of the fifty states. A 7-cents-a-gallon increase would have moved Kentucky up to nineteenth place. The last time the gas tax had been raised was during the Collins administration in 1986, when it went up a nickel. As it turned out, my timing was terrible, as gas prices spiked in early 2000. The house Democrats were against increasing the tax during an election year, so I eventually dropped it from my legislative agenda.

Regarding my desire to fund more road projects, I talked house Democrat Pete Worthington into sponsoring a plan to use existing money in the Transportation Cabinet's coffers on current road projects. The Transportation Cabinet routinely deposited the total cost of a road project in a bank account, even though the project might not be completed for several years. In 1999 I knew the Transportation Cabinet had more than $669 million in the bank for ongoing but uncompleted construction projects. I estimated that as much as $325 million could be used for new projects without interfering with those ongoing projects. That money was just sitting in the bank, accumulating interest, which seemed like a waste to me. The money collected from the following year's gas tax would replenish whatever I "borrowed" from the Transportation Cabinet's existing bank account. Whenever I brought up the need for more money in the Road Fund, legislators would refer to that huge bank balance and ask, "What do you need more money for?" I wanted to eliminate that line of reasoning.

It took a lot of persuading on my part to convince transportation secretary James Codell to give us access to some of that money. Historically, the Transportation Cabinet's finance management practices have been very conservative, and it has been reluctant to part with its money. I verbally harassed Codell at every opportunity until he finally relented, and I was able to fund additional road construction projects without raising the gas tax. As the old adage states, "Where there's a will, there's a way." Well, as a county judge and as governor, I had the will and, in most cases, I found a way. By the time I left the governor's office in 2003, the Transportation Cabinet's bank account had decreased to less than $100 million, but construction projects hadn't slowed down one bit.

In addition to early childhood development, adult education, and tax reform, I had several other legislative priorities in 2000. These included:

- Collective bargaining for public employees
- Smart growth encompassing land-use planning and urban sprawl
- Promotion of safe water resources
- Minority affairs, including an effort to increase minority employment in state government and state contracts with minority businesses
- Restoration of a competitive health insurance market through the establishment of a high-risk pool called Kentucky Access
- Improved infrastructure, including roads and water delivery systems

The $14.4 billion two-year budget proposal I presented to the General Assembly in January called for substantial increases in funding for education, including an additional $120 million for the Bucks for Brains program, as well as increased funding for health care, state employees' salaries, and brick-and-mortar projects around the state. My tax reform plan would raise an additional $144 million a year through what I termed "revenue recovery." In my budget speech to the legislature, I noted that Kentucky had the eighth-lowest tax burden in the nation, and I asked the legislators if they wanted Kentucky to be ranked the eighth-worst state in the country. I warned that if they wrote another "safe" budget that didn't require a change in the tax code, that wouldn't move Kentucky forward. I challenged them to have the courage to join me in advancing the state into the new century.

I combined my proposed spending and funding initiatives in one bill because I didn't want the legislature to approve the spending plan without passing the means to fund it through genuine tax reform. I thought my approach was logical, but David Williams told the media my budget proposal was "unusual." He said combining spending and funding in one bill made it more complex to deal with, and he pointed out that previous governors had presented their revenue plans separately from their budgets. House speaker Jody Richards wasn't happy with how I presented my budget proposal either, and he broke with tradition by not cosponsoring the bill. In fact, the legislature eventually divided up the spending and funding parts of my budget proposal and created two separate bills.

Education was the focus of my entire administration, so in addition to my early childhood development and adult education initiatives, I proposed that the General Assembly commit $23 million in the next biennium to improve training for teachers in Kentucky. Moreover, I proposed removing the Educational Professional Standards Board (EPSB) from the Kentucky Department of Education and making it an autonomous body that reported directly to the governor. My daughter Bambi was a teacher, and she was shocked to learn that education majors in Kentucky colleges were not being taught the standards prescribed by KERA. These colleges were still teaching their students methods from the 1970s. In my opinion, the EPSB had become too cozy within the Department of Education, and that relationship had to end. I thought making the EPSB an independent entity was the best way to do that.

In my State of the Commonwealth speech, I talked about my sincere desire to double the funding for mental health care. I decided to add this item to my legislative agenda after visiting several Kentucky facilities that cared for patients with mental disabilities. My visit to the Home of the Innocents in Louisville had a particularly traumatic effect on me. Some of the children were bedridden and had been placed in the facility because their families couldn't take care of them properly. Many homeless people have mental health issues, particularly veterans who suffer from post-traumatic stress disorder (PTSD). After visiting several of these facilities, I was determined to increase aid for mental health care. To my surprise, I received a standing ovation from members of both political parties when I mentioned this in my speech. This show of support moved me, and I had to wipe away a few tears before I could continue. At that moment, I knew I would have no difficulty passing that part of my legislative agenda, which was very gratifying.

Regarding possible tax reform legislation, I wasn't naïve. I knew that getting legislators to vote for any kind of tax increase is difficult, even in the best of times. I knew it would be even more difficult now that the Republicans controlled the state senate. In addition, fourteen senators and just under fifty house members would be facing either primary or general election challengers in 2000. They knew their opponents would certainly use it against them if they voted to raise anybody's taxes. However, I thought tax reform was still possible and at least worth a try.

Before the session started, Williams expressed confidence that if anyone could take the lead on tax reform and push it through the legislature, it was me. He indicated that he and his senate Republican caucus were ready to work with me because it would not be an easy task. Early in the session, I actually got more resistance from the house Democratic leadership. They wanted to deal with tax reform in a special session rather than the regular session because the legislative agenda was already too crowded, and tax reform was a complex issue. In my opinion, the issue wasn't that complicated, and somewhat surprisingly, Williams told the media that he thought tax reform could be passed during the regular session. As a result, I pressured the house leadership to put tax reform on the agenda.

I think Williams's first instinct, which reflected his *real* beliefs at the time, was to cooperate in a bipartisan manner to move Kentucky forward, just as he had in 1990 when he voted for KERA and the tax to support it. Prior to the start of the 2000 legislative session, he and I were in a "good government" frame of mind, and I had no reason to believe he would deviate from that. Maybe I *was* a little naïve about how fast political postures can change in Frankfort.

Williams kept assuring us that if the house passed a tax reform bill, the Republican-controlled senate would follow suit. "You pass it, and we'll pass it," he said numerous times, and we believed him. The house Democrats never would have stuck their necks out and voted to increase taxes if they knew the bill had no chance of passing in the senate. There is no point in taking that kind of political whipping when there's no reward. Even with Williams's support, I knew substantive tax reform would be an uphill fight, but if we were successful, the rewards for Kentucky would be worth the cuts and bruises incurred along the way.

I didn't want a bill that merely worked around the edges of tax reform. I believed the 2000 legislative session could be a once-in-a-lifetime opportunity to mold Kentucky's future. I thought the stars were aligned to pass a law that would transform Kentucky's tax structure and put the commonwealth on a solid financial foundation heading into the twenty-first century. I thought real tax reform would lead to new revenue streams and economic growth. I had tremendous political momentum coming off my landslide reelection and a quiver full of political capital that I was willing to expend to pass meaningful tax reform. I was serious, and I thought the legislature was too.

Although I approved all the individual components, I did not draft the tax reform bill by myself. It took a team of people that included Crit, Skipper, Jim Ramsey, and Budget Office and Revenue Cabinet staff members. It looked like a system that would result in greater revenue as the economy grew. I unveiled our proposal at a news conference held at the Farnham

Dudgeon Civic Center in downtown Frankfort. I had invited the members of both legislative chambers to attend, but only fifteen showed up. Undeterred, I sent all 138 legislators a video of the presentation I gave that day.

Designing a *fair* tax system is not the same as designing a *politically acceptable* tax system. The real trick is getting the plan passed by the legislature. My initial tax reform initiative included taxing specific services such as dry cleaning, haircuts, car repairs, watch repairs, shoe repairs, out-of-state-telephone calls, and satellite television services—things that couldn't easily be sent out of state. I also wanted the legislature to study the possibility of taxing mail-order catalog and out-of-state online merchandise sales. Although selling products online is a federal issue involving interstate commerce, I wanted to bring the issue to the attention of our representatives in Washington, DC, because states lack the authority to tax that growing revenue stream. A company in Texas that sells merchandise online to Kentucky consumers uses some of Kentucky's infrastructure free of charge, while Kentucky businesses have to pay taxes to support that infrastructure, which isn't fair.

My tax reform initiative, which emerged as HB 996 after the house separated it from HB 502, the budget bill, would have removed 200,000 to 300,000 poor Kentuckians from the tax rolls and cut the taxes of 950,000 other Kentuckians; another 275,000 would have seen little change in their taxes. However, 412,000 of the wealthiest Kentuckians would have paid higher taxes, and there was fear that this tax hike would drive some of them out of the state.

Representative Charles Siler, a Republican from Williamsburg, was a director of the Williamsburg National Bank. He was a good, honest, stand-up guy. He told his colleagues on the floor of the house that he was proud to be one of the few Republicans who had voted for the tax increase in 1990 that funded KERA, even though it cost him his seat when his constituents voted him out of office in the next election. (He was later reelected.) However, he didn't regret that vote because it had helped improve education in the state and in his district. He said it would be wrong for him and his Republican colleagues to vote *against* the tax reform bill but *in favor* of a budget bill based on the tax reform bill's increased revenue. That speech so moved Greg Stumbo that he walked over to Siler, shook his hand, and told his house colleagues that they would *not* be committing political suicide if they voted for my tax increase.

I think Williams was sincere when he told me in December 1999 that he would support substantive tax reform. Before the 2000 legislative session began, he told the media that he and his caucus intended to cooperate with the Democrats in the house and the governor's office and that they would not be obstructionists. However, I guess I can understand Williams's change of heart. He was in a tough spot. He had risen like a phoenix in the Republican caucus after being relieved of his preferred committee assignments and treated like a pariah when he bucked senate minority leader John Rogers and voted for KERA in 1990. As a "reward," Rogers gave him the smallest office in the senate, which was not much bigger than a closet. Nor had Williams joined the Republican caucus and the five dissident Democrats to oust Eck Rose from the senate president's chair in 1997, and he had not voted for Larry Saunders as Rose's successor. Prior to 1999, Williams was an outcast in his own caucus.

I wasn't privy to the inner workings of the Republican caucus, so I have no idea how Williams managed to redeem himself and be elected senate president in 2000. His redemption was truly remarkable, and I give him credit for his perseverance and innate political ability. Not many politicians could survive being ostracized by their own party members and then emerge as that party's leader! Williams was politically perceptive and had leadership ability, but he let his new power and position go to his head. I also suspect that Senator Mitch McConnell had a lot to do with the Republicans' position.

The 2000 legislative session was Williams's first as president of the senate, and his hold on that position was somewhat tenuous. At that time, he didn't have the power to dictate to his caucus. Later on, he would. Early in the session he inadvertently expressed his insecurity when he said, "Now, Governor, you can't get out in the state and campaign against the members of my caucus." I replied, "David, I'm going to be a Democrat. I'm going to support my party. But when the election is over, I can work with whoever wins." I'm sure that's not what he wanted to hear, and it may have added to his insecurity.

In the days and weeks after my State of the Commonwealth address, Williams made speeches around the state claiming that he was now against tackling tax reform because it was just a ruse by the Democrats to raise everybody's taxes. Republicans always demagogue the tax issue. In reality, they don't want any less out of government; they just don't want to pay for governmental services. When Republicans are in charge in Washington, they spend like crazy and raise the annual deficit and the overall national debt. They're against governmental spending only when the Democrats are in charge. Funny how that works! Their claim that raising taxes stifles business growth and that government can stimulate business activity by issuing broad-based tax cuts has no validity factually or historically. That economic theory has *never* worked!

After mercilessly flogging us Democrats over the tax reform issue out in the state, Williams sang a different tune when he got back to Frankfort. He told me, "Don't worry. I have to say that stuff to mollify the Republican base, but I'll be there for you when the bill comes up. I've got the votes, but *you*, as the governor, have to sell it." He even gave me the names of the people in his caucus who would vote for it. I thought Williams was posturing when he told the media that although my tax reform proposal wasn't exactly dead on arrival in the senate, it was green around the gills.

From my perspective, Williams made a mistake by not telling me beforehand that he could no longer support tax reform. That would have been the honorable thing to do. He should have come to me and said, "Governor, I know what I told you. But there is no support in my caucus for your tax reform plan and therefore I can't support it." I would have been disappointed, but I would have understood. Unfortunately, he didn't do that. Instead, he played along as if tax reform could pass in the senate and then called me a liar when I told the media about his prior commitment to support tax reform.

In my opinion, Williams deliberately misled the public by claiming that the Democrats wanted to raise everybody's taxes. He intended to use that issue as political fodder in the November elections so the Republicans could hold on to their majority in the state senate. Power is an aphrodisiac, particularly when you experience it for the first time, as Williams and the senate Republicans did in 2000. Williams's focus became maintaining control of the senate. Whether tax reform was needed to help Kentucky move forward didn't figure in his political calculation. The only thing that mattered was holding on to political power, regardless of the cost to the state.

I believe people ought to be able to see some tangible proof of how their tax dollars are being spent. I'm a big supporter of pork-barrel politics as long as it's not a waste of money. Pork, as I define it, is a visible capital project that's a good use of money, but perhaps not particularly important, that is added to the budget by one or more legislators. Pork greases the wheels of government. What one legislator regards as pork might be another legislator's indispensable project. I think individual legislators ought to be able to tell their constituents, "I got you this fire station" or "I got this road fixed" or "I got you this Little League baseball field and public park." They need to be able to show that taxpayers got something in return for their tax money. Tip O'Neill, the late Speaker of the US House of Representatives, often said, "All politics is local." And he was right!

I didn't know Williams had double-crossed me until the house passed HB 996, a scaled-down version of my original tax reform bill, in early March by a vote of fifty-seven to thirty-nine. I should have had an inkling that something was up when the Republican representative from Morgantown, Woody Allen, who voted against the bill, called it a "Democratic tax bill" and predicted it would "never see the light of day" when it was sent to the Republican-controlled senate. He said the Democrats would find themselves "out on a limb, and you will hear the saw and it will be a long fall!"

In early March the house passed the state budget bill, predicated on the assumption that the $178 million tax reform bill would also pass. Early the next day, David Williams, Dan Kelly, and Richie Sanders sat stone-faced in my office and, despite Williams's previous assurances that the tax reform bill would pass in the senate if it passed in the house, bluntly told us that they were against it. At that moment, Crit, Skipper, and I knew we'd been had. Williams had deliberately led us into a political trap and was proud of his chicanery, and that made us mad. Crit said, "David, that's *not* what you told us yesterday!" He chuckled and replied, "Well, that was yesterday."

There was a time when legislators might lie to the press or lie to their constituents, but they didn't dare lie to the governor or to their fellow lawmakers. If they promised to vote for a piece of legislation, they didn't go back on their word. And if they did, there would be very real consequences. When I realized that Williams had *deliberately* lied to us, he lost all credibility as president of the senate with me. He sacrificed his personal integrity to gain a temporary political advantage.

This was the first budget proposal any modern Kentucky governor had presented to a politically divided General Assembly, so the 2000 legislative session was a test of how the new divided government model was going to work. I had consulted senate Republicans and given them the opportunity to contribute to my initial proposal, but when the budget bill arrived in the senate, Williams, Kelly, and Sanders set about "pruning" it. They had already killed HB 996, the tax reform plan that was the budget bill's financial foundation. The problem was that the Republicans had no experience leading one of the legislative chambers, and they had no idea what they were doing.

As a result, Williams and I got into an unfortunate war of words. He flatly told the media there would no tax increases passed during the 2000 legislative session. I responded by telling the media, "We have presented our program to move Kentucky forward. The house modified it a little bit, and now the Republicans have an opportunity to articulate their vision for the future, and we will have to wait and see what that is. They will find, just as we have found, that the options are tough. They're going to use smoke and mirrors, but let's wait and see the whole package." Williams self-righteously proclaimed that the budget bill the senate Republicans sent to the house would be more than adequate. Instead of allowing the senate Democrats to offer amendments to the Republicans' budget proposal, as he had promised, Williams quickly adjourned the senate over the Democrats' objections.

The Republican version of the budget bill cut funding for public schools by $21.5 million, and it cut nearly $16 million from a teacher quality initiative and many other programs and projects that would have benefited Kentucky. Strangely, the senate version of the budget managed to find enough money to hire nine additional full-time employees for the offices of the Republican leadership. Democratic senator Marshall Long compared the Republican budget proposal to a pile of manure. Benny Ray Bailey said the Republican version of the budget was like peeling an onion because it brought tears to his eyes. On the day of the senate floor debate on the budget, I attended a rally by county, city, and state government employees against the Republicans' version in the capitol rotunda two floors below the senate chamber. Echoes from the rally reverberated in the senate. I told the protesters, "If it's a pig's ear, I'm going to call it a pig's ear! The house passed a silk purse, and the senate has turned it into a pig's ear!" The crowd responded with thunderous whooping and hollering.

After a party-line vote of twenty to seventeen, with one absentee (Gary Johnson), the senate passed the Republican version of the budget. I called it "absurd and simplistically irresponsible" because it didn't contain any new revenue streams. I told the media that Williams had put politics over people. He was more interested in using substantive tax reform as a political weapon than in moving Kentucky forward. By this time, Williams and Kelly had decided to jump on Grover Norquist's bandwagon (founder and president of the antitax organization Americans for Tax Reform) and demonstrate that, if left to their own devices, they would reduce the size of state government until it could be drowned in a bathtub, and they wouldn't raise taxes come hell or high water.

The budget bill ended up going to a conference committee in an effort to reconcile the differences between the house and senate versions. At one point during the conference committee's deliberations, senate A&R Committee chair Sanders got so confused and frustrated that he requested a meeting with Crit. Almost crying, he asked, "Can you help us straighten this out?" So Crit and Jim Ramsey worked with the senate Republicans and got the process back on track. The conference committee finally came up with a budget that was acceptable to everyone, or at least one we could live with.

The senate Republicans agreed to pass the tax reform bill, but not in its entirety. Instead, the Democrats and Republicans reached a compromise that imposed a 6 percent tax on interstate phone calls and a 6 percent access fee that long-distance telephone companies paid to local phone companies. In exchange, Williams got the house leadership to agree to decrease unemployment insurance taxes paid by businesses. Therefore, Williams was able to call the tax reform and budget deal "revenue neutral." After the session ended, I signed the bill into law.

In reality, the Republicans had a tough choice: either vote for a tax increase to balance the budget or go home and explain to their constituents why money had been cut for water and sewer lines and other projects those communities desperately needed. They were damned if they did and damned if they didn't. Nobody could declare total victory, and nobody lost face during the negotiations. By the way, Williams's district received more than $12 million in that budget. Republicans like pork too, when they are the recipients!

Tax and revenue experts predicted that the tax increases would generate $89.4 million over the biennium, while the cut in unemployment insurance taxes would result in a loss of $75 million, for a net increase of just $15 million—a drop in the bucket in a $14 billion biennial budget. However, money generated by those tax increases went into the General Fund. The cut to unemployment insurance taxes came from a different fund, and frankly, unemployment insurance will cost whatever it's going to cost. That fund may have been running a surplus at the time, but Williams didn't really save the business community any money. He may have delayed the payout from one year to the next, but it wasn't a permanent cut because the unemployment insurance fund has to pay for itself.

I knew that, so I was more interested in the revenue side of the budget compromise. Instead of the $178 million my original tax reform proposal would have generated, I received half that amount. I wasn't ecstatic about the budget compromise, but I wasn't too unhappy either. You can do a lot of good things with $89.4 million! Early childhood development and adult education were the focus of my second term, and I intended to designate some of that additional money to those areas.

There will always be conflict between the executive and legislative branches of government, whether the leadership is from the same or the opposite political party. That is normal and healthy. I hadn't always seen eye to eye with Greg Stumbo or Eck Rose, even though we were all Democrats, so I knew there would be some conflict over public policy now that the Republicans were in control of the state senate. But I hadn't expected Williams to take that natural conflict to a personal level. I told the media about my pre–legislative session meeting with Williams in December 1999, when he promised that he and his caucus would support substantive tax reform and an increase in the gas tax. When the media asked Williams about our December meeting, he didn't deny the *substance* of what I said; instead, he attacked me *personally.* He claimed I had been inebriated at the meeting and said it was not the first time he had seen me in that condition. That was an out-and-out lie. I admit I had a drink during the evening meeting, but I was not drunk. I offered David a drink, which he normally would have accepted, but he said he couldn't because he had gout. I was shocked by this personal attack, which amounted to character assassination. Honest policy differences and standing up for one's position are to be expected in a healthy democracy. However, this attack was harmful not only to me but also to the state. I was the chief executive, and as such I represented Kentucky to the nation and the world. After his accusations, I considered our relationship irreparably broken. I mostly worked with and through Dan Kelly and had little to do with Williams, although I never refused when he requested a meeting.

I devoted almost 20 percent of my State of the Commonwealth speech to collective bargaining for public employees. When the press asked house speaker Jody Richards and senate president David Williams about collective bargaining's prospects in the 2000 legislative session, they both reacted as if they were passing a hot potato back and forth. Richards said he looked forward to receiving a collective bargaining bill from the senate. Williams responded that it was his understanding that house Democrats would submit a bill. Collective bargaining for public employees obviously had the support of organized labor, while municipal and county officials and the Chamber of Commerce generally opposed it. In reality, I knew that collective bargaining had little chance of being passed by the legislature, but I wanted organized labor to know I still supported collective bargaining and wasn't afraid to state my position publicly. I was also looking ahead to 2004, when I thought I might be running against Jim Bunning for the US Senate, so I was shoring up my support within organized labor.

There is no doubt that Republican control of the state senate affected my legislative agenda and the legislative agenda of the Democratic house leadership. For example, in early March Greg Stumbo filed House Bill 992, intended to adjust the workers' compensation law passed during the 1996 special session. Under the revised law, workers' compensation insurance costs had decreased by 41 percent, saving Kentucky employers more than $300 million. But even industry officials called the legislature's 1996 changes draconian, and I agreed that the 1996 revisions went too far, so I supported Greg's effort to amend the law. The intent of HB 992 was to increase benefits to injured workers who were permanently disabled, expand programs to retrain disabled workers who were unable to return to their old jobs, double the death benefits paid to deceased workers' families, change the evaluation process for black lung cases, and adjust limits on attorneys' fees to address complaints that workers were getting inadequate legal representation. The bill also sought to maintain a competitive environment to control employers' costs.

The House Labor and Industry Committee amended HB 992 to increase benefits for some injured workers. Walt Turner, commissioner of the Kentucky Workers' Compensation Program, said the amendment might double the increase in program costs from 8 percent up to 16 percent. During the floor debate, several amendments to increase benefits were defeated because of the fear that extreme changes to the existing law would jeopardize the bill's passage once it reached the Republican-controlled senate. I didn't support these amendments, and HB 992 couldn't pass in the house without my help. J. R. Gray, a house Democrat from Benton, said HB 992 was the worst workers' compensation bill he had ever voted for in his life, but it was the strongest bill the Republican-controlled senate would consider. Even Johnnie Turner, a Republican from Harlan who had been an army medic during the Vietnam War, said HB 992 did very little to help injured workers, and he said that Kosovo refugees received more consideration. The house passed HB 992 by a vote of seventy-one to twenty-seven.

Prior to the Republican takeover of the senate, if the Democrat-controlled house had passed a bill that the Democrat-controlled senate didn't like, the leaders of the two chambers would hammer out a compromise in a conference committee. Obviously, with the senate now controlled by Williams and his Republican caucus, the house couldn't assume that the senate would even bring a bill out of committee, let alone put it up for a vote on the senate floor. Therefore, the house Democrats had to factor in how the senate Republicans would react to every single piece of legislation they passed. As a result, the house often sent a watered-down version of a bill to the senate. In the case of HB 992, Stumbo was a workers' compensation attorney, so naturally, he was on the side of the workers. The Republicans almost invariably represented business interests. Therefore, Stumbo was just being practical. Rather than sending the senate a bill that tried to correct all the flaws of the workers' compensation law, he sent a version the Republicans might be willing to entertain and possibly pass. When the legislative branch is divided politically, it makes a huge difference.

Even the Republicans realized that the 1996 revisions had gone too far, as they had heard complaints from businesses around the state. However, they drafted a substitute to HB 992 written by Senator Katie Stein from Fort Thomas, and Williams and Kelly tried to rush it through the senate. Stein introduced her substitute bill at an 8:00 a.m. committee meeting without giving the senate Democrats time to read it, and Kelly scheduled the floor vote for later that same afternoon. The substitute bill barely passed. Initially, it failed on the senate floor because Republicans Lindy Casebier and Tom Buford voted with the Democrats. However, Kelly went to work on the two senators and managed to get Casebier to change his no vote to an abstention, which made the vote seventeen to seventeen. Then Virgil Moore, who hadn't voted yet, voted yes, so the substitute bill passed by a vote of eighteen to seventeen, which meant it would go to a conference committee.

Businesses supported Stein's substitute bill. I condemned the substitute bill, and so did organized labor. Among other things, Stein's bill deleted both the provision intended to help coal miners with black lung and the provision that doubled death benefits from $25,000 to $50,000. House negotiators eventually agreed to the senate version, but only after I promised the Democrats that within twelve months I would call a special session to revisit the issue.

I made it clear during the debate on HB 992 that in eastern Kentucky, the November election would be a referendum on that bill. Williams claimed it was unfair of me to blame the Republicans for diluting the original intent of HB 992. He then castigated me for politicizing the issue, saying the revised workers' compensation law I had urged the legislature to pass in 1996 was the cause of the problem. He was partially correct. The 1996 revision had indeed gone too far. However, I had thrown my support behind the house version of the bill in an effort to correct those mistakes. Steve Earl, the political action director for the United Mine Workers, said he thought the issue would cause major problems for Republicans in the coal districts. In fact, I believe the Republicans' dilution of HB 992 was a major factor in the Democrats holding on to two eastern Kentucky senate seats that fall. HB 992 didn't gut the 1996 revisions, and I think we ended up with a more reasonable law, but it wasn't what we really needed.

Another item on my 2000 legislative agenda was fixing the 1994 health insurance law by establishing a high-risk insurance pool. Twenty-eight other states had already done so, and I thought it might be a solution for Kentucky too. Insurance commissioner George Nichols III was a supporter of the idea. People with costly medical conditions and serious or chronic illnesses would be separated from the rest of the state's insurance market and buy their insurance from a high-risk pool called Kentucky Access, which replaced the Guaranteed Acceptance Program (GAP). The goal was to entice insurance companies that had left the state to return and offer health insurance to most people at lower premiums. The state administered the new program, and it was financed by utilizing almost $40 million from the tobacco settlement over the biennium.

Some feared that having a high-risk pool would stigmatize people with serious or chronic conditions and that the coverage cap of $1 million was inadequate for many illnesses such as leukemia or AIDS. Some were afraid that insurance companies would be more than happy to force taxpayers to cover care for the sickest patients, creating a bottomless hole in the state budget. A number of experts argued that it would be more cost-effective and more inclusive to just expand the Medicaid program. They claimed the high-risk pool would benefit only insurance companies, while expanding Medicaid would help Kentuckians, particularly low-income individuals, and would pump $130 million into the state's economy. In making my decision to back the high-risk pool, I relied on the expertise of insurance commissioner Nichols. The bill passed by just one vote in the house and one vote in the senate. In the end, the high-risk pool didn't work as intended, and it was supplanted by the federal Affordable Care Act, passed in 2010 during the Obama administration. Health insurance is a national issue, and it can't be adequately addressed at the state level.

In early March 2000 Dan Kelly and I held a news conference to announce a plan to bring safe drinking water to all Kentuckians within twenty years. We called it the 2020 Plan, and its goal was to make public water available to 95 percent of Kentucky homes by the year 2020. When Dan and I met to discuss legislative priorities, he told me his number-one goal was to increase Kentuckians' access to clean water. Dan had been the city attorney in Springfield, which supplied all the water for rural Washington County, so he was thoroughly versed in the subject of water distribution. Having been a county judge myself, I certainly understood the importance of providing clean water to every Kentucky community. I pointed out that my legislative agenda for the upcoming session was already pretty full, and Dan, exercising his new power as majority floor leader in the senate, expressed a desire that I find time to address the water issue. I had a good relationship with Dan, who was a reasonable man, and we both knew that water was an important issue, so I agreed. We wouldn't always see eye to eye, but I was happy to work with Dan when I could, and this was one of those times.

The plan took shape in Senate Bill 409. Eleven thousand miles of water lines would have to be laid, at a cost of about $1.5 billion, to bring safe drinking water to the 102,000 Kentuckians who lacked access to a clean, sustainable water supply. During our news conference, I pledged to support an expenditure of $50 million in seed money over the next two years, and I proposed routing that money through the Kentucky Infrastructure Authority (KIA). I based the plan on my experience in Pike County, where there had been five or six community water districts when I became county judge. Only one of those districts actually had a water system, and even that one was dysfunctional much of the time. Early in my first term as county judge, I merged all the community water districts into one central water district, which increased service and improved efficiency. Today it is the largest rural water district in the state. It has a professionally run water treatment plant and is a multimillion-dollar operation.

Under SB 409, the area development districts would establish water management areas within their borders to facilitate the development of a regional plan to deliver clean water. Water delivery can't be left up to each community or even each county because there has to be a water source. Sometimes the most efficient way to serve a community is to obtain water from another county. For example, Knott County utilizes Carr Creek Lake as a water source, so we built a regional water supply system that serves Knott, Letcher, and part of Perry Counties. Water districts need logical planning at a regional level to avoid inefficiency and duplication.

The bill also called for water plans to be reevaluated at the county level every five years, with the development districts in charge of prioritizing water infrastructure projects. SB 409 set up an account with the KIA to develop incentive programs to encourage water systems to coordinate water delivery and to merge and provide water service in unserved and underserved parts of the state. The KIA assigned every part of Kentucky to a water district and required each district to serve its entire area. For example, a district's water storage tanks had to be large enough to serve the entire territory, and its water lines had to be large enough to reach the remotest part of its territory.

I induced Roger Recktenwald, director of the Big Sandy Area Development District, to head the KIA. We had worked together in Pike County, and Roger made the program work better than expected. To fund the water plan, we used community development block grants and abandoned mines money, both of which are federal programs the state can use for infrastructure projects such as water and sewer lines. We also used coal severance tax revenue and other budget appropriations to achieve our goal.

Thanks to SB 409, I believe Kentucky provides a greater percentage of its residents with clean water than any other rural state in the country.

More than 95 percent of Kentuckians now have access to potable water. That has led to economic development benefits and has been a boon to the housing industry. In fact, the water plan was such a success that some people resent it because it enabled suburban expansion into rural areas. Fayette County, for example, is trying to preserve its green spaces and therefore would prefer to discourage suburban sprawl.

Dan Kelly deserves equal credit for the water plan. We did it together. It is one of the initiatives I am most proud of. I have long believed that all Kentuckians deserve good water and a good road leading to their residence, no matter where they live in the commonwealth.

During the 2000 legislative session, Republicans passed Senate Joint Resolution (SJR) 57, which reclassified the Ten Commandments as a historical text instead of a religious document. Williams and Kelly thought I would veto the bill and thereby walk right into the political trap they had set for me. The new designation allowed the Ten Commandments to be posted in schools and public buildings along with other historical documents, such as the Magna Carta, the US Constitution, and the Kentucky Constitution. House Democrat Tom Riner, who was a Baptist minister, sponsored an amendment that required the state government to proclaim the Ten Commandments the foundation for all Kentucky laws and called for the placement of a seven-foot-high monument of the Ten Commandments next to the Floral Clock outside the State Capitol Annex Building.

The US Supreme Court had already declared that posting of the Ten Commandments in public schools and on public property was unconstitutional, so I was not about to fall for the Republicans' political ploy and veto the resolution. It was not my job to decide the constitutionality of the Ten Commandments bill, so I confounded Williams and Kelly and went ahead and signed SJR 57, knowing that the American Civil Liberties Union would challenge it in court and certainly win. The press attacked me, but I knew that many Kentuckians supported the language contained in SJR 57, and the Republicans were hoping to use my veto as a wedge issue in the November elections. I don't like playing political games, but that doesn't mean I don't know how!

I have always supported the doctrine of separation of church and state. When I was lieutenant governor, Congressman Scotty Baesler told me that, based on his experience in Washington, the gravest danger facing the country was Christian fundamentalists' influence on the Republican Party. He wasn't the only one who foresaw that danger. Barry Goldwater, Republican candidate for president in 1964 and icon of the modern conservative movement, famously said, "Mark my word. If and when these preachers get control of the [Republican] Party, and they're sure trying to do so, it's going to be a terrible damn problem. Frankly, these people frighten me. Politics and governing demand compromise. But these Christians believe they are acting in the name of God, so they can't and won't compromise. I know! I've tried to deal with them!"

As the 2000 legislative session came to an end, tempers flared, particularly in the senate. Both sides of the aisle were still adjusting to the new political reality of a Republican majority in that chamber. Williams had filed Senate Bill 2 to prevent state campaign contributors from being awarded government contracts, and it had stalled in the house's State Government Committee. Williams accused the Democratic leadership and me of being in league with special interests and claimed we had no desire to turn off the money spigot. Senate Democrats had given Williams the nickname "Little Newt," after former US House Speaker Newt Gingrich, whom the media had criticized for slashing the budgets of social programs and for his "scorched earth" political style.

In late March Williams publicly accused me of trying to oust him as senate president. He claimed I had talked to at least two senate Republicans about putting together a coalition to remove him as president, and he warned that I had made a serious mistake by meddling in the senate's internal workings. I responded that several senate Republicans had approached *me* to express their dissatisfaction with Williams. Given David's reversal on tax reform and his lies to the press, I would have been derelict in my duty as governor if I didn't at least explore his own party's complaints about him. As it turned out, there wasn't sufficient dissatisfaction with Williams's leadership in the Republican caucus, so I dropped the issue. However, I told the media that Williams had changed since his days as a senator in the minority party. David didn't deny that, and he told the press that I had changed too. He was right. I now regarded him as the leader of the opposition, so my conduct toward him had necessarily evolved to fit these new circumstances. In my opinion, he had made a naturally contentious relationship between the executive and legislative branches worse by being untrustworthy and thin-skinned.

Another issue that emerged late in the 2000 session involved legislative pensions. It required some very cagey subterfuge, and although the vast majority of legislators later claimed they had been kept in the dark, I'm sure the leaders of both chambers understood exactly what was going on and gave the perpetrator a wink and a nod. Republican senator Albert Robinson added an amendment to House Bill 389, a routine bill that created a medical benefits plan for judicial and legislative retirees who lived out of state and couldn't participate in the regular health care plan. Lo and behold, Robinson's under-the-radar amendment almost *doubled* legislators' retirement benefits!

Other legislators were aghast and claimed they had no idea what Robinson's amendment did. (I'm reminded of the scene in *Casablanca* when Captain Renault, played by Claude Rains, exclaims that he is shocked to find that there is gambling at Rick's Café.) Afterward, the legislators pointed fingers of blame at one another for this dastardly act from which they all profited handsomely. Williams even tried to blame me and senate minority leader David Karem. Even though all twenty Republican senators had voted for the bill, Williams claimed I let it pass so that I could beat Republicans over the head with it during the fall election campaign. He said Karem had actually asked for the vote that got the substitute bill out of committee and then made the motion to put the bill on the consent calendar so it didn't have to be voted on separately on the senate floor. Karem took offense, accused Williams of rewriting history, and demanded an apology. I think Robinson received the go-ahead to tack on his amendment from Williams and Kelly, who were trying to ingratiate themselves with their caucus. In my experience, Republicans only pretend to be fiscal conservatives, particularly when Democrats are in charge.

I initially wanted to veto the bill, but I changed my mind when William Lambert, chief justice of the Kentucky Supreme Court, wrote me a letter and explained that my veto would hurt hundreds of judicial and legislative retirees who lived out of state and were in desperate need of health care coverage. Therefore, I told the media that it wasn't my job to decide how much legislators should earn in their official capacity. In the end, the voters would hold them accountable. If legislators wanted to double their pensions, they would have to justify that decision to their constituents. Critics might say that I ducked the issue, and they would be right. At the end of the day, I saw no advantage in getting on the wrong side of legislators whose support I would need in the future, particularly with the opposition party in charge of the senate.

On the last day of the 2000 legislative session, as midnight approached and everyone was punch-drunk with exhaustion, both legislative chambers passed House Bill 936, the annual legislative sessions bill, introduced by Jody Richards. It had been tied up in the senate, and everyone considered the bill dead, but then Williams suddenly decided to bring an amended version out of committee. Interestingly, Kelly opposed the bill and said, "It will cause us to become a body of continual sessions." HB 936 called for a thirty-day legislative session in odd-numbered years that would end by March 30.

The senate amendment required a supermajority in each chamber to pass budget or tax bills during the short session. I publicly opposed the bill because it allowed the legislature to tackle any topic during the thirty-day sessions instead of the usual business involving the oversight of gubernatorial appointments and administrative regulations. When Williams discovered that he was one vote short of passing the bill, he threatened to sing Merle Haggard's country-and-western song "Rainbow Stew" until he got the one vote he needed. He promptly received that vote because everybody wanted to go home and nobody wanted to hear him sing. Once the amended version of HB 936 made its way to the house, it quickly passed, and all the legislators made a beeline for the exits before anybody had an opportunity to examine what they had done. An exhausted Richards called me at 1:00 or 2:00 in the morning to tell me that he "thought" the bill had passed.

Leading one of the legislative chambers was a new experience for the Republicans, and there was a learning curve. Although I had a good relationship with Dan Kelly, my relationship with David Williams only got worse. Over the next two years, Williams and his caucus got stronger. They were able to articulate their policies to better serve their own political causes, but those policies were not necessarily in the best interests of the average Kentuckian. In my opinion, Republicans are very good at demagoguery. They're good at winning elections but not very good at governing because, historically, their policies don't work.

Overall, I thought the 2000 legislative session had been relatively productive, despite the Republican-controlled senate. I didn't get everything I wanted, and the Republicans didn't get everything they wanted either, but together we managed to pass a budget we could all live with. We were still trying to figure out how this new power-sharing arrangement would work, and both sides had suffered some scrapes and bruises. I was hopeful that Williams, Kelly, and Sanders had learned from their experience and that we would develop a better working relationship. I was optimistic that the senate Republicans and house Democrats had mastered the art of compromise. If so, the rest of my second term should proceed smoothly, and I should be able to accomplish most of my agenda. As it turned out, my optimism was misplaced.

It seemed that Williams and Kelly had learned an entirely different lesson: the art of obstruction. Power was new to them, but they quickly learned how to use it. Near the end of the legislative session, Kelly told the media that the most important word in the English language is *no*, and that reflected the Republicans' attitude toward compromise and cooperation with the house Democratic leadership and the governor's office going forward. As we were about to find out, Williams and Kelly had become better organized and more skilled at obstructing progressive legislation that would have moved Kentucky into the twenty-first century. If I had known what the Republicans' strategy was going to be, I would have asked for a Kevlar helmet and flak jacket for Christmas that year.

Unfortunately, a national economic recession had begun by the time the 2000 legislative session ended. Without passage of the original version of HB 996, we wouldn't be able to generate substantial new revenue. When the new fiscal year started on July 1, we were already cutting the budget the legislature had passed in March.

I have to mention that Benny Ray Bailey's political career came to an inglorious end in May 2000. The reward for his 1997 Machiavellian effort to chair the senate's A&R Committee and remove Eck Rose as senate president proved to be short-lived. In the May 2000 Democratic primary, Johnny Ray Turner defeated Bailey by more than seven percentage points in the Twenty-Ninth District, where Bailey had won by more than twenty-two percentage points in 1996. I must admit that I inadvertently contributed to that defeat. In 1999 I was making a speech in Hazard in Perry County, which is next to Benny Ray's home county of Knott but not in his district. He was in attendance and, in an effort to give him some credit, I complimented him on his help with a Perry County project. I commented that "it was almost like Perry County had two senators." Turner's campaign consultant turned that statement into a horrible negative ad about Benny Ray. If that didn't beat him, it certainly contributed to his defeat.

Glenn Freeman, another Democratic member of Bailey's cabal, also met defeat in that primary at the hands of Dr. Dan Mongiardo in the Seventeenth District.

First meeting of the Agriculture Development Committee, which I chaired. We disbursed the tobacco settlement money to farmers in the form of grants to encourage the growing of alternative crops. (Courtesy of Kentucky Department for Libraries and Archives, Archives and Records Management Division)

My last administrative team, including me, Judi, my administrative cabinet, and a few other important administrators, was divided equally between men and women. (Courtesy of Kentucky Department for Libraries and Archives, Archives and Records Management Division)

14

Jousting with Republicans while the Nation Goes to War

After the 2000 legislative session, the public relations battle between the two political parties began in earnest. The *Lexington Herald-Leader* and the *Louisville Courier-Journal* took the Republicans to task for being obstructionists and standing in the way of real tax reform. It was a "good government" argument on the part of the newspapers. David Williams and Dan Kelly responded with the erroneous "political" argument that they had stopped the Democrats from increasing everybody's taxes. Ellen Williams, the able chairperson of the Kentucky Republican Party, claimed that her party had prevented half a billion dollars of irresponsible taxes, the introduction of casino gambling, and an increase in the gas tax. That was not true, but the message resonated with voters. (In fact, the house Democrats had stopped my gas tax increase.) "Good government" positions don't attract many votes, but rejecting tax increases sure does, and that was the only goal of US senator Mitch McConnell and state senate president David Williams. They were concerned only with winning the next election—raw power for the sake of raw power, no matter the cost.

Despite Republican obstruction during the 2000 legislative session, we made progress in a couple of areas, one being civil rights. House Bill 347, which required Kentucky's public schools to close in observance of the Reverend Dr. Martin Luther King Jr.'s birthday, passed in both chambers, and I signed it into law. Similar bills had met a lot of resistance in previous sessions, and I believed it was the right time to follow the example of other states and establish a state holiday to honor King, thirty-two years after his assassination in Memphis.

I believe my civil rights record is a strong one. I appointed minorities to my cabinet because I understood the importance of the state government demonstrating racial diversity to the people of Kentucky. I also instructed my cabinet secretaries to hire as many qualified minorities as possible, and they did a good job following my directive. As a result, I think I had a good relationship with the Black community in Kentucky.

However, I didn't stop there. At a conference in mid-April, I signed an executive order to end the practice of racial profiling by all law enforcement agencies in Kentucky. I took this step after a bill addressing this issue sponsored by Gerald Neal, a Black legislator from Louisville, died in the Senate Judiciary Committee during the 2000 session. Lexington police chief Larry Walsh was aware of and troubled by this problem in his department, and Louisville mayor Dave Armstrong acknowledged that some police officers blatantly targeted Black drivers for traffic stops. I also instructed the Kentucky State Police and local law enforcement agencies to collect data on the race and gender of people who received traffic citations. The numbers demonstrated that minorities received disproportionately more citations than whites. I was not naïve enough to think that racial profiling would suddenly stop. But I thought publicizing the issue and raising awareness would make everyone more conscious of it, which might lead to a reduction in the practice. Today, a larger percentage of Black people than white people recognize me, and I believe it's because of my efforts to help the Black community.

It was a presidential election year, and I suspected that the Democratic nominee, Vice President Al Gore, who hailed from neighboring Tennessee, was in for some tough sledding in Kentucky. The state was obviously becoming more conservative, and some of his positions were decidedly liberal. As a Democratic governor, I had to demonstrate at least nominal support for Gore, even though his positions on coal, gun control, tobacco, and abortion were contrary to public opinion in Kentucky.

At some point during his second term as vice president, I met with Gore in his office in the Executive Office Building, located right across the White House driveway. I was there to talk about coal, and he brought out a large graph illustrating how the earth's temperature was rising, going back as far as the last ice age. I told him, "You better be careful, Mr. Vice President. One of these days, you might be begging us to burn more coal to warm the earth back up so we don't freeze to death." He, of course, blamed the rise in temperature on fossil fuels such as coal and oil, and he may be right. But it wasn't a good issue to discuss in the coalfields of eastern and western Kentucky. As the campaign progressed through the summer of 2000 and into the fall, polls indicated that Gore was not well liked in Kentucky. Even among Kentucky Democrats, support was lukewarm.

In 1992 Bill Clinton beat George H. W. Bush in Kentucky by just over forty-eight thousand votes, and in 1996 he beat Bob Dole by an even smaller margin of just over thirteen thousand votes. Four years is a lifetime in politics. That was a different Kentucky, a different candidate, and a different time, and I knew that in 2000, Kentucky wasn't trending well for the Democratic Party. Gore was unlikely to beat George W. Bush in the state, and I saw no need to beat a dead horse. In fact, the Gore campaign didn't think he could win in Kentucky either, so I wasn't asked to do much of anything. As chair of the Democratic Governors Association, I was one of the cochairs of the Democratic National Convention held at the Staples Center in Los Angeles in August. During my non-prime-time speaking slot at the podium, I told a nearly empty convention center that Bush had flunked out of college—he often referred to himself as a C student—whereas Gore would be the "education president." Given Gore's unpopularity, I didn't hold any in-state fund-raisers for him, and Bush ended up winning in Kentucky by more than fifteen percentage points.

Rather than trying to get Al Gore elected president, I devoted my time to regaining control of the state senate and getting a couple of Democrats elected to Congress. The state legislative elections were important because, with completion of the 2000 census, legislative redistricting would be on the General Assembly's agenda in the next full session. Whichever political party controlled the state house and senate would be responsible for drawing the district lines for its chamber.

During the fall campaign, David Williams accused me of handpicking Democratic candidates to challenge Republican senators in an effort to return the state senate to Democratic control. Fourteen senate seats were up for grabs, seven held by Republicans and seven by Democrats, and some experts predicted that the Democratic Party might pick up two or three Republican-held seats. Williams accused me of employing a host of dirty tricks, including withholding state funds for construction projects in Republican districts. When the press informed me of those charges, I responded that Williams was being ridiculous and had apparently lost his mind.

Admittedly, I did encourage Democratic candidates to run against incumbent Republican senators. For example, I recruited Bill Corum, president of an electric cooperative and a supporter of mine, to run against Virgil Moore in the Fifth Senate District. I also recruited Lawrence Kuhl, a banker, to run against Albert Robinson in the Twenty-First Senate District because I thought Robinson was vulnerable after the media's exposure of his amendment to double legislators' pensions. As the titular head of the Kentucky Democratic Party, it was my job to support the party's candidates. It was my duty as a Democrat to help my party retake control of the state senate, and heading into the 2000 election, my staff and I still didn't recognize how conservative Kentucky had become.

However, I *never* used state funds allocated for construction projects to obtain political advantage in an election. That would have crossed the line between the governor's political role as the leader of his party and his governing role as chief executive of the state. Williams's accusations were misleading at best, and regarding my use of state funds as a cudgel, they were downright false. After that, things got ugly between us.

Prior to Williams's election as senate president, he often stopped by the governor's office to have private conversations with Skipper and me. He was our eyes and ears in the Republican caucus. He advised us how his caucus was likely to react to some of our proposals. Williams was smart, mild-mannered, and congenial. One day during my first term I said, "David, you ought to plan on running for governor after I'm out of office. The next governor is going to be a Republican. Democrats will have held the office for thirty-two years. That's just too long." He responded, "Governor, I don't want to be governor. I just want to be the president of a Republican-controlled senate." I thought he was crazy. I knew there was going to be a Republican governor, but I never thought Republicans would control the senate. How little I knew.

After Williams became president of the senate, the power associated with that office changed him dramatically, and he became someone I didn't recognize. I always aimed my criticism at David Williams the *political leader* of the state senate, not David Williams the *person*. At least, that was my intent. Apparently, he didn't interpret it that way.

Williams's worries about the outcome of the November elections turned out to be unnecessary. Despite my recruiting efforts and my alleged "dirty" campaign tactics, the Republicans held on to their slim twenty-to-eighteen majority in the state senate. If those results were any indication, my "dirty" campaigning was not very effective.

After the election, Williams said he was ready to let bygones be bygones, but I was through dealing with him on a personal basis. He had repeatedly proved to me that I couldn't trust him. I still interacted with Williams when I met with the senate leadership as a group. I was courteous, but I addressed him as "Mr. President" rather than by name, which had been my custom in the past. He had not only burned his bridges with me; he had also blown up the pilings! He might not have liked me personally, but he should have respected the office I held.

The congressional elections that November were of little interest to me. My major focus was the state legislature. Nevertheless, I supported almost all the Democratic congressional candidates. When requested, I raised a little money for them and showed up at their campaign events. The only one I didn't support was Sydney Jane Bailey, who called herself the "Basket Lady" because she always carried a basket wherever she went. I didn't know her, and neither did anybody on my staff. She ran against Hal Rogers for the Fifth Congressional District seat. She may have been a nice woman with the best of intentions, but she had no chance to win against Rogers. She wound up losing by more than forty-seven percentage points. I may have voted for Hal myself in that election; I don't remember.

I supported Brian Roy, a former Marshall County sheriff and former US marshal, who ran against Ed Whitfield, the Republican incumbent in the First Congressional District. I thought Roy was a good candidate, and I raised money and campaigned for him. However, his defeat by sixteen percentage points made me realize that Kentucky was becoming—or had already become—a deeply red state. In northern Kentucky's Fourth Congressional District, I campaigned for incumbent Ken Lucas, who was running against Republican Don Bell. Ken was a college fraternity brother of mine, and I had appointed him Boone County judge/executive. He was a little more conservative than me, but he had to be to run for Congress in northern Kentucky. Ken won easily, beating Bell by almost nine percentage points.

I also raised money and campaigned for Eleanor Jordan, a Black woman from Louisville who had served in the Kentucky House of Representatives before I appointed her ombudsperson of the Cabinet for Families and Children. She was running against Republican incumbent Anne Northup in the Third Congressional District. I didn't think Eleanor had much chance of winning, even though the Third District had several Black precincts and a strong union presence. The reality was that the working-class white people who lived in the district just weren't ready to vote for a Black woman. Even though I supported Eleanor, and President Bill Clinton came to Louisville to campaign for her, she lost by more than eight percentage points.

One of the most important outcomes of the 2000 election was that the voters approved (by four percentage points) the constitutional amendment allowing annual sessions of the state legislature. Annual legislative sessions are a good thing. The legislature's job is to make public policy decisions, and in a rapidly changing world, that is practically a full-time job.

During the 2000 legislative session, the General Assembly passed, and I signed into law, the Kentucky Innovation Act to attract high-tech startups and help the state transition away from its traditional agricultural, coal, and textile economy. The tobacco settlement agreement had been the death knell for Kentucky's tobacco farmers, the coal industry was slowly declining, and the North American Free Trade Agreement (NAFTA) had opened the floodgates for textile manufacturers to relocate their operations to Mexico and Central America, where labor was much cheaper and environmental regulations were less stringent or nonexistent. The Kentucky Innovation Act created the New Economy Program and established the Kentucky Innovation Commission to advise lawmakers on how to make the state more competitive in a knowledge-based economy.

The New Economy Program was designed to encourage high-tech start-ups to come to Kentucky. For more than a decade, Kentucky had offered a 40 percent tax break to investors in high-tech start-up companies. However, only three investment partners had actually claimed the credit, which I found particularly confounding and frustrating. The tax break meant that an investor could establish a million-dollar qualifying company in Kentucky for $600,000. As a former business owner myself, I thought that was a great incentive, but it hadn't spurred the kind of investment the legislature had envisioned.

I appointed a four-person search committee, led by state budget director Jim Ramsey, to find someone to head the New Economy Program. Dr. William Brundage came highly recommended. Brundage, who had a PhD in microbiology from Louisiana State University, had served as president and CEO of the Enterprise Florida Technology Development Board from 1993 to 1997, before his employment as head of the Kansas Technology Enterprise Corporation. Therefore, he came to Kentucky with a lot of experience and expertise. His first task was to determine where Kentucky stood in the new high-tech economy. We could then compare our state's strengths and weaknesses to other states to determine where and in what to invest. One problem was that Kentucky was a very venture-capital-poor state, which put it at a distinct disadvantage.

Once we had identified Kentucky's strengths and weaknesses, I tasked Brundage with developing a business plan that outlined how the state could build a high-tech economy and what it would cost. I knew Kentucky's universities would play a key role. We needed to create a large pool of highly educated workers, and we needed to increase the number of scientific researchers in the state. It was Brundage's job to figure out how to accomplish that.

As part of his business plan, Brundage suggested that we create a handful of innovation and commercialization centers to help entrepreneurs access technology, develop business plans, conduct market research, find qualified management, and raise money. I totally supported that plan, and we established about half a dozen centers around the state before I left the governor's office. The idea was to give high-tech start-ups a physical location to begin their operations and provide them with secretarial and janitorial staff, as well as office equipment such as desks, telephones, copiers, and fax machines, until they were financially able to stand on their own two feet. Some of these high-tech start-ups were just getting off the ground when I left office. With Ernie Fletcher's election as governor, funding for these centers ended. Only he knows why he did that, but I'm guessing that petty partisan politics played a role.

In my State of the Commonwealth address to the General Assembly in early January 2001, I listed tax reform, workers' compensation reform, environmental cleanup, and mandatory solid waste collection as my top priorities for the legislature's first thirty-day session. When I mentioned the need for comprehensive, revenue-neutral, bipartisan tax reform, I received a standing ovation from the majority of legislators. The one legislator who sat on his hands was David Williams, who told the media he was not interested in passing tax reform, period.

Not long into the legislative session, Williams managed to embarrass me after the *Louisville Courier-Journal* published a story about a $30 million discretionary fund called the Highway Construction Contingency Account (HCCA). It had been created in 1990 during Wallace Wilkinson's administration, and it had never been audited. The newspaper reported that Mountain Enterprises, owned by Leonard Lawson, a political supporter of mine, had received 40 percent of those funds. It also reported that since my election in 1995, I had spent 19 percent of the money on projects in Pike County, where I'm from. Many legislators were unaware that such a fund existed, and Williams told the media that I had turned the HCCA into a slush fund to reward my political friends and supporters. He vowed that, going forward, he and his caucus would oversee spending from that account. The truth was, Williams was right, *if* someone wanted to look at it that way. Technically, the secretary of the Transportation Cabinet controlled the HCCA, but the secretary reported to me. The HCCA was my fund to use as I saw fit, and I spent the money on road projects wherever I identified a need. Most of those projects happened to be in eastern Kentucky in general and Pike County in particular, where Lawson's company controlled the majority of the blacktopping jobs. Money from the HCCA was spent wherever it was needed. It wasn't about doing Lawson a favor. It was about helping the people who needed it most.

I had a lot of friends and supporters who were county judges, and if they needed $100,000 for a worthy road project, I was happy to help them. As a former county judge, I understood how important roads are. Lawson benefited because he happened to be the only road contractor in eastern

Kentucky with the capacity to supply the necessary blacktop. So technically, I suppose you could call the HCCA a slush fund that I used to help some of my county judge friends and supporters. I certainly had more of those in eastern Kentucky than elsewhere, but as far as I know, all the money went toward worthy and necessary road projects and involved no graft or corruption. If that was the wrong thing to do, I plead guilty without remorse.

Due to the *Courier-Journal*'s exposé on the HCCA, Williams sought to impose greater legislative oversight of the executive branch of government. For example, he sponsored Senate Bill 60 during the 2001 short session, which would have required the governor's executive orders dealing with the reorganization of government or official state policy to be cataloged and postponed for thirty-five days from their effective date. The bill also would have given subpoena power to legislative committees, along with the power to compel testimony, under oath, through a majority vote of the committee; increased senate membership on several house and senate oversight committees; prohibited the use of emergency administrative regulations to impose or increase fees or taxes; and created a new joint committee to oversee spending by the Transportation Cabinet. The Democratic leadership in the house had no problem killing SB 60.

I ended up suing the legislature when Williams claimed that the General Assembly had the power to review executive branch regulations. In early January 2002 Franklin County Circuit Court judge William Graham ruled that the General Assembly's method of overturning administrative regulations was unconstitutional, and he took away the legislature's veto power. This might have seemed mundane to the average person, but it was an important constitutional and administrative issue. The legislature has a constitutional oversight role over the executive branch, but it can't take actions that lie solely within the executive branch's purview. Executive orders, which usually clarify an existing law, are such actions. If a governor issues an executive order that the legislature thinks is contrary to an existing law, the legislature can sue the executive branch and let the court issue a ruling. If the legislature disagrees with the court's ruling, it can clarify the law during its next session, and there's nothing the executive branch can do about it. In this case, Williams was trying to encroach on the executive branch's power, not the other way around. Williams's purpose in sponsoring SB 60 was to enhance the Republican Party's image of being for good government.

Williams had apparently anticipated Judge Graham's ruling because he had already drafted Senate Bill 1, which revised the legislature's regulatory review process. Rather than voting on regulations one at a time, the General Assembly would vote on regulations in a batch. SB 1 also contained some provisions that encroached on the executive branch's power, including greater oversight of executive orders. In reality, I think Williams was just exerting his power as senate president and trying to demonstrate his political strength to his caucus and to me.

In early September 2001 house minority leader Jeff Hoover and senate president Williams sent yet another signal that they intended to interfere in the executive branch's business. They questioned why I had hired forty-seven people—adding to the sixty-three employed in the governor's office since my first term started in 1996—and doubled the payroll. Over the years, I had added ten special functions to my office pertaining to agricultural policy, early childhood development, domestic violence, and others, as well as reopening Kentucky's office in Washington and undertaking two economic development initiatives in Appalachia. Hoover and Williams thought I might be trying to control functions previously managed by existing state agencies to circumvent legislative oversight. They also wondered why twenty-three of my office staff earned salaries of $80,000 or more. Hoover questioned whether I was adding to my office staff as a form of political patronage. He and Williams indicated that they intended to scrutinize the budget of the governor's office during the 2002 legislative session.

In reality, by transferring staff from state agencies to the governor's office, I streamlined the chain of command. For those issues in which I had a personal interest, I wanted someone nearby to reduce the response time needed to answer a question or get something done. By having someone with expertise right in my office, I didn't have to go through a cabinet secretary and wait while the secretary drilled down through layers of bureaucracy to find someone who had the answer I needed. I didn't have the patience for that. I admit that I wasn't averse to bypassing the chain of command and following my gut instinct, which usually turned out to be right. I was a hands-on administrator, so I didn't have too much respect for the chain of command in the first place. I wasn't adding to the size of the state government by increasing the staff in the governor's office, but I was transferring more responsibilities to my office. It had nothing to do with circumventing legislative oversight, as Hoover and Williams charged.

During the 2001 legislative session, I asked Greg Stumbo to sponsor House Bill 132, yet another attempt to fix the workers' compensation law. The intent of HB 132 was to relax the disability restrictions on coal miners suffering from black lung. It would have required either evidence of breathing impairment or X-ray evidence of lung problems, but not both, to diagnose black lung. The bill also promoted the presumption that if miners had at least fifteen years on the job, their disability was undoubtedly the result of mining coal, with the coal industry shouldering the increased cost of benefits. Even with these provisions, organized labor criticized the bill for not going far enough. HB 132 passed in the house by a vote of sixty-four to thirty-two, after house Republicans tried unsuccessfully to water it down.

However, once HB 132 reached the senate, Katie Stine, the Republican chair of the Economic Development, Tourism, and Labor Committee, said the bill was too complex to study during the short legislative session. She refused to bring it up for a vote in her committee, even though I appeared before the committee and pleaded for the bill's passage. I believe she got her marching orders from David Williams, who told the media that HB 132 was just my attempt to appease labor groups and my critics in eastern Kentucky. The next day, after lobbying by labor leaders and Democrats, two Republicans agreed to join the eighteen Democrats in a procedural move that would have forced a floor vote on HB 132. However, Williams got wind of what was about to occur and quickly adjourned the senate. I thought his conduct was shocking and unconscionable.

I never understood why Williams's opposition to me always seemed so personal. If he was trying to protect businesses by keeping workers' compensation insurance costs low, he should have just said so. His actions indicated that he had adopted Mitch McConnell's "scorched earth" political strategy. HB 132 was dead as a doornail, and workers' compensation reform would have to wait until the next legislative session.

Near the end of January 2001, I unveiled the solid waste plan I wanted to implement statewide. I persuaded Larry Clark, a Democrat from Louisville, to sponsor House Bill 237, which called for every county to offer universal, mandatory garbage pickup by January 1, 2003. I thought that would give all 120 counties more than eighteen months to prepare. To ensure compliance, counties that didn't participate would be penalized by losing state grants and 10 percent of state road plan money.

When HB 237 got to the senate, Republicans resisted it for a reason that actually surprised me. Majority floor leader Dan Kelly said HB 237 was unfair because it required the counties to come up with the money to collect garbage and clean up dumps. Instead, he suggested that the state fund the dump cleanup program to the tune of $35 million over a five-year period. He later suggested that the state could finance the plan by selling $26 million in bonds or by dipping into the state's $30 million HCCA, the same money Williams had characterized as my slush fund. I guess it's okay to use a slush fund if it scores political points for Republicans.

When HB 237 came out of the senate's Agriculture and Natural Resources Committee, chair Ernie Harris had stripped the mandatory garbage collection provision. This emasculated the bill because it wouldn't get to the root of the state's solid waste problems. The Republicans' version also stuck the state with the cost of cleaning up illegal dumps. Democratic senator Marshall Long, who was respected in both legislative chambers, ridiculed the Republican version as "garbage." I told the media the Republicans had chosen the most expensive way to address the issue, and their plan wouldn't work. I knew what I was talking about because, as county judge, I had ridden on the back of a garbage truck in Pike County. I said the house Democrats would never pass the Republican version of the bill, and even if they did, I would never sign it. Because the bill had a revenue component, it needed twenty-three votes to pass in the senate during the short session, not a simple majority. Fortunately, the Republican version of the bill failed on a straight party-line vote, twenty to eighteen. Williams told the media that he had offered a compromise—agreeing to require mandatory garbage collection in counties that showed no progress in cleaning up dumps after three years—but I had rejected it. That was true: I rejected his proposal because he refused to clarify what he meant by "no progress." I hadn't just fallen off a tobacco wagon. I was well aware that Williams was a sharp attorney with more than a working knowledge of legalese. I wasn't a lawyer, but the phrase "no progress" seemed to offer a lot of wiggle room, so for me, it was no deal! HB 237 didn't pass in 2001, even though Kentucky had an estimated three thousand illegal dumps. After the short session ended, I took the media on a tour of five of those illegal dump sites, three of which just happened to be in Williams's district.

The first thirty-day legislative session turned out to be a bust. Not one significant piece of legislation was passed. The senate Republicans had tossed my two main agenda items—workers' compensation reform and mandatory garbage collection—in the wastebasket. Senator Tim Shaughnessy called the session a disaster, but I preferred to classify it as an adjustment period. We were still learning how to negotiate a divided government with the Democrats controlling the house and the Republicans controlling the senate.

During the 2001 legislative session, two things became clear. First, I was not going to have any kind of working relationship with senate president David Williams, who was trying to exert power rather than influence. Exerting *influence* is being willing to compromise: you get something, and I get something. Exerting *power* is what dictators resort to when they have no influence. In my opinion, Williams never understood the difference. Second, it became clear that the house Democratic leadership and the senate Republican leadership did not like or trust each other, which was going to make bipartisan compromise difficult if not impossible going forward.

At the end of March I signed an executive order that created the Certi-fied Clean County Program to temporarily circumvent the legislative pro-cess when it came to illegal dumps. My executive order gave Kentucky counties incentives to clean up illegal waste sites, and I promised to reim-burse 75 percent of the direct expenses incurred by participating counties. I decided to take Kelly's advice and funded the program by tapping into the HCCA and redirecting discretionary money in the Kentucky Infrastructure Authority Fund. When state inspectors determined that a county no longer had any illegal dumps, it would be certified a clean county. We installed "Certified Clean County" signs along roads, which officials considered a badge of honor. Those signs told everyone traveling through the county that it was an environmentally friendly place. Even though I've been out of the governor's office a long time, I still see some of those signs today.

Primary and secondary education was another issue that caught my interest in 2001. President George W. Bush's inauguration took place on January 20, 2001, and within his first month in office, he called a meeting at the White House for more than a dozen education leaders from around the nation, including six governors. I was very flattered to be included in that group. After listening to what President Bush and Secretary of Educa-tion Rodney Paige had to say, I was very pleased that one of the adminis-tration's first initiatives would involve elementary and secondary education. Both the president and the secretary appeared to be well informed regard-ing the problems faced by schools, particularly in states like Kentucky. I agreed with their approach, which advocated less detailed micromanage-ment and decision making from Washington and more flexibility to let the individual states attain their own educational goals. I was optimistic and hopeful that federal help was on the way.

Not long afterward, President Bush introduced his No Child Left Behind (NCLB) initiative—based on the idea that individual results in the classroom could be improved by setting high standards and implementing measurable metrics to reach defined objectives. To receive federal funds for schools, states had to test all students at individual grade levels and dem-onstrate improvement over time. There was one problem: states were per-mitted to develop their own standards and tests to assess basic skills. Unfortunately, many states made their tests too easy to avoid a loss of fed-eral funds.

Every year in late February, the National Governors Association (NGA) held its annual meeting in Washington, and it was customary for the sit-ting president to meet with the governors to discuss federal-state relations. This was an opportunity for the president to hear firsthand the challenges faced by each state, and it allowed the president to give the governors a heads-up about the administration's planned initiatives that would affect them. In our meetings with President Clinton, we had sat around tables in the State Dining Room at the White House. The press took photographs before being ushered out by the press secretary. Then Clinton and the governors spent a couple of hours having a frank discussion about national policy and events taking place in the individual states. The Bush White House intended to change that format. President Bush would make a short speech and then exit, leaving his staff to carry on the discussion with the governors. This gave us the impression that we weren't important enough to warrant more time with Bush. There was almost an open revolt among the Democratic governors, and some of the Republican governors didn't like it too much either. We made such a ruckus that President Bush agreed to make a short speech and then take a few questions.

My optimism about NCLB had evaporated by the time the NGA met the following year. We realized that federal funds would not be forthcoming to support the remedial programs needed to implement NCLB. As a result, the Republicans knew this would be a rough session for the president. At the start of the question-and-answer period, President Bush recognized only Republican governors, and they asked about international affairs and other subjects with little relevance to the duties of a governor, in an effort to avoid NCLB. Democratic governor Ronnie Musgrove from Mississippi stood up at every opportunity, eager to ask a question, but Bush never recognized him. After several attempts, Ronnie decided to keep standing so the president had no choice but to recognize him. "Okay, Ronnie," Bush said, "what's your question?" Ronnie stated, "Mr. President, the best I can figure is that you've given us money to test all of these students to *discover* their deficiencies, but no money to *correct* those deficiencies." Bush replied, "Well, that's exactly right! We're going to find out what you're doing wrong, and then we're going to make you straighten it out." That pretty much ended the question-and-answer session.

NCLB also had a school voucher component that I disliked because it put the interests of individual children above the interests of society as a whole. A voucher system only increases society's division into the haves and the have-nots. When the wealthy and the intellectual elites take their children out of public school, they are no longer interested in funding public education; this leads to a deterioration of the public school system, to the detriment of society. Of course, Republicans tend to support voucher systems because they *want* society to be ruled by an aristocracy. I don't think that's the best system of government in what purports to be a democratic republic.

Once I really understood NCLB and how it was going to be administered, I realized it wasn't as good as I had originally thought. Under the Kentucky Education Reform Act (KERA), we were already doing the testing required by NCLB. Since each state could establish its own testing standards, there was nothing to prevent a state from establishing low standards to make itself look good. Under KERA, Kentucky had some of the highest standards in the nation, and we didn't want to compromise them. Therefore, Kentucky ran the risk of losing federal funds because it had higher standards than most other states! It was an unfair and inequitable law. NCLB wasn't the progressive program for education it could and should have been.

By the spring of 2001, the Consensus Forecasting Group (CFG) predicted at least a $117 million budget shortfall in fiscal year 2001 and a $300 million shortfall by the end of fiscal year 2002. In addition to dipping into the Rainy-Day Fund for the first time since it was created, I told all state agencies to prepare for a 2 to 4 percent budget reduction. I wanted to spare primary and secondary education as well as higher education from budget reductions, but otherwise, I favored across-the-board budget cuts, which probably wasn't the best approach. I should have analyzed state programs to determine which ones were not worth continuing, but I took the expedient route and called for cuts to all non-education-related parts of the state budget.

In mid-May I decided to fulfill a campaign pledge to organized labor to allow union representation for public employees. I knew the Republican-led senate would never agree, so I signed an executive order that allowed the more than thirty thousand state employees to choose unions to represent them on a new governor's advisory council. My executive order didn't require the collection of union dues, negotiation, or binding arbitration, so it was really just a first step in getting public employees into the collective bargaining process. However, my action drew sharp criticism from the Republicans, who said I was circumventing the legislative process. This was not true. I was just formalizing a new method of communicating with my employees. I thought it was important to honor my commitment to state employees, even if my executive order lacked teeth. I still didn't believe public employees should be able to strike, but I strongly believed they had a right to be represented by a union. My executive order gave unions a foot in the door, and the Public Employee Alliance of Kentucky, a pro-union organization, immediately sent those thirty thousand state employees an informational pamphlet that explained the benefits of unionization. Many state employees eventually joined the Kentucky Association of State Employees (KASE), but enrollment was strictly voluntary.

On September 10, 2001, I hosted a meeting of the Southern Governors' Association at the Marriott Griffin Gate Hotel in Lexington. Vice President Dick Cheney was a featured speaker, and he touted President Bush's huge tax cut. Cheney claimed the tax cut protected Social Security and Medicare, and anyone who said otherwise was misleading senior citizens. I thought Cheney was being disingenuous. We now know that Bush wanted to privatize Social Security, and he pushed his Medicare Part D prescription drug plan through Congress but didn't allocate any additional money for it. Some well-respected economists and political pundits speculated that the Republicans' real intent was to bankrupt Medicare as a way to abolish it, and I agreed with them.

The Republican mantra is to tell the American people not what they *need* to hear but what they *want* to hear, while distorting the truth. The Republicans have perfected this to an art form, as proved by their rhetoric on President Bush's tax cuts. They wrapped themselves in the American flag and told the American people that the tax cuts would pay for themselves by encouraging economic growth. That was bunkum then and it is bunkum now, in my opinion. That economic theory has never worked. The Republicans know it, but they keep trying to sell it to the American people, and for some reason, the people keep falling for it, despite ample evidence to the contrary. So far, Democrats have been unable to convince the American people that the theory of trickle-down economics is a cruel hoax, but I still hold out hope.

While in Lexington, Vice President Cheney also attended two Republican fund-raisers, one for the Republican National Committee and another for Congressman Ernie Fletcher, who later succeeded me as governor. As the official host of the conference, I spent only a few minutes in casual conversation with Cheney before I introduced him, but I know for a fact that terrorists attacking our country was not on our minds on September 10. Later that day, Cheney flew back to Washington.

September 11, 2001, is a date seared in the national memory, as is December 7, 1941, and November 22, 1963. I arrived at the Marriott Griffin Gate Hotel for the start of the second day of the conference, and as I was going over the day's agenda with three or four other governors, somebody entered the room and said a plane had crashed into one of the towers of the World Trade Center. I remember saying, "Oh, that's awful." We assumed it was a small private plane and went back to work. A few minutes later, another person rushed in and said a second plane had crashed into the other tower of the World Trade Center. We all jumped up and went to a small room with a television set. A few minutes later we learned that another plane had struck the Pentagon.

At that moment, all hell broke loose! We realized the country was under attack, but nobody knew who was responsible or when the attack would end. The sixteen other governors and their spouses wanted to leave for their home states immediately. Most of them had flown to Lexington in government planes, but the federal government had grounded all commercial and private aircraft. There was no way for the other governors to get home unless they were from a nearby state and had driven to the conference. I had the governors and their spouses taken to Kentucky State Police headquarters at the old Ramada Inn in Frankfort. From there we established a relay system, utilizing each state's police force or highway patrol to transport the governors to the next state, moving them one step closer to home. It was a great example of teamwork and interstate cooperation during a national emergency.

I couldn't believe that people turned commercial airliners into weapons and deliberately sacrificed themselves and thousands of innocent people for a cause I couldn't begin to accept or understand. I was horrified, and I felt powerless as I watched the Twin Towers collapse. It was eerie not to see or hear a single aircraft in the sky. It wasn't until the next day that I began to feel rage. I knew that whoever the terrorists were, they would pay a terrible price for what they had done. Before September 11, many people were unaware of the threat posed by Islamic terrorism. Kentucky had many vulnerable targets that would be attractive to jihadists. The military stored nerve gas at the Bluegrass Army Depot in Madison County. Uranium was stored at the Paducah gaseous diffusion plant. Ashland Incorporated had many oil and natural gas storage tanks around the state. Louisville and Cincinnati had international airports.

The State Capitol Building and Annex had a token law enforcement presence. We simply weren't very security-minded back then, but 9/11 changed everything. Although the odds of an ordinary citizen being in the wrong place at the wrong time during a terrorist attack are astronomical, nobody is truly safe. After a day or so, it became apparent that the attacks were over. It was time to get the nation and Kentucky back to a more normal routine.

The annual labor-management conference held at Kentucky Dam Village in mid-September seemed like a good way to let Kentuckians know that we needed to restart our lives and get moving again. Unaware that all civilian aircraft were still grounded in the wake of 9/11, we boarded the state plane and flew to western Kentucky with no problem. However, before we took off to fly back to Frankfort, the pilot contacted the air traffic controller in Memphis to identify our plane and our destination. The air traffic controller practically shouted, "Civilian aircraft are grounded! Nonmilitary aircraft are not permitted to fly at this time! You could be shot down!" I don't know how we flew from Frankfort to Kentucky Dam Village undetected, but the Memphis controller was *not* happy with us. He wouldn't give us permission to fly, so we waited at the airport for an hour or so while the pilot did some fast talking with the Federal Aviation Administration (FAA) in Washington. We were just about to get a motel room to spend the night when the FAA finally gave us permission to fly back to Frankfort. We might have been the only civilian aircraft in the air in the entire United States that day, and I wouldn't have been surprised if our plane was shadowed by a couple of fighter jets. Within a few days, the airways opened again as the federal government tried to get the country back to normal.

A few weeks after 9/11, the chairman of the NGA, Governor Parris Glendening of Maryland, organized a tour of Ground Zero in New York City for a dozen or so governors. We all traveled by commercial aircraft to demonstrate that flying was safe. Ground Zero was a sobering scene, and the wreckage of the Twin Towers was still smoldering. I'm an engineer, so I understand the nature of steel structures. An intensely hot fire can weaken steel, and with that much jet fuel burning in a confined area, the steel holding those buildings together just gave out. When one floor collapses onto the floor below, it creates a cascading event, and the weight of five, ten, fifteen stories crushes the floors below, and the downward momentum stops only when it reaches the ground. Osama bin Laden was an engineer, but I doubt that he expected the Twin Towers to collapse. Fewer than a dozen men armed with box cutters and a rudimentary understanding of how to pilot an airliner killed more Americans than the Japanese killed at Pearl Harbor and shut down the entire country.

When President Bush called for a National Day of Prayer and Remembrance for those killed in the terrorist attack, I had to wipe away tears as I thought of all those families who had lost loved ones. When I addressed hundreds of people at the state capitol, I told them that, as outraged as we were, we shouldn't lash out at Muslims or people of Middle Eastern descent. Many of these people were our friends and neighbors, and they were just as outraged as the rest of us. Threats had been made against a Frankfort pizza shop owner who was of Middle Eastern heritage, and I made it a point to publicly order pizzas from that shop to drive home the message. I think the vast majority of Kentuckians conducted themselves honorably.

After the 9/11 attacks, I supported President Bush's invasion of Afghanistan to topple the Taliban regime, root out al-Qaeda, and capture or kill Osama bin Laden. However, that was happening on the other side of the world, and I still had a state to run. Due to the economic shock wave generated by 9/11, the CFG predicted that the unemployment rate in the state, which had been 3.8 percent in 2000, would jump to 6.6 percent in 2002, and economic growth would be a meager 1.8 percent. Kentucky's economy hadn't been that bad since 1983. This wasn't the kind of news I wanted, but it was the message I received. The 2002 legislative session wouldn't be a lot of fun, but I was looking forward to it anyway.

15

From the Mountaintop to the Valley and Back Again

The economic downturn meant that I was facing another bare-bones budget situation heading into the 2002 legislative session. Therefore, I kept my agenda to a minimum. I asked the legislature to approve a cost-of-living increase for teachers and funding for the three Kentucky scholarship programs. I also proposed to increase the state's bonding authority by $220 million. Of that $220 million, I wanted to use $100 million for school construction and the remaining $120 million to fund the Bucks for Brains initiative. Those were my priorities.

When I proposed the 2002–2004 budget, critics said I put the burden of the budget shortfall on the backs of state employees. First, they claimed that I cut the state's contribution to the state employees' retirement fund by $30 million, reducing the state's contribution rate from 5.89 percent to 3.76 percent of workers' salaries. This wasn't accurate because we used an unexpected windfall from another source to replace a portion of the state's obligation. When Blue Cross/Blue Shield went public, it was required to disburse its equity to policy holders. Because the state pension fund had purchased health insurance policies for state employees from Blue Cross/Blue Shield, it received $61 million of equity. At my recommendation, the General Assembly accepted that revenue as credit against the state's obligation to the pension fund.

Next, critics charged that I cut the mandatory 5 percent annual cost-of-living raise for state employees to 2.7 percent. That was true. However, I was the only governor since John Y. Brown to honor the 5 percent raise, and I did it in the first six years I was governor. In fact, inflation had been very modest during those six years, and state workers' pay and benefits had almost reached parity with the private sector.

Looking back, the budgets adopted for fiscal years 1999–2000 and 2000–2001 included almost unprecedented amounts of new money. However, my other three biennial budgets were tight—or at least they turned out that way. The budget passed in the 2000 legislative session was a good one, but the revenue didn't meet expectations.

I recently analyzed annual revenue in the Kentucky General Fund for the past several years and discovered some interesting things. Governor Wilkinson averaged an 11 percent annual increase in the General Fund during his four years in office. However, even though the legislature passed an almost $1 billion tax increase to fund KERA, it did not fully fund the higher cost of public education in Kentucky over the long run. Governor Jones averaged a 5.6 percent annual increase in the General Fund. During my administration, revenue increased 5.4 percent per year in my first term and 3.8 percent per year in my second term. State revenue actually declined from 2001 to 2002—the first time anyone in Frankfort could remember that happening. Ernie Fletcher had it good financially. His average annual revenue increase was 8.3 percent. Steve Beshear served during difficult financial times: average annual revenue increased only 1.3 percent in his first term and 2.5 percent in his second term. Kentucky had another negative revenue growth year in 2010. Matt Bevin didn't fare much better, with an average annual growth rate of 3 percent. The fact is, Kentucky's revenue-generating structure is wholly inadequate, but no one is willing to stand up and admit it. That does not bode well for Kentucky's future.

One of the major issues facing the legislature in 2002 was redistricting. David Williams and Dan Kelly had asked me to call a special session after the thirty-day 2001 session ended. I refused to do so until the house and senate reached a consensus on their redistricting plans, which they hadn't done. I wasn't going to call a special session so the lawmakers could argue amongst themselves at the taxpayers' expense.

The Republicans filed lawsuits in Franklin County Circuit Court and US District Court in Louisville in an attempt to obtain a court-ordered redistricting deadline, which the courts declined to impose. At the beginning of the 2002 legislative session, Kelly went so far as to accuse me of stalling to prevent the Republicans from gaining more seats in the General Assembly, which simply wasn't true. General Assembly redistricting was strictly a function of the legislative branch, not the executive branch. Once the 2002 legislative session began, I had no role in or influence over the redistricting issue as it pertained to the state legislature.

Congressional redistricting was another matter entirely, and I did get involved in that, particularly as it pertained to the Third Congressional District. The Republicans wanted to expand that district into Oldham County, which leaned Republican. Congresswoman Anne Northup and the state senate Republicans wanted to solidify her grip on her US House seat, and the Democrats, me included, wanted to prevent that. Jack Conway, who worked in my office, was planning to run against Northup, and I didn't want to put his candidacy behind the eight ball right off the bat. In the end, we managed to keep the Third Congressional District contained in Jefferson County, but Northup still beat Conway by more than three percentage points in November.

As the filing deadline for the legislative races approached at the end of January 2002, David Williams's paranoia was front and center when he found himself facing a Republican opponent in the primary. Williams blamed me for recruiting Brien Freeman, an attorney in Corbin and the son of former Democratic state senator Glenn Freeman, to run against him. He claimed I had promised to raise $100,000 for Freeman's campaign, but the truth was, I didn't even know that Freeman was seeking Williams's seat. Williams later claimed that an unnamed person from my office had offered him a deal: I would "persuade" Freeman to drop out of the race if Williams supported House Bill 768, sponsored by Democratic representative Jim Callahan from Wilder, to allow video slot machines at racetracks. Crit publicly denied any involvement by anyone in my administration, and Freeman himself denied any knowledge of it. There was no way Freeman was going to beat Williams, with or without my help. I wouldn't have wasted my time trying to defeat Williams; he was too popular and had too many family and political connections. He was just playing to his political base, trying to generate publicity by claiming to be a victim of my vindictiveness and grabbing a cheap headline or two.

Regarding HB 768, I was aware that racetrack owners and presidents were lobbying for video slots. Alex Waldrop, president of Churchill Downs, told the media that the state would get $1.7 billion from slot machines over a six-year period, based on the bill's provision that gave the state 35 percent of the profits. He said HB 768 was the legislature's best chance to avoid deep budget cuts. Williams threatened that if the house Democrats passed the slots bill, he would assign it to an unfriendly committee in the senate and kill it. He even went so far as to say that deals offered to individual legislators by my staff and horse industry lobbyists reminded him of the 1992 BOPTROT scandal. I don't know about the lobbyists, because they didn't work for me, but I can guarantee that nobody from my office offered any under-the-table deals. I purposely kept a low profile on this issue because I knew that any attempt on my part to influence legislators would backfire, and Williams would relish the opportunity to publicly humiliate me.

I don't think Williams opposed the video slots bill on philosophical or moral grounds. I think he was protecting a particular gambling establishment on the Indiana side of the Ohio River that he was known to frequent. That casino was making money hand over fist from Kentucky gamblers and didn't want to compete with video slot machines at Kentucky's race-tracks. I told the horse-racing people that if they could get Williams to support HB 768, I'd be happy to get on board, but it was not in their best interest for me to lead the charge. In the end, Jody Richards and Greg Stumbo decided there wasn't enough support to bring the bill up for a vote in the house.

The main controversy that emerged near the end of the 2002 legislative session was over House Bill 507, the state budget bill. In January I had submitted what amounted to another bare-bones budget. In fact, Harry Moberly, chair of the House A&R Committee, said he had never seen such a challenging budget in his twenty-three years as a legislator. Since there was little discretionary money to fight over, the house passed my $14.4 billion two-year budget bill practically intact by a vote of ninety-six to one.

Richie Sanders, chair of the Senate A&R Committee, told the media the senate wouldn't be making many changes to the house version of the budget bill, and Kelly echoed that comment. They were right. With only minor revisions, HB 507 passed easily in the senate with bipartisan support. I thought the budget bill was on its way to easy approval. However, when the conference committee met to iron out the differences between the house and senate versions, a major sticking point arose.

The house version of the budget bill contained $9 million to continue public financing of gubernatorial campaigns. During a meeting of the conference committee, Williams and Kelly drew a line in the sand and demanded the elimination of that $9 million before they would agree to a compromise. They knew the house Democrats would never agree to an outright repeal of the public financing law, so they decided to starve it of cash instead. During the conference committee negotiations, Williams and Kelly stuck to their guns and wouldn't budge, and neither would the house Democrats. That is why we ended the 2002 legislative session on April 15 without a state budget.

After the legislature adjourned, the public relations war began as each side blamed the other for the state budget impasse. Nine million dollars might sound like a lot of money, but in a $14.4 billion two-year budget, it really wasn't. The Republicans inflated the figure by saying that if everyone who was considering a gubernatorial candidacy actually ran, the state might have to pay as much as $30 million in 2003. Theoretically, they were correct. The law limited each candidate to $1.2 million for each race, but it did not limit how many people could run. The $9 million in the budget might be enough to finance no more than two candidates in each primary and two in the general election. Kelly said schoolteachers should receive a raise before political candidates received a dime. That message resonated with the Kentucky Education Association, as well as with many voters. The impasse became a game of political chicken between Democrats and Republicans.

Kelly claimed the house Democrats received their marching orders from someone on the first floor of the capitol, meaning me. He was wrong. I supported the Democrats' effort to preserve the campaign finance money in the budget, but I wasn't leading that parade. I was going to be out of office after the next election. Richards was running in the Democratic gubernatorial primary, and he wasn't a wealthy man, so I'm sure that played a role in his defense of the public financing law, but I never discussed it with him. The Republicans were standing fast in preparation for the 2003 gubernatorial campaign, and it appeared that Sixth District congressman Ernie Fletcher would be their candidate. They didn't want Fletcher hindered by any campaign spending limit.

I was content to play a supporting role and take some of the heat off the house Democrats for the state budget impasse. I told the media that I would veto any budget bill that didn't include public financing for gubernatorial elections. But the truth was, if the house Democrats had agreed to legislation that defunded the public financing law, I would have signed it.

I called the legislature back to Frankfort for a special session seven days after the regular session ended, in an attempt to resolve the budget issue. On the second day of that session, I met with the house and senate leadership in my office to try to settle the dispute. I made it clear that I would not agree to a major change in public policy without adequate public input and debate, so I offered a compromise. As the law stood, all gubernatorial candidates were eligible for public financing if they agreed to the law's spending limits. I proposed to limit public financing to $9 million, no matter how many gubernatorial candidates entered the race. Williams and Kelly were willing to accept the compromise, but the house Democrats on the conference committee, particularly Larry Clark from Louisville, were tired of the Republicans' bullying tactics, so they refused to budge, and the meeting adjourned.

Subsequently, at the daily conference committee meetings, the Democrats and Republicans just stared at each other without saying a word until, after an hour or longer, they mutually decided to adjourn the meeting. Since the special session was costing taxpayers $45,000 a day, both sides agreed that continuing the session was pointless, so both chambers adjourned and everybody went home. The special session had been an abject failure, and we were still without a state budget. However, the new fiscal year didn't start until July 1, so there was plenty of time for the senate Republicans and house Democrats to reach a compromise. I believed the house Democrats held the moral high ground and that Williams and Kelly would blink first. I was wrong.

After the special session collapsed and the legislators went home, I publicly praised the house Democratic leadership for standing up to Williams and Kelly. The Republicans took to the airwaves and kept repeating their slogan that public financing was nothing more than "welfare for politicians," which, to their credit, was very effective. Kentucky had become politically conservative, and people were much more receptive to Republican messaging than we realized. In fact, Republicans are generally much better at messaging than Democrats. Democrats tend to be wedded to the facts, whereas Republicans are very good at sloganeering and hammering home a message without much regard for the truth, in my opinion. Williams and Kelly apparently figured they had a winning message, so they were willing to wait out the Democrats, no matter the cost to the state.

As the new budget cycle drew closer, I had several options. One option was to allow a cooling-off period of several weeks and then call the legislature back for another special session to try to reach an agreement before the July 1 deadline. But with no movement by either side, I didn't expect to see a different result until the legislators felt pressure from their constituents. And that wouldn't happen until people started to experience pain in the form of reduced or terminated state services.

Another option was to shut down the state government on July 1 and keep it closed until the legislature passed a budget or the courts ordered us to do something. Constitutionally, the state legislature has only one major obligation and function: pass a state budget. Theoretically, one could argue that if the legislature didn't pass a budget, there would be no money to run the state government, so the governor would have no choice but to close it down completely. Once constituents stopped receiving their welfare checks, black lung benefits, state pension checks, or food stamps; contractors couldn't get their buildings inspected; hunting and fishing enthusiasts couldn't buy licenses to pursue their sports; and convicted criminals were released from jail, legislators would be compelled to reach a budget agreement—and fast! However effective this strategy might be, I didn't think the people of Kentucky should be hurt just because their elected representatives couldn't agree on whether to publicly fund the gubernatorial campaign finance law. If the courts ruled that the state government couldn't operate without a budget, I would shut it down, but I wasn't going to take that step on my own. If the courts had forced the state government to close, I think the Republicans would have suffered politically because they were the ones refusing to fund an established law. Whether they agreed with the law or not, they were obligated to either fund it or repeal it. I could have initiated a strong statewide campaign to pressure the senate Republicans to fund the law, but I don't know how it would have played out. My goal was to spare Kentuckians who relied on government services the pain of a government shutdown.

Another option was to shut down parts of the state government while continuing to operate essential services, such as the state prisons, the Kentucky State Police, and the welfare and food stamp programs. That wasn't a viable option because I considered all of state government essential. If a state government agency wasn't essential, the legislature wouldn't have funded it in the first place, although I suppose one could argue that the state parks could have been closed.

Instead of choosing one of these options, Crit, Skipper, Jim Ramsey, and I decided to try to run the state government by executive order. We were well aware of the important constitutional issues, but we believed we were on solid legal ground. Ben Chandler had previously issued an opinion that, in the absence of a state budget passed by the legislature, a governor could continue to spend public funds for government operations for the protection and welfare of the public, as directed by the state constitution and legal statutes. We thought that sounded like a broad interpretation, and we decided to run with it.

Since the campaign finance law had been the only sticking point during the conference committee meeting, we decided to operate the state government based on the parts of the budget to which the legislators had already agreed, which, for all practical purposes, was most of it. It wasn't like we were going to be spending the state's money frivolously. As governor, the decision was mine, and I made it quickly. I didn't agonize over the legality of my action, although I was certainly aware of the constitutional questions involved. My staff and I identified the problem, weighed the options, and agreed on a solution. Then I made a command decision and issued the executive order. I firmly believe that the buck stops with the guy at the top, and in state government, that's the governor. Once I made the decision, it was up to my deputies to carry it out, and in this instance, they kept the state government running on all cylinders without missing a beat.

I believed then, and I believe now, in the coequality of the three branches of government. I wasn't trying to wield the dictatorial power of a Louie Nunn, Wendell Ford, or Julian Carroll. The legislature had set a bad precedent for future legislatures by refusing to fulfill its fiduciary responsibility to the people of Kentucky, and I was determined to mitigate the damage. I was determined to keep the state government operating normally until a court told me to stop.

After I released my spending plan by executive order, state treasurer Jonathan Miller, with my blessing, filed a lawsuit in Franklin County Circuit Court to determine whether he could continue to issue state checks. Williams asked that he be allowed to join in the lawsuit, and because this involved a constitutional question, we had no objection. On several occasions, Williams had told the press that he had no problem with me spending state money to keep essential government services running. He understood that I was merely adhering to the parts of the budget the conference committee had agreed to.

There were several other legal ramifications related to running the state government by executive order that I intentionally did not address. Normally, when the legislature passes a state budget, it includes language that suspends more than one hundred existing laws for the two years the budget is in effect. For example, a 1982 law capped state employment at thirty-three thousand employees. The legislature had suspended that law in nearly every budget since its enactment, and by 2002, there were more than thirty-seven thousand state employees. Therefore, if the legislature didn't pass a budget by July 1, four thousand state employees would have to be laid off or fired. I wasn't going to do that unless a court told me I had no choice. And, as noted earlier, state employees were required by law to get an annual 5 percent raise—a law that had often been suspended in the past—and my proposed budget included only a 2.7 percent raise. Unless the legislature passed a budget, it could not suspend these laws, which might place me in legal jeopardy. And according to Denis Fleming, legal counsel for the governor's office, I did not have the unilateral legal authority to suspend these laws.

In mid-July the house Democrats offered a compromise when they agreed to apply the public financing law only to primary elections, not general elections. The compromise also would have banned spending on gubernatorial campaigns by the two political parties. I told the press I would support the compromise, although it was not my preferred plan. However, the senate Republicans refused to budge; they still insisted on the total abolishment of public financing for gubernatorial campaigns. The nonpartisan CFG predicted a $176 million deficit in fiscal year 2003, and that grim forecast made the Republicans' "welfare for politicians" slogan even more appealing. The truth was, the Republicans were winning the public relations battle, and there wasn't much the Democrats could do about it. The budget standoff became a fall campaign issue in the state legislative races, with both sides blaming the other for the impasse. However, public opinion polls indicated that the majority of voters favored the Republican position.

Before the Franklin County Circuit Court reached a decision on the lawsuit filed by Miller and Williams, the house Democrats blinked. In November they agreed to eliminate the $9 million for gubernatorial campaigns from the state budget. However, I believe that if the court had ruled, it would have decided that, outside of public safety (whatever that is), I didn't have the authority to spend state money before the legislature passed a budget. But as long as people kept receiving their state services, the vast majority of Kentuckians didn't care about the constitutional issues.

While this drama unfolded in Frankfort over the summer and fall, I continued to prepare for my political future. In early May I attended a fundraiser in Washington for state treasurer Jonathan Miller's reelection campaign. Former vice-presidential candidate Joe Lieberman, Indiana senator Evan Bayh, and President Clinton's former chief of staff Mack McLarty were headliners at the event. Jonathan was a rising star in the Democratic Party and had worked in Washington for Vice President Al Gore. Nevertheless, it was quite unusual for a minor officeholder from a small state like Kentucky to have a fund-raiser in Washington with A-list politicians in attendance. In his remarks as host of the event, Lieberman encouraged me to run for the US Senate. He looked right at me and said, "Governor, whatever we can do to convince you to run for the Senate, we're going to do it. You're a winner, and we'd love to have you here." Afterward, I told the media that I wouldn't mind moving to Washington. At the time, I was riding high in the public opinion polls in Kentucky, and I was full of confidence.

On September 17, 2002, whatever political future I might have had went up in smoke, and even worse, it almost cost me my marriage. On that day, Mark Hebert at WHAS-TV in Louisville broke the story of my affair with Tina Conner. Tina and her husband, Seth, owned a five thousand-acre farm in Hickman County in far western Kentucky. They also owned the Birch Tree Nursing Home in Clinton, the county seat. I had become acquainted with the Conners during my 1995 gubernatorial campaign, when they hosted a reception for me at their home. Like the hundreds of other people I got to know during the campaign, I considered them friends and supporters who were interested in politics and good government. Tina became my political contact person in Hickman County, and she eventually became much more than that.

After the story broke, I knew that I had destroyed not only my political career but also my marriage to Judi. Telling her the truth was devastating.

Judi packed up and went home to Pikeville for several months. With time and effort, we managed to repair our relationship, and Judi eventually came back to Frankfort. The details of our personal struggle are too painful to share, but I'm more than willing to discuss the political fallout.

For months, every time I appeared in public, members of the media asked about my affair with Tina and I tried to answer their questions as honestly as I could. I understood that they were just doing their job. In fact, I never held it against Mark Hebert for breaking the story. He is a fine reporter. However, I didn't think my personal indiscretion affected my ability to run the government. I had definitely been wounded politically, but I wasn't dead, and I intended to continue to lead the state. It took about a month to regain my political equilibrium and confidence as I got used to the new personal and political reality I had created. I knew that I was toxic politically, so I stated publicly that I would not get involved in state politics or campaigning. And obviously I would not be running for a US Senate seat. The truth was, my political career had probably ended months prior to my affair becoming public knowledge, when I began to advocate for a tax increase to avoid severe budget cuts. By itself, either one could be the kiss of death for a Kentucky politician.

In late March 2003 the Executive Branch Ethics Commission charged that I had used my official position to benefit Tina Conner. It alleged that I had helped ST Construction Company, owned by Tina and her husband, get state certification as a disadvantaged business enterprise, which gave it preferential treatment in the awarding of subcontracts for highway construction. Transportation secretary Codell said this wasn't true. The commission also claimed that I was personally involved in the decision to create a job in the Transportation Cabinet for one of Tina's friends. That was true, although I didn't think it was illegal. In addition, the commission charged that I had appointed Tina to the State Lottery Board and her husband to the State Agricultural Development Board for personal reasons. I had already accumulated approximately $300,000 in legal expenses to defend myself, and I wanted to put the entire mess behind me, so rather than fight the allegations, I paid the $5,000 fine assessed by the commission and moved on.

The Republicans took advantage of my scandal in their television ads during the fall 2002 campaign. Anne Northup beat back Jack Conway's challenge in the Third Congressional District, where my approval rating had declined by fifteen percentage points since my affair came to light. The Republicans also picked up another member in the state senate when they took Marshall Long's seat after he decided not to seek reelection. This gave the Republicans a twenty-one–to–seventeen majority.

When the legislature's short session began in January 2003, budget projections were the worst they had been in fifty years. Given that fact, in my annual State of the Commonwealth address I went ahead and promoted the idea of raising taxes on cigarettes, packaged alcohol, and businesses. David Williams described my speech as vague and told the media I had failed to provide leadership. My intention was to encourage the house and senate leadership to develop a dialogue and build a consensus on how to tackle the budget crisis. Even former governor Louie Nunn (a Republican) said he couldn't understand why the senate Republicans wouldn't work with me and the house Democrats to solve the state's budget problems. He understood that unless we resolved our budget issues during the 2003 legislative session, the next governor, who would likely be a Republican, would be left with the mess and would probably have to raise taxes or make draconian budget cuts. That would cripple the Republican Party's chances of retaining the governor's office for the next twenty years. After his election in 1967, Nunn had raised taxes, and it cost him his political career. The taunt "Nunn's Nickel" followed him for the rest of his political life. If taxes had to be raised to solve the budget crisis, Nunn preferred that this be accomplished when a Democrat was still in office.

However, in my opinion, Williams wasn't particularly eager to see a Republican elected governor in 2003. He wanted to be the most powerful Republican in Frankfort, and he wouldn't be if the next governor was a Republican. Therefore, Williams saw no need to provide the incoming governor with additional revenue, whether that person was a Democrat or a Republican. There was no incentive for Williams to increase taxes.

During the 2003 legislative session, it was obvious that the budget had to be amended. Williams and Kelly indicated that they were unwilling to start negotiating until I had submitted my budget amendment proposal. The revised budget I submitted to the legislature in early February called for $570 million in new revenue over the next biennium, obtained by raising taxes on cigarettes, packaged alcohol, and businesses. In my budget speech to the legislature, I said I had been "to the mountaintop of cutting the very heart and soul out of government, and I've returned sickened, saddened, and resolute. I can stomach no more." I told the legislators they could "pay now or pay later. *Statesmen* will step to the plate and pay now. *Politicians* will make the people pay later." Without new revenue, "the people of Kentucky will see what an emasculated government really looks like. I already know. You must now decide. If we raise no taxes, we will put Kentucky back a generation. If we raise taxes a little, it will be like a narcotic, masking the pain but not curing the disease. Those who can't see my vision for Kentucky can have the ugly budget with no new taxes. If you can't see very far, ugly doesn't look too bad. If that is to be the future of Kentucky, that future will be your legacy, not mine." The response to my speech was stony silence. House Democrat Joe Barrows later told the media that my budget proposal was irrelevant. Harry Moberly and Jody Richards said my tax increase proposal would be dead on arrival. Williams said my proposal insulted him. He didn't mention the people of Kentucky or the other state senators. Nor did he mention that I had invited his input into the budget's design and he had declined.

My proposed business tax involved a three-pronged increase. First, I proposed to eliminate the state corporate income tax. It was too easy for multistate corporations to shift profits to states with low or no corporate income taxes. I would circumvent that dodge by imposing small taxes on corporate activity that couldn't easily be shifted to other states, such as hiring Kentucky labor. Second, I proposed a small property tax increase for businesses. Third, I proposed a very small corporate sales tax, based on the amount of sales made in Kentucky. Businesses couldn't hide these figures, and I thought the tax increases were reasonable. However, I encountered election-year resistance from the senate Republican leadership, as well as criticism from a member of my own party, Ben Chandler.

Chandler had been trying to indict me for seven years, since my 1995 campaign. He also sued me in an attempt to prevent the early release of nonviolent offenders from state jails and prisons as a cost-saving measure. Franklin County Circuit Court judge William Graham initially ruled against Chandler but agreed to consider further arguments. As a gubernatorial candidate in the upcoming 2003 election, Chandler vowed not to release prisoners early and not to raise taxes. I understood that Ben was boxed in politically. He had to run for governor in 2003 or get out of politics, and if he ran, he had to separate himself not only from me but also from the Democratic establishment that had run state government for more than thirty years. Although I *understood* why he took those positions, I didn't *appreciate* them. I fired off a letter to him that stated, "Evidently, you have discovered a way to get us through this crisis with no new revenue and no cuts to services that affect the health, safety, and well-being of our people. I request that you share that plan with me and the legislature. In fact, I insist that you share it with us." I wasn't going to let Chandler use me as a punching bag to help his gubernatorial campaign. After seven years of legal harassment, my frustration with him had reached its limit.

A few days after I gave my budget speech to the legislature, a *Courier-Journal* editorial called for me to resign because my affair had caused too much political damage and I was no longer able to lead the state. In my opinion, the newspaper was more concerned with the upcoming gubernatorial election and keeping the governor's office in Democratic hands, and it obviously thought the best way to do that was to get me out of the way and off the front page. That editorial surprised and disappointed me because the *Courier-Journal* had always been supportive of me and the majority of my policies.

I had no input when the conference committee met to iron out the differences in the house and senate budget proposals. I was frozen out, and although I understood that I was in no position to help anyone politically, it still hurt. I remember submitting an idea to Larry Clark, who had been a friend and a political ally, and not even receiving a response. The budget the legislature passed essentially eviscerated the lieutenant governor's office. It took away the lieutenant governor's automobiles, mansion, security detail, and chief of staff, which saved the state about $2.5 million a year. The budget the legislature passed in the 2003 session was out of balance and wouldn't meet the needs of the state, but there was nothing I could do about it. Crit had resigned by that time to run for state auditor, and budget director Jim Ramsey was now president of the University of Louisville, so I had lost my eyes and ears on the conference committee.

When I signed the legislature's budget bill, the lawsuit involving the constitutionality of operating the state government by executive order became moot, and Judge Graham dismissed it shortly thereafter. The answer to that constitutional question would come later when the legislature again failed to pass a state budget during Ernie Fletcher's time as governor.

After the legislative session concluded, I considered calling another special session to tackle comprehensive tax reform but decided against it because of my lame-duck status and lack of interest in both chambers. Fortunately, due to President George W. Bush's massive tax cut, the state received an unexpected windfall of $276 million in federal money, which eased our budget shortfall. We used half the money to cover a projected deficit in the Medicaid budget, and the other half came to the state in the form of a flexible grant. That funding was not recurring money, so it didn't solve the underlying structural problem in the state budget, but it was enough to soften the effect of the budget cuts in the near term.

At the end of May, at the urging of state senator Ernesto Scorsone, I issued an executive order that prohibited discrimination against state government employees or job applicants on the basis of sexual orientation or gender identity. I knew the next governor could rescind the order, but it was the right thing to do. Louisville, Lexington, and Covington had already enacted fairness ordinances.

As my second term wound down, I gave only fleeting thought to my legacy as governor. Louie Nunn's legacy was the sales tax increase and mental health reform. Wendell Ford's legacy was the reorganization of state government and the coal severance tax. Julian Carroll constructed many buildings and highways, increased teachers' pay, and reformed the bail bond industry. John Y. Brown Jr.'s legacy was allowing the state legislature to assume its rightful position as a coequal branch of government and laying off thousands of state workers he later had to hire back. Martha Layne Collins's legacy was bringing Toyota to Kentucky. Wallace Wilkinson's legacy was the state lottery and passage of the Kentucky Education Reform Act on his watch. Brereton Jones's legacy was the gubernatorial succession amendment and health insurance reform, even though the latter was ultimately unsuccessful. I think my legacy will be workers' compensation reform, higher education reform, and the Bucks for Brains initiative.

As the election of a new governor approached, I was ready to leave Frankfort and go home to Pikeville. I had succeeded in doing almost everything I hoped to achieve, with the exception of comprehensive tax reform. Overall, I was pleased with the accomplishments of my two administrations and my record as governor, my personal shortcomings aside. Being governor is a wonderful job, but after eight years, it was time to leave.

The day after the November election, I invited Ernie Fletcher and his soon-to-be chief of staff, Daniel Groves, to the governor's office. We talked for about forty minutes. I congratulated Fletcher on his victory and told him I would help in the transition any way I could. I tried to explain how the political game had changed, but evidently, he didn't listen. Still, it surprised me when Fletcher and his Republican cohorts so cavalierly tried to abuse the merit system as if it were 1967. They tried to oust merit system employees to make room for political appointees, and it ruined Fletcher's political career and his administration. Ernie was an honorable person, but he surrounded himself with political novices full of hubris who thought the rules didn't apply to them. They found out differently.

I don't think Fletcher realized what was happening until it was already out of control, and by then, it was too late. Ernie was a sincere, honest, trustworthy man, and he and his wife, Glenna, treated Judi and me with respect. I don't remember him ever criticizing me by name, and I appreciated that courtesy. During Ernie's first year in the governor's office, the press would call me for comments about something he did, and I refused to take the bait. Finally, the press got the message and quit calling. Don't get me wrong: I didn't always agree with Fletcher's approach to public policy—after all, he was a Republican, and I was a Democrat—but I had been given my time in the center of the ring, and now it was Ernie's turn.

As governor, I tried to advance the ideals of my party at the state and national levels. From the early days of my governorship, I actively sought leadership roles at the regional and national levels. Early in my first term, my staff created a list of state-related organizations that I could join and perhaps lead to counteract Kentucky's image as an economically and culturally backward state and to enhance its national image. In 1997 I became chair of the Southern Growth Policy Board and chair of the Southern Regional Education Board. In 1999 I became chair of the National Education Goals Panel and the Education Commission of the States. In 2000 I became the state cochair of the Appalachian Regional Commission, chair of the National Commission on the High School Senior Year, and chair of the Democratic Governors Association. In 2001 I became chair of the Southern Governors Association, and in 2002 I became chair of the National Governors Association (NGA).

Kevin Goldsmith, who coordinated my national leadership roles for most of my eight years in office, recently reviewed my career with the leaders of some of these organizations. The comments of Raymond Scheppach, executive director of the NGA during my governorship, are indicative of the reputation I established in Washington:

> During my 27 years as the executive director of the National Governors Association . . . , I had the distinct privilege of working with over 300 of the nation's governors. One governor stands out, however, in his ability to rally the other governors as well as other groups in Washington D.C. to urge members of Congress to pass critical legislation. That was Governor Patton of Kentucky, who chaired the NGA from July 2002 to August 2003.
>
> His ability was recognized early when in 1997 he was the chair of the NGA Economic Development Committee, which had jurisdiction over infrastructure. During his tenure, he created the TRUST coalition, which was a huge coalition of state and local governments and private sector corporations which led the fight in 1997 to reauthorize the surface transportation bill. It was a massive bill that reauthorized all transportation programs from highways to transit transportation. Looking back, it was a remarkable achievement to hold together such a diverse group and to get the bill enacted by the Congress and signed by the President.

Speaking to the General Assembly is always an important occasion. (Courtesy of Kentucky Department for Libraries and Archives, Archives and Records Management Division)

Later during his chairmanship, the economy weakened in the United States between the third quarter of 2002 and the first quarter of 2003. President Bush sent to Congress an economic stimulus plan, which was primarily tax cuts for individuals and corporations. There was no fiscal aid for states in the President's initial bill. Governor Patton, as the NGA Chairman, was again able to rally all the nation's governors as well as a large number of other groups to support a $40 billion fiscal aid package for state and local governments as an amendment to President Bush's bill. The amendment with the aid package passed and the entire bill was signed into law on May 23, 2003. Again, this was a remarkable display of leadership.

On a more personal note, the governor was a pleasure to work with as he understood both policy and politics and most important, he was a man of integrity who also had a sense of humor.

Near the end of my term, I served on the board of the James B. Hunt Jr. Institute for Educational Leadership and Policy Foundation Inc., established by former North Carolina governor Jim Hunt, who was also a devoted promoter of education. That appointment supported my national reputation as an education governor. As I prepared to leave Frankfort, I

The Kentucky Derby is Kentucky's day in the sun. Here I'm presenting the trophy to the owner of the 2002 winner, War Emblem. (Courtesy of Kentucky Department for Libraries and Archives, Archives and Records Management Division)

hoped that Ernie Fletcher and his administration would add to Kentucky's national reputation for educational reform at all levels.

After the public inauguration ceremonies concluded on December 8, Judi and I said our final good-byes to our staff and then left for the long drive home to Pikeville. I was looking forward to beginning a new chapter in my life.

I am arguably the most traveled elected state official in Kentucky's history. Throughout my thirteen years in Frankfort, I visited all 120 counties every year, first as chair of the Kentucky Democratic Party and then as lieutenant governor and governor. During election years when I was running for office, I visited every county twice—once during the primary election and again during the general election. I can truthfully say that I have been in every county in Kentucky at least sixteen times.

I didn't know what the future would bring, but I was determined to meet it head-on and do something that was meaningful. Going home and watching television was not part of my plan. I was determined to make a difference somewhere.

16

Life after the Governor's Office

When Judi and I arrived back in Pikeville as private citizens, we quickly fell into our old routine.

Then, on Christmas morning 2005, we suffered the greatest tragedy of our lives: our fifteen-year-old granddaughter, Judith Paige Johnson, had died during the night of bacterial meningitis. The family had shared Christmas Eve dinner and exchanged gifts. Paige, as we called her, wasn't feeling well and laid down on the couch with her head in my lap. She seemed to have a slight fever, but the thought that she was seriously ill never crossed my mind. She was like a daughter to both Judi and me, and in fact, we had legal custody of all three grandchildren at the time. Paige was an innocent child, and her death crushed us. I was going to give her my Ford Explorer when she got her driver's license. No parent should have to bury a child, and Paige was ours. When our son Jan Harvey Johnson, Paige's father, recently died of pancreatic cancer, we had months to prepare, but still, it is a shock when it happens.

In the spring of 2006 our son Chris and daughter Nicki acquired a lease on some coal their uncle Nick Cooley had inherited from their grandfather Jake Cooley. The coal market was strong at the time, so they decided to mine the coal. They had a small amount of money to invest in the operation, and I signed a note for the rest. I became very involved in helping Chris establish and operate the mine. That experience took me back to the old days, and I enjoyed it tremendously. Chris, who lived in Lexington, stayed with me in my town house during the week, and it gave us an opportunity to work together for the first time in our lives. I was sensitive to the fact that I was working *for* Chris. I made an occasional suggestion, but it was Chris's operation, and he was the boss.

The mine worked out well and made good money for a year or two. Once the original mine had nearly played out, the rational move would have been to close it, sell the equipment, and put some money in the bank. However, we were having one of those booms that occur in the coal business once every ten years or so, and there was another seam of coal about sixty feet above the one Chris was mining. It was only about thirty inches thick (generally, that's the thinnest a seam can be and still be mined profitably), but the price of coal was so high that I knew he could make a lot of money in just a year or two. I helped Chris negotiate a contract with Addington Coal Company, a large and reputable company based in Ashland. I knew the owners, and they had supported me in my races for governor. The price we negotiated for the coal was about twice what Chris had been getting. The new mine was also very close to a railroad, so he could sell the coal himself after the one-year contract with Addington expired.

The coal from this new mine needed to be "washed," a process that removes rock from the coal. I assumed the role of engineer and designed and supervised the construction of the washer. I bought the used equipment needed to build it. I had three people working for me, and I occasionally picked up a cutting torch or a welder and actually did some hard work myself—not bad for a seventy-one-year-old man! I really enjoyed that.

In April 2009, just about a month before I would have finished building the washer, Addington notified Chris that it was canceling the contract. Chris sued, but the company filed for bankruptcy, and there wasn't anything more he could do. The coal boom of six months earlier had disappeared, and the coal industry's collapse began in earnest. There was nothing to do but abandon the entire project. The lawsuit was recently settled for a substantial amount, but it didn't cover all the money lost.

I had stayed away from Frankfort since leaving office, but that changed in June 2008 when Governor Steve Beshear appointed me to the Council on Postsecondary Education (CPE), which I had created in 1997. In January 2009 I was elected chair of that organization. At the time of my appointment to the council, it was searching for a new president, and we interviewed three candidates. Bob King from New York stood out. He was an attorney by education. He had served three terms in the New York legislature and had been elected county judge/executive in Monroe County, which includes Rochester. He served as director of the State Office of Regulatory Reform under Governor George Pataki and then became the governor's budget director. He had also been chancellor of the State University of New York (SUNY). At the time, he was president of the Arizona Community Foundation and was on the board of A. T. Still University, an osteopathic medical school in Kirksville, Missouri. I thought King was the clear choice to head the CPE, and the rest of the council agreed. He understood politics, government finances, and postsecondary education administration. He was the right age, had the right kind of personality for the job, and was a Republican, which was a plus because that party held the majority in the Kentucky Senate. King understood the importance of the legislature and was eager to get to know the members. During the 2009 legislative session, he asked me to introduce him to the state legislators, and most of them treated me well, even the Republicans. King quickly realized that Kentucky was a conservative state. He observed that a Kentucky Democrat looked a lot like a New York Republican. We got along great.

Judi and I had taken an interest in Pikeville College for many years, and it had been a major recipient of our philanthropic support for the past two decades. Judi had attended the college, as had her parents. I had been on the board for more than thirty years. We realized that people in the mountains needed access to higher education close to home, and we were concerned about the college's financial health. During my first year in the governor's office, I had played a major role in getting Pikeville's osteopathic medical school approved and funded. As governor, I was able to obtain the support of some influential people for this rather radical idea.

After I left the governor's office in December 2003, the college named me a distinguished lecturer and gave me an office on the same floor as the president's office to house my political memorabilia and give me a place to work, if I so desired. Governor Fletcher intended to refurbish the governor's office in the capitol, and the state agreed to "loan" the college almost all the old furnishings. In fact, I brought the old green carpet, which had been in the office since Martha Layne Collins was governor, home with me when I left Frankfort. The college also provided an office for Judi and her memorabilia right across the hall from mine.

In 2008 it became apparent that Pikeville College was in financial trouble. One of the problems was that the administration was awarding too many scholarships (institutionally funded) and exceeding the scholarship budget. Board chairman Terry Dotson appointed a three-person committee to investigate the problem, and I was one of the three. The first thing we did was examine the athletic program. Once the costs of coaches, travel, scholarships, and the like were added up, there wasn't much left to pay for academics. We had to change that. We looked at the women's basketball program, which cost approximately $175,000 a year, not including academics. Only three of the eleven players paid tuition, totaling $33,000; the student-athletes paid about $9,000, and Pell Grants (federally funded scholarships) and state scholarships paid the rest. Unfunded institutional scholarships paid the remaining $142,000. The men's basketball program had about the same ratio of income to expenses but an even larger deficit. Surprisingly, the football program was not as badly out of balance, but it still didn't generate enough income to support the academic side of the college.

The college allocated each coach a certain amount of money for scholarships. The coaches awarded the majority of the scholarship money to just a few athletes, so their rosters were too small to ensure good teams. Other than men's basketball and men's and women's bowling, Pikeville's athletic programs were not very competitive in the MidSouth Conference, which includes Georgetown, Linsey Wilson, Campbellsville, University of the Cumberlands, Union College, Kentucky Christian University, and other colleges in Ohio, West Virginia, Tennessee, and Georgia. The MidSouth Conference is the power conference in the National Association of Intercollegiate Athletics (NAIA), the small-college equivalent of the National Collegiate Athletic Association (NCAA).

Our committee met with the staff and asked, "Exactly what is it you don't understand about a budget?" The problem was that *we* didn't understand how the system of awarding college scholarships works. Most colleges begin to recruit students a year ahead of time. By about January, they start offering scholarships. Most students shop around at different colleges, and many get several scholarship offers. Obviously, they can't accept all of them, so colleges have to estimate how many offers will be turned down and how much their offers can exceed their scholarship budgets and still come out even. Pikeville College had consistently exceeded its scholarship budget. But because the coaches and the admissions department, which administered academic scholarships, awarded large scholarships to just a few individuals, they were running out of money before recruiting enough students to fill the classrooms. Our committee didn't know this and just ordered the staff to stay within the budget. In the spring of 2009 the college stopped offering scholarships very early and ended up with surpluses in many of the scholarship accounts. It also ended up with a dramatically reduced enrollment: 673 in the fall of 2009.

In 2008 Hal Smith, president of Pikeville College, informed the board that he was retiring. The board conducted a national search for his replacement. Michael Looney took over as president in January 2009 but left precipitously that August, just before the fall term began. It had not been a good year for the college. Enrollment was down dramatically, and the college was losing a lot of money.

A day or two after the news broke that Looney was leaving, I got a call from a young man I didn't know, James Hurley, who asked to meet with me. I had no idea what he wanted, but I agreed. When Hurley arrived at my office at the college, he explained that he was the principal of Belfry Middle School in Pike County. He said, "I want you to help me become the president of Pikeville College." I was a little shocked, and it took me a minute or two to reply. "What really ought to happen," I said, "is that I should become the president of Pikeville College, and you should come here and help me do it." Without hesitation, he said, "I'll do that!" The conversation wasn't much longer than that.

I needed to approach this issue very delicately. Rather than speaking directly to board chairman Terry Dotson, I casually mentioned to another board member, Bill Baird, that it was going to be almost impossible to find a good president under the circumstances, and we didn't have time to go through a long search process. I said I would be willing to take the position for a year, if that's what the board wanted. A day or two later, Dotson called me and said, "Let's have lunch." We discussed the situation, and the outcome was that I agreed to serve as Pikeville's president at no pay for a year, during which time we would try to improve the college's financial position and, in the process, attract a qualified candidate.

At the time, the college president was a member of the board of trustees, but I thought this was wrong. (It is still a common practice at many colleges.) The president is an employee of the college, and if the board needs to discuss the president's performance in executive session, the president shouldn't be there. But if the president is a board member, it's awkward to exclude him or her. So I resigned from the board.

I didn't know much about college administration, but I knew it was different from business and different from government. For one thing, colleges have a tradition of faculty involvement in their governance, particularly as it pertains to the academic aspects of the institution. I didn't know how that worked, so I struck a deal with Tom Hess, the college's interim dean and a tenured professor: I would pay the bills, and he would run the academic part of the college. Hess served very effectively in that capacity until he went back to the classroom in 2020.

James Hurley was a big reason why I thought we could succeed. James had been a star basketball player at Pikeville about a dozen years earlier, and that's where he met his future wife, Tina. She had been a star player on the women's basketball team. James grew up in Perry County, and Tina grew up in the Peter Creek section of Pike County, and they were both very dedicated to the college. I appointed Hurley vice president of enrollment management, and we analyzed how to get the college back on a sound financial footing. Because the college is essentially a tuition-supported institution, enrollment is important. I consulted some of my postsecondary education friends, and they advised me that we needed at least a thousand students in the undergraduate program to support a good liberal arts curriculum.

Pikeville had a large athletic program, and student-athletes constituted about half the undergraduate enrollment. But because many of them
were receiving athletic scholarships, the athletic program was a financial
drain on the college.

In contrast, the medical school paid its own way. It had about three
hundred students, or seventy-five students in each of the four classes,
which is small for a medical school. We generally had about thirty-five
hundred applicants for a first-year medical school class, so it wouldn't be
hard to increase enrollment to generate more revenue. The problem was
that we didn't have room for any additional medical students.

Many people think the college's dramatic progress during the four
years I was president was some kind of miracle. But it was just smart planning and hard work by a lot of people. Hurley and I were determined to
save the institution we both cared about. We focused on increasing undergraduate enrollment and hired another alumnus, Gary Justice, as director
of admissions and financial aid. Justice deserves much of the credit for
the dramatic rebound in undergraduate enrollment. We also wanted to
increase revenue by offering new undergraduate programs, but first we had
to improve what we already had.

Hurley and I completely redesigned the scholarship program. We
modified athletic and activity scholarships and expanded them to encom-
pass other extracurricular activities, such as dance, choir, and academic
teams. We limited the average size of athletic scholarships, generally to
$3,000, but the coaches could award scholarships in different amounts—
giving one athlete $1,000 and another $5,000—as long as they averaged
$3,000. These athletes and most other students also received academic
scholarships, based on the students' ACT scores. The better the score, the
bigger the scholarship. All the institutional scholarships, both athletic and
academic, were unfunded and therefore actually discounts.

Students from low-income families were eligible for federal Pell
Grants, the size of which depended on several factors, such as family size
and income. At the time, the maximum Pell Grant was approximately
$5,000, and many of our students qualified. Kentucky students eligible for
Pell Grants were also eligible for two other state scholarships: a $1,000 Col-
lege Access Program (CAP) scholarship, available to any Kentucky student
attending an accredited nonprofit or public college in Kentucky, and a
$3,000 Kentucky Tuition Grant (KTG), for Kentucky students attending
accredited nonprofit independent colleges. These state scholarships were
funded by proceeds from the state lottery, and because there might be
insufficient money to cover all eligible students, they were awarded on a

first come, first served basis. We made sure that our students and those we were trying to recruit applied early. Students eligible for the full Pell Grant, CAP, and KTG received close to $9,000, which was about the average per-student cost of Pikeville's undergraduate program if we had full enrollment. Students eligible for these three scholarships also received the Pikeville Promise, which paid their remaining tuition. In addition, the Kentucky Education Excellence Scholarship (KEES), based on academic performance, provided $250 to $2,000 a year, which students could use for books, dormitory rooms, meals, and other expenses.

Tuition at Pikeville was approximately $17,000, but we borrowed from the tradition of good-old American capitalism: we doubled the price and then gave customers a 50 percent discount. In academia, that's called the discount rate, and most independent colleges in Kentucky discount their listed tuition by about 50 percent. In 2012–2013, the last year I was Pikeville's president, the actual tuition income averaged $9,000 per undergraduate student. Kentucky students paid close to $3,000, and out-of-state students paid around $5,000.

Hurley and I recruited potential students from eastern and central Kentucky high schools. Having taught in Bullitt and Jefferson Counties, James knew most of the superintendents, principals, coaches, and guidance counselors in the Louisville area, as well as in eastern Kentucky. High school administrators were always happy to let a former governor talk to the seniors and juniors. My talks were generally about the value of obtaining a postsecondary education, and I encouraged students to consider Pikeville College.

We also realized that many students transfer after their first year or even their first semester of college, so we contacted students we had recruited but who had enrolled elsewhere to see whether they wanted to transfer to Pikeville College. When I was president, more students transferred *to* Pikeville College than transferred *out*.

Hurley and I had set a goal of having 1,000 undergraduates enrolled by the fall of 2012. We had 967 in the fall of 2010, 1,201 in 2011, 1,245 in 2012, and 1,313 in 2013, my last year as president.

Shortly after my appointment as college president, I discovered that we had received a $500,000 grant from the J. Graham Brown Foundation in Louisville to outfit patient exam rooms used to train medical school students in what I would call bedside manner. As part of the medical school curriculum, students examine actor-patients exhibiting the symptoms of certain diseases, and it is the students' job to diagnose them. This exercise required rooms outfitted with examination equipment and a sound system, and an adjacent room where the professor could monitor the students through a one-way mirror. Pikeville didn't have such facilities. Our students went to an osteopathic medical school in West Virginia for this training, but they weren't making good grades on the relevant section of the examination administered by the national medical board. Pikeville had already engaged an architect to remodel the first floor of Spilman Faculty Residence Hall, which was very close to the Armington Building, where the medical school was located. The estimated cost was $1.5 million. We already had the Brown Foundation grant for $500,000, and I persuaded Governor Steve Beshear to recommend us for a $500,000 grant from the Appalachian Regional Commission (ARC) to help fund the project. I was confident we could raise the other $500,000.

As a former member of the board of trustees, I knew the administration had been considering expanding the medical school for some time. I asked the dean of the medical school, Boyd Buser, how much we could increase the size of the first-year class (seventy-five at the time), and he recommended adding fifty students. I asked him what would be required to expand the program by fifty students per class, and he said he needed one larger lecture hall, as well as more classrooms and laboratories. I did the math: if we could admit two hundred additional students (fifty per class), the increase in annual tuition income would be close to $6.5 million. The additional cost of educating an extra two hundred students would be nowhere near that. I then suggested renovating all four floors of Spilman Hall to accommodate the increased enrollment in the medical school. A few weeks later, the estimate came back: $4.5 million to modify Spilman Hall and build a stand-alone lecture hall in the parking lot next door.

At about the same time, I learned that Pikeville Medical Center was undergoing a major expansion, with financing from the Rural Development Administration (RDA) through the US Department of Agriculture. The medical center was getting a large forty-year loan from the RDA at no more than 4 percent interest. My friend Tom Fern, with whom I had worked in Frankfort, was the head of rural development in Kentucky. I asked him about the RDA program, and he said Pikeville College met the eligibility requirements, and approval wouldn't be a problem. We wouldn't have to start making payments until one year after the building was finished. We already had $1 million, so we needed an additional $3.5 million to pay for the renovation. At 4 percent interest over forty years, that would cost the college about $180,000 a year. With an additional $6.5 million in tuition coming in, we could afford that.

As the architect explained his plan, he pointed out that Spilman was a forty-five-year-old building with low ceiling heights and other shortcomings that the renovation wouldn't solve. But if we tore it down and built a new structure on the same foundation, using the same design he and the faculty had approved, it would add only $2 million to the cost. At 4 percent interest for forty years, the additional cost to the college would be only $100,000 a year. No problem!

I also knew the college was earning approximately $100,000 a year by renting Spilman Hall apartments to faculty. Why tear down a building that was generating $100,000 a year at very little cost? I wondered how much it would cost to locate the new building on the down-street side of the Armington Building instead of on the Spilman Hall site. We could connect the new building to Armington with an elevated walkway. According to the architect, the new plan would cost about $7.5 million, or just $2 million more than building on the Spilman site. The numbers still worked! I later learned we were eligible to participate in the federal government's New Markets Tax Credit Program. Going ahead with the new building turned out to be a no-brainer!

Dotson called a meeting of the board of trustees' executive committee to discuss the situation with the architect. There had been ongoing discussions about needing more room for the undergraduate program, and the architect suggested that we could frame out an extra floor in the new building for about $1 million and then finish it at a later date. One committee member said that at 4 percent interest for forty years, we should build two additional floors, and the board approved. Now we were up to $9.5 million.

Then Dean Buser objected to having half the medical school in one building and half in another. He suggested building one structure large enough to house the entire medical school; then the medical school's space in the Armington Building could be used to handle the increase in undergraduate enrollment. That put the total cost at $12 million. Hurley added that a new cafeteria would be a great recruiting tool, which would cost another $2 million. Then a committee member asked why we were spending so much money on a building in the back of the campus, where few people would see it. We had long talked about adding a new building on the hill in the front of the campus, which would probably cost only $2 million more. By the time the committee was finished, the cost of the project had soared to $16 million, but the numbers still made sense.

After the new building's design was completed, we hired a construction manager to supervise the project. He reviewed the plans and gave us the bad news: construction would cost $20.5 million, not $16 million. Now we had to get serious, because that was a lot of money! However, Tom Fern assured us that we could get an RDA loan for that amount. Besides, board members' enthusiasm for the project had grown. After the addition of $5 million for fixtures and furniture, the executive committee authorized the project, and we negotiated a loan with the RDA for $24.5 million. (We still had the $1 million from the Brown Foundation and ARC.)

Board member Jim Booth, who was in the coal business, wanted to name the building the Coal Building, and the executive committee approved. We had the usual cost overruns, which brought the final price of the building to about $35 million, but we managed to raise about $10 million for the project from supporters of the college. The increased medical school and undergraduate enrollment put the college on a firm financial footing. In my last year as Pikeville College president, we ran an operating surplus of almost $1 million.

I stayed on as chair of the CPE until December 2011, when the issue of Pikeville College becoming a state college surfaced. My position as college president and chair of the CPE constituted a conflict of interest. Pikeville's potential status as a state college was discussed during the 2012 legislative session, but it didn't receive much support. Not becoming a state college actually worked to Pikeville's benefit. It retained the freedom to chart its own course and create entities such as the Kentucky College of Optometry. It also plans to establish a college of dentistry by 2025.

In the fall of 2011 Hurley and I worked on another initiative. I learned that the US Department of Education defines a university as an institution of higher learning that offers graduate degrees. A medical degree is a graduate degree, and Pikeville College had a medical school, so Pikeville College was actually a university! Did we want to change the name of the school? We posted the debate online and generated a heated discussion. Many older alumni and supporters objected to the change. Younger people, particularly students, were in favor of the college becoming a university. If so, what university? I wanted to change the name to Central Appalachian University because it was the only university actually located in central Appalachia, and I thought it was parochial to call it the University of Pikeville or Pikeville University.

This discussion occurred after the University of Connecticut (UConn) and the University of Massachusetts (UMass) won NCAA basketball championships and our men's basketball team won the NAIA championship that year. One student posted this suggestion online: "Let's name it the University of Pikeville and call it UPike!" That name caught on like wildfire. It didn't take me long to realize that the train was leaving the station, so I got on it. Most people in Kentucky who are familiar with postsecondary education know that UPike exists.

Hurley and I worked well together. He was industrious and capable, and he cared about the institution. After working with him for about a year,

I recognized that he would make a good college president. However, he didn't have a doctoral degree. Neither did I, but I knew the faculty wanted my successor to have a doctorate. I told Hurley that if he earned his doctorate, I would recommend to the board of trustees that he replace me as president. He started working on his degree, and it took him almost three years to earn it. When I notified the board that I was stepping down as president in July 2013, it hired him as my successor without conducting a national search. For me, it had been a satisfying four years.

Hurley asked me to stay on as chancellor, a nonadministrative, public relations–type position, and I agreed. I attend fund-raising events and alumni meetings and greet potential students and their parents on campus. I also occasionally speak to classes and groups in eastern Kentucky. I am a member of twelve boards or commissions—some local, some regional, and some statewide—as part of UPike's public service mission. However, since 2020, the COVID-19 pandemic has severely limited my activity.

James Hurley left the university in 2015 and is now the president of Tarleton State University, a member of the Texas A&M University system in Stephenville, Texas. He played an integral role in the dramatic improvement of the University of Pikeville. One way or another, I have been able to recognize and entice capable and dedicated people to work with me, which is the secret to my success in life.

In the past, I've been invited to speak to a number of high school graduation classes. That is a critical time in the transition from childhood to adulthood. Many of my graduation speeches went something like this: "Don't be afraid of failure. If you have never failed at anything, you have never tried anything that is very difficult. At this stage in life, even if you are valedictorian, you haven't succeeded enough to ensure your success in life. And if you are at the other end of that scale, you haven't failed enough to ensure that your life is a failure. It is up to you. You are now in charge of your life. You are an adult. Now is the time to commit yourself to hard work and an ethical lifestyle. But you still need more education!"

Judi and I sold our house in Pikeville and bought a town house that we still maintain, but after a year or two, we moved into the President's House on the UPike campus. It's a great atmosphere and very convenient. The President's House is a residence the college bought years ago, and it's too small to do any serious entertaining, but it's all Judi and I need. The university's board decided to build a new residence for the president that's more appropriate to the position.

As of 2023, I read and write a lot during a typical day spent in my office. I have written—or at least started writing—twenty-nine essays on a variety

In my fifth career as president of the University of Pikeville, I led a major expansion project that included construction of the Coal Building to house the Kentucky College of Osteopathic Medicine. (Author's collection)

My friends from across the state funded a statue of me at the foot of the iconic ninety-nine steps that access the main campus of the University of Pikeville. I have always been reluctant to see my name on buildings, bridges, and highways, but this was an honor I really appreciated. (Author's collection)

of subjects, some on politics, some on government, and one work of fiction that I hope to finish someday. I have spent a lot of time working on this book with the help of Jeffrey Suchanek. At one time, I hoped to be important enough to write about subjects that other people would be interested in reading. I don't know if I've reached that level of importance, but I have learned that writing is hard. I don't have trouble formulating ideas in my mind, but I do have trouble translating them into words on paper. My typing could use improvement, and so could my grammar. I appreciate the University Press of Kentucky for publishing this volume.

I will finish by saying that I've had a blessed life. I've failed in many ways, large and small, but I've succeeded more often than I have failed. I had an idyllic childhood because I didn't know how big the world was. My parents used the right amount of love and discipline. My sisters were great companions. I was successful in business. I was successful in government. I was successful at the University of Pikeville. I helped raise a great family that I'm very proud of. Judi and I have a great relationship and are great partners. What more could a man want? I feel that I have more to do, but if the Lord calls me home tomorrow, I won't complain.

Afterword

A First Lady's Story

I have referred to Judi's contributions to my life and my public service throughout this narrative, but here I want to review her accomplishments in more detail. Judi had an influential position as First Lady of Kentucky. She could have used that position to hobnob with the elite and the glamorous, but she chose to serve the abused, the neglected, and the women and children of Kentucky.

Judi's parents taught her that serving other people was a noble calling. They led by example and influenced Judi's character well into her adult years. Her mother, Esta Craft from Letcher County, was a social worker; her father, Roy Conway, was in law enforcement. Roy and Esta met while they were both attending Pikeville College. Roy was a state representative from Pike County before World War II. During the war, he worked on the Manhattan Project to develop the atomic bomb and received a citation from the government. After the war, he operated a furniture store in Pikeville. In 1949 he was elected sheriff of Pike County, which was a lawless place at the time. Gambling, prostitution, and bootlegging were rampant. Roy campaigned on a platform of cleaning up corruption and proceeded to do that. In the process, he made many enemies, including some politicians who had been profiting through kickbacks from the criminal element. In July 1950, after only six months in office, Roy received a telephone call reporting criminal activity going on out in the county. Two men shot him as he left the house. He died in his wife's arms, with Judi and her three sisters looking on. Judi was ten years old.

After Roy's murder, Esta sold the furniture store and agreed to serve as acting sheriff until the next election. Then she bought a local grocery store. After a few years, she sold the grocery store and became a social worker. Esta taught her girls about compassion for others, particularly those facing hardship in their lives. Some nights, Esta would bring a family home with her because they weren't safe under their own roof or had nowhere else to go.

The looks on their faces were a blend of gratitude for the sanctuary and fear of the abuse they had escaped. Those faces made a huge impression on Judi.

Judi was active in her community. She was a member of the Pikeville Junior Women's Club and the Pikeville Women's Club. She graduated from Pikeville High School and attended Pikeville College, where she studied bookkeeping. She worked for several coal companies and later owned and operated the AnPat Landscaping and Gardening Company in Pikeville.

One of the great joys of my life came in 1977 when Judi agreed to be my wife. We joined our families—my two children from my first marriage, Nicki and Chris, and Judi's two children from hers, Bambi and Jan Harvey. Judi was not just my wife but my full partner in the public service that embodied my career. She was an invaluable asset when I ran for Pike County judge; when I served as chair of the Kentucky Democratic Party, lieutenant governor, and governor; and during my time as president and then chancellor of the University of Pikeville (formerly Pikeville College). More people than I'd like to admit have told me that Judi was better at working a crowd than I ever was. I'm inclined to believe them. I have always admired Judi's authentic love of people.

The meaningful contributions Judi would ultimately make as First Lady of Kentucky began when she served on the Attorney General's Task Force on Child Sexual Abuse while I was lieutenant governor. She would attend task force meetings and come home at the end of the day tearful and full of the stories told by the survivors of abuse. She urged me to promise that if we were ever in a position to help survivors and their families, as we would be in the governor's office, we would try to make life better for them.

While on the task force, Judi got acquainted with Carol Jordan, who would become her close partner in reform efforts during my gubernatorial administration. Carol had worked in the fields of domestic violence, sexual assault, and child abuse for more than a decade. She later worked for the president of the University of Kentucky, Dr. Lee T. Todd, and they created the nation's first academically based interdisciplinary research center focusing on violence against women. Judi and I always saw that program as a way to protect the legacy of our work on behalf of women and children.

As governor, I saw that we needed a formal structure to improve the state's response to domestic violence, sexual assault, and child abuse. That led me to create the Governor's Office of Child Abuse and Domestic Violence Services, and I named Carol as its founding executive director and Judi as a special adviser. Judi was involved in every aspect of that office's work, and she made a profound difference.

When I first met Carol in 1995, she was a member of a legislative task force on domestic violence chaired by Senator Jeffrey R. Green, and she wanted my endorsement of their legislative package. Both Judi and I were impressed with the proposals, but one bill they were asking me to support raised a key question. Kentuckians had heard me say many times that my first budget as governor would be "structurally balanced," and when we got to Frankfort, we found that the budget would also be very tight, meaning that there was practically no money for new programs. Carol acknowledged my commitment to a balanced budget but publicly voiced her support for the innovative Victim Information and Notification Everyday (VINE) program created in Louisville after a young woman named Mary Byron was murdered by an abuser just released from police custody. VINE was a top legislative priority for the task force, and Carol asked me to fund it. I hesitated as I pondered how to answer, and then Judi said, "Yes, we'll do that." It was the first of many times Judi obtained state funding for programs she cared about.

Judi made her mark in a unique way with the Kentucky General Assembly. She and Carol would go to the Capitol Annex at the beginning of every legislative session to brief the Democratic and Republican leadership on all the bills in their legislative package for the year. She also testified before multiple legislative committees, carrying her persuasive message to those who would vote on the more than twenty bills she and her various task forces and councils proposed. I may be biased, but I have never seen any First Lady work the legislature like Judi did. Her partnership with Carol led to the passage of progressive legislation pertaining to child abuse, sexual assault, and domestic violence. Some of the laws were controversial, but that never bothered Judi. Her only concern was whether women and children would be better off.

On several occasions, Judi accepted invitations by her bills' sponsors to sit in their seats on the house or senate floor when her proposal came up for a vote. I have no hard evidence that this ever happened, but I often wondered whether Judi quietly cast that legislator's vote as she sat there smiling. In the house, they voted electronically at their desks.

Judi would occasionally go to the floor of the chamber and discuss her bills with the legislators. I told her, "Judi, you can't lobby a legislator on the floor. They'll throw you out of there." She responded, "Then they'll just have to throw me out!" They never did, but I know some of them wanted to.

Judi also started the practice of giving awards to the sponsors of her bills at the end of the legislative session. That sounds like a nice thing to do, but it was not without controversy. Judi never cared whether the sponsors of her bills were Democrats or Republicans. She liked me to accompany her to these award ceremonies, and while I was happy to do that, several of these events led to some awkwardness. One time, Judi and I traveled to a rural part of southeastern Kentucky to recognize a Republican senator who had sponsored one of her bills. As the Democratic governor, I was involved in the effort to unseat him in the next election. When Judi took the podium and began praising the senator, I leaned over and whispered to him, "Congratulations, but don't think I'm not going to continue to work against you in the election." The senator smiled and whispered back, "Governor, I would expect nothing less." He won reelection anyway.

Judi was extremely persuasive when she lobbied individual legislators. On one occasion, a member of the Republican leadership added an amendment to one of Judi's bills, much to her chagrin. Judi and Carol showed up at his office early the next morning and waited for him to arrive. When he did, he politely, and I dare say bravely, invited them in. Judi smiled broadly and said, "Now, honey, I hear you want to put a bad amendment on my bill. I'd like Carol Jordan to explain to you why that's a problem." After Carol's explanation, the legislator looked at Judi and said, "Okay! Okay! I'll take the amendment off your bill, but I think I've been had." Judi just laughed and said, "Well, honey, if that's true, it couldn't have been done by two nicer women." Incredibly, Judi's bill passed without any amendments. Her unique, down-home style changed legislators' minds without offending them. She had a real gift.

Judi's effectiveness as an advocate for legislation was even mentioned in an article that appeared in the *Lexington Herald-Leader*. The article claimed that Judi was having more success with her legislative priorities than I was having with mine. Truth be told, that was true!

Judi and I decided early on that an important part of my administration would be improving protections for women and children. Being big believers in partnerships to accomplish major reforms, we reached out to Kentucky's domestic violence shelters and developed a close relationship with the Kentucky Cabinet for Women and Children (later the Cabinet for Health and Family Services). Judi personally visited a number of shelters across the state, and we both visited the Women's Crisis Center in northern Kentucky, one of the first shelters in the state. It still offers lifesaving services to women and children. These visits encouraged us to redouble our efforts to help families harmed by violence.

Judi joined the Kentucky Coalition Against Domestic Violence (KCADV), created in 1981 as the Kentucky Domestic Violence Association, and the Kentucky Association of Sexual Assault Programs (KASAP), founded in 1990 as the Kentucky Rape Crisis Center Association, to help establish an annual statewide conference on violence against women. The conference attracted hundreds of advocates and other professionals from Kentucky and other states to participate in state-of-the-art training on domestic violence, sexual assault, and child abuse. Judi spoke at that event each year while I was in office. After we left the governor's office in 2003, the two coalitions continued the conference, and they celebrated twenty years of successful conference events not long ago.

In 1996 Judi learned that the KCADV and its member organizations had created what purported to be the nation's first certification program for advocates working in domestic violence shelters. Proud of the coalition's emphasis on providing only high-quality services for domestic violence survivors, Judi hosted a unique graduation ceremony for all the newly certified women's shelter staff at the governor's mansion each year.

In 2002 Judi also used the governor's mansion to host an important reception to recognize Domestic Violence Awareness Month. She and Carol created the White Ribbon Campaign, which acknowledged men in Kentucky who had contributed in important ways to ending violence against women. Through this campaign, Judi publicly thanked judges, law enforcement officers, prosecutors, university presidents and researchers, legislators, and other current and former statewide elected officials who had made a difference in the fight against domestic violence. They all wore white ribbons at the event and spoke about the need to end violence against women.

During the first month of my administration, to give Judi a means to recommend policy and legislative changes, I signed Executive Order 96-68 to create the Governor's Council on Domestic Violence and Sexual Assault. I formally named Judi chair of the group. A year later, as the council continued its work, former governor John Y. Brown Jr. contacted me and asked that we "put him to work" as part of the effort to address domestic violence. Governor Brown became a strong supporter of expanding domestic violence shelters after his sister "Boo" was assaulted by someone she knew. Brown stayed by his sister's side throughout her assailant's trial, and he offered to do more to end the scourge of domestic violence. We wanted him to play a highly visible role, so I appointed him cochair of the council. Brown said, "It has always been my conviction that this society is made up of laws that protect everyone according to a sense of justice, fairness, protection, and equality, but when I witnessed my sixty-six-year-old sister beaten up by a man, it crystalized for me that our society still treats domestic violence as though it was a different crime."

The council made numerous legislative recommendations, including the following:

- Create civil protective orders for stalking victims
- Expand the triggers for victim notification of an offender's release from prison
- Notify victims when offenders attempt to purchase a firearm
- Create local domestic violence coordinating councils
- Expand the types of licensed professionals in Kentucky who must receive training on domestic violence, sexual assault, and child abuse
- Strengthen the Sexual Assault Nurse Examiner Program

Advocates for victims of rape and sexual assault watched Judi and her task forces and councils make substantial reforms during my two administrations. In September 1999 I created a first-of-its-kind task force to study the state's response to sexual assault. Given Judi's great leadership ability, I named her the honorary chair and asked Representative Joni Jenkins and commonwealth attorney Steve Wilson to be cochairs. Joni was an outspoken legislative advocate for women and worked for many years as an advocate for rape victims at the Center for Women and Families in Louisville. Steve was a well-respected prosecutor from Bowling Green and served for a number of years on the Kentucky Prosecutors' Advisory Council. I gave this task force a short deadline to accomplish its work so that we could present legislation to the 2000 General Assembly. Judi met the deadline and brought me a strong package of bills that included:

- Repealing the inadmissibility of marital rape charges in custody cases
- Removing the one-year reporting requirement for marital rape and sodomy
- Designating the date-rape drug gamma hydroxybutyrate (GHB) a Schedule I controlled substance
- Allowing rape crisis centers and children's advocacy centers to conduct forensic sexual assault examinations
- Creating a civil right of action for stalking victims
- Extending the rape shield law to civil cases

In addition to making her presence known in the halls of the Capitol Annex, Judi influenced the state budget on behalf of the programs she cared about. During my two administrations, funding for domestic violence programs and rape crisis centers increased 42 percent and 129 percent, respectively. In addition to recurring General Fund monies, we allocated $1 million in capital construction funding to allow domestic violence shelters to improve their facilities.

Judi received many accolades for her work against domestic violence and child abuse. There had never been such a committed and effective advocate for these causes in Frankfort. These are just some of the awards she received:

- Kentucky Coalition Against Rape and Sexual Assault 1996 Outstanding Legislative Advocacy Award
- Kentucky Domestic Violence Association 1996 Committed to Peace in Kentucky Homes Award
- Kentucky Commonwealth Attorneys' Association 1997 Outstanding Leadership Award
- Lexington YWCA 1997 Smith-Breckinridge Award (which required Judi to make a speech in front of one of the largest groups she had ever spoken to)
- Center for Women and Families in Louisville Year 2000 Woman of Distinction Award
- Office of Victims of Crime (Washington, DC) 2001 Annual Award

In 1998 Vice President Al Gore visited Kentucky and presented Judi with a $3 million check from the STOP Violence Against Woman program of the US Department of Justice. Gore said Judi was doing more to advance the cause than any First Lady in the nation. One of her proudest moments as First Lady was the ceremony that named the shelter for women and children in Whitesburg after Judi's mother: the Esta Craft Conway Shelter for Abused Women. In 2003 Judy's portrait joined others on the wall called "Women Remembered," and it still hangs in the Kentucky State Capitol.

Judi's growing expertise on the experiences of women and children in Kentucky's court system led her to support the Kentucky Supreme Court's effort to create family courts. In her book on my administration, Fran Ellers quoted Kentucky Supreme Court chief justice Robert Stephens: "If I was the father of the family courts, Judi was the mother." Judi attended the opening of several family courts in jurisdictions across Kentucky, and in 2002 she attended a graduation ceremony held by one of the state's first drug courts.

Judi's desire to strengthen Kentucky's courts led to her involvement in judicial appointments. As governor, I was interested in appointing more women to the bench. Judi and Carol often provided the names of qualified women, many of whom I appointed during my two administrations. In 1999 Judi and I hosted a first-of-its-kind reception at the governor's mansion for all women judges in Kentucky. Judi also made recommendations for circuit and family court judges and one justice of the Kentucky Supreme Court.

As the new century approached, Judi and I turned our attention to child abuse in Kentucky. In the late 1990s a man was convicted of killing one of his children, and the Cabinet for Families and Children took steps to revoke his parental rights to his other children. Shockingly, Kentucky law prevented the state from taking that action. In short, Kentucky law required that a child satisfy the statutory definition of an "abused child" before the state could terminate a parent's rights. Although this wasn't the intent of the law, it essentially meant that the state could protect only previously abused children. The fact that the father killed one of his children did not protect the victim's siblings. Judi and I couldn't live with that, so we worked with Representative Tom Burch and Carol to propose House Bill 142 in the 1998 legislative session. Our child protection legislation was ultimately successful, and it strengthened the state's ability to protect its children.

Another legislative effort championed by Judi was a bill that allowed abused children's court testimony to be videotaped, rather than requiring them to face their abusers in court. This was one of Judi's commonsense bills, and she was a passionate advocate. However, some legislators questioned whether it contravened the Kentucky Constitution by not allowing a defendant to face his or her accuser. Judi rose to the challenge with her usual energy when fighting for Kentucky's children. Her senate sponsor was again Jeff Green, and they made an indefatigable team. Judi's bill is now law, and the children of Kentucky are better off because of it.

Judi also raised public awareness about child abuse every April by forming a partnership with the Prevent Child Abuse Kentucky organization and hosting blue-ribbon receptions at the governor's mansion. She even succeeded in bringing together University of Kentucky basketball coach Tubby Smith and University of Louisville basketball coach Rick Pitino to tape a public service announcement about the prevention of sexual assault.

Beyond correcting weaknesses in the law, Judi and I wanted to find a new, innovative model for Kentucky's child protection system. We asked Carol to help us draft this new model. At the time, Kentucky had three Children's Advocacy Centers (CACs)—one in Lexington, one in Louisville, and one in northern Kentucky. As we analyzed the three centers' work, we believed we had found our new model. At the heart of the new approach was creating a central location where all the professionals involved in the protection process, including police, social workers, therapists, and prosecutors, would gather to interview the abused child. Using the CAC model, we established a child-centered agency with highly specialized professionals in every one of Kentucky's sixteen area development districts. Judi was able to secure a $2.5 million federal grant to purchase forensic medical examination equipment for the CACs across the state to improve our response to abused children. The names of the CACs Judi visited reflected how she felt about these programs: Home of the Innocents, the Healing Place, Child Watch, and Children First. I couldn't have been prouder when the CAC in Pikeville serving eastern Kentucky was named Judi's Place for Kids.

Judi also secured a significant amount of money for CACs from the state's General Fund, just as she did for the domestic violence shelters and rape crisis centers. Judi didn't stop there. As the CACs began to perform forensic medical examinations of abused children, she pushed through a reform that allowed the CACs to become Medicaid providers and bill for those services. Judi also convinced me to sign an executive order that allowed Kentucky's victims services agencies to participate in the state government's retirement system.

Judi's efforts on behalf of the commonwealth's children drew national and international attention. She hosted Britain's Princess Anne at a family and children's program in Lexington. In 1998 Tipper Gore, then the wife of Vice President Al Gore, accepted Judi's invitation to speak at a conference on child abuse prevention. Judi gave Tipper a specially designed rag doll, a project she had implemented to raise public awareness of child abuse. Additionally, the National Center for Missing and Exploited Children implemented one of Judi's favorite projects, which allowed Kentucky to create its own Amber Alert System to locate missing or kidnapped children. Judi's advocacy on behalf of children was recognized by the Kentucky Council on Child Abuse, the Kentucky Council for Exceptional Children, the Exploited Children Help Organization, Children First, the Sunshine Center, the Family Place, the Center for Women and Families, and the Barren River Area Child Advocacy Center.

I first learned that Judi was involved with legislation related to women's health during the 1996 legislative session, when she stopped me in the hall of the capitol and told me about a bill pertaining to breast cancer that had just been passed by the General Assembly. Through her assistant, Kay Harrod, Judi had been contacted by a woman with breast cancer whose insurance carrier wouldn't pay for the particular treatment she needed.

Judi worked with state senator Ernesto Scorsone and the Kentucky Commission on Women to pass a bill that required insurance companies to pay for that treatment. Judi made sure the legislation had an emergency clause so the woman she had talked to could receive that vital treatment immediately. I ran into that woman after I left office, and she let me know that Judi had probably saved her life.

With the help of Kay, Judi initiated the annual Celebration of Hope. Every year after the Kentucky Derby, Judi invited women who had survived breast cancer to a gala luncheon and entertainment program to celebrate their successful treatment. It was held outdoors under a tent on the grounds of the governor's mansion, which had also been used to host our Derby guests. The event eventually became so large that it was relocated to the Farnham Dudgeon Civic Center in downtown Frankfort. By the end of my administration, more than twelve hundred women attended this annual event. Kentucky First Ladies Glenna Fletcher and Jane Beshear continued the tradition after I left office.

Judi was so concerned about the well-being of cancer patients that she visited them in the hospital and wrote them personal notes of encouragement. During my two administrations, Judi chaired a task force on breast cancer, which led to a recommendation to create an Office of Women's Health and Mental Health in the Cabinet for Health Services, as well as a law requiring insurance companies operating in Kentucky to pay for breast reconstruction for breast cancer patients. Judi originated five pieces of legislation concerning breast cancer patients and created the nation's first Breast Cancer Commission to support victims of the disease. She was recognized for her advocacy by the Susan D. Komen Breast Cancer Foundation, the Kentucky Cancer Program, and the Brown Cancer Center.

Judi lent a passionate and persuasive voice to her causes, but what most people didn't know was that she was terrified of public speaking. Her staff wrote her remarks, and she would spend at least two weeks memorizing every word. She also learned how to use a teleprompter, which takes even the most polished politicians some time to master. However, as soon as Judi began to speak, her nervousness subsided. Once she allowed her genuine passion for the cause to take over, she always captivated her audience.

Judi's many other accomplishments include honorary doctorates from Pikeville College and Morehead State University. The University of Kentucky named an endowed chair in her honor for the study of violence against women. She was appointed chair of Kentucky's initial Native American Commission. Two of her ancestors were Cherokee, and she has

In her role as First Lady, Judi was active on behalf of those who did not have a voice in government. Pictured with her is former governor John Y. Brown Jr., who helped with her initiative to fight violence against women. (Courtesy of Kentucky Department for Libraries and Archives, Archives and Records Management Division)

always been concerned about the welfare of Native Americans. In 1998 she earned membership in the Daughters of the American Revolution and was very active in that organization while we were in Frankfort. She was appointed cochair, with former governor Martha Layne Collins, of an economic summit on women. She served on the Kentucky Commission on Women, which secured a place for the pictures of important women in the history of Kentucky in the halls of the capitol. She was named 2002 Woman of the Year by *Kentucky Monthly* magazine.

Since we returned to Pike County, Judi has continued her activism. She is a member of the Pike County Tourism Commission and is currently serving as its chair. She serves on the board of the Westcare Emergency Shelter and Rehabilitation Program, which operates three facilities in Pike County. That organization recently converted a former schoolhouse on Marrowbone Creek into a modern facility for women recovering from drug addiction and named it after Judi. She is also on the board of Judi's Place for Kids and has served on the Pike County Fine Arts Commission, Pikeville Main Street Program, and Kentucky Heritage Commission. She was

Judi was always enthusiastic about the issues she was involved in. (Courtesy of Kentucky Department for Libraries and Archives, Archives and Records Management Division)

the 2007 recipient of the Paul Harris Fellows Award, bestowed by the Pikeville Rotary Club, and the Tony Turner Award from the East Kentucky Leadership Conference. The Pediatrics Department of the University of Pikeville Medical School recognized Judi for her work on behalf of children. In 2019 Bernheim Forest included Judi in its exhibit of the ten most important women in Kentucky, which includes a mural of each woman displayed in various places in the arboretum.

As we were leaving Frankfort for good, Judi said: "Over the years, I've become more comfortable with myself. There are things I've done that I never would have thought I could have done. I leave this [governor's] office as a stronger person than when I came, by helping other women become stronger too. I'm very pleased and proud to have been the First Lady of Kentucky. I feel it is a great honor to serve the people of Kentucky."

I could not have asked for a better life partner than Judi. I probably don't deserve her, but she has been my rock in many ways. I will be forever grateful.

Acknowledgments

I would like to thank the president of the University of Kentucky, Eli Capilouto; the dean of the University of Kentucky Libraries, Doug Way; and former dean Dr. Terry L. Birdwhistell for their administrative and financial support of the Paul E. Patton Oral History Project. In particular, I would like to thank the staff of the Louie B. Nunn Center for Oral History, including director Dr. Douglas A. Boyd, oral history archivist Kopana Terry, oral history reference librarian Jennifer Bartlett, processing archivist Danielle Gabbard, and former oral history reference librarian Judy Sackett. I would also like to thank the UK Office of Philanthropy for its help in raising the necessary funds to transcribe the interviews on which this book is based. To those who contributed to that cause, I humbly thank you. Without the transcripts, there would be no book. In addition, I want to thank Kevin Goldsmith, who worked with Andrew "Skipper" Martin to research some aspects of my two administrations that helped refresh our memories. In particular, I want to express my appreciation to archivist Robin Smith at the Kentucky Department for Libraries and Archives for her assistance in locating information pertaining to my two terms as governor. Thanks also to Ashley Runyon and her staff at the University Press of Kentucky, who made the publication of this book uncomplicated and painless. Special thanks go to Dr. Amanda Slone, assistant provost and associate professor of English at the University of Pikeville, for her expert editorial skills in polishing the book's text.

Thanking the many people who aided me along life's journey, including my political career, would be an impossible task, so I will not even attempt to do so, for fear of leaving someone out. Many of those people to whom I am indebted are mentioned throughout this book. Skipper Martin, Jim Ramsey, and Crit Luallen top the list, but all my cabinet secretaries and my staff in the governor's office have my utmost gratitude. Whatever success I had as governor, I owe it all to them. You know who you are, and I am grateful beyond words. To all the state employees who worked throughout the commonwealth during my two terms as governor, know that I appreciated your dedication and perseverance, and I tried to improve the quality of your lives through pay raises, better working conditions, and respect.

I could not have accomplished what I did without the care and support of my family. I have not been the perfect son, husband, or father, but my family sustained me through good times and bad, even when I didn't deserve it. They have my undying love and respect.

Paul E. Patton

Kentucky Remembered: An Oral History Series

Series Editors: James C. Klotter, Terry L. Birdwhistell, and Douglas A. Boyd

Books in the Series